CUSTOM DRAPERIES
IN INTERIOR DESIGN

CUSTOM DRAPERIES
IN INTERIOR DESIGN

MARY NEAL
Davis-Neal, Inc.

ELSEVIER
New York · Amsterdam · Oxford

Elsevier Science Publishing Co., Inc.
52 Vanderbilt Avenue, New York, New York 10017

Sole distributors outside the United States and Canada.
Elsevier Science Publishers, B.V.
P.O. Box 211, 1000 AE Amsterdam, The Netherlands

©1982 by Elsevier Science Publishing Co., Inc.
Second Printing, 1983.

Library of Congress Cataloging in Publication Data

Neal, Mary, 1920–
    Custom draperies in interior design.

    Bibliography: p.
    Includes index.
    1. Drapery in interior decoration. I. Title.
NK2115.5.D73N4   747'.5   81-19564
ISBN 0-444-00640-0   AACR2

Illustrations Joanne Otepka
Desk Editor Danielle Ponsolle
Designer Virginia Kudlak
Compositor The Composing Room of Michigan, Inc.
Printer Halliday Lithograph

Manufactured in the United States of America

CONTENTS

PREFACE

Why should anyone who operates a workroom feel compelled to write a book about custom draperies? Believe me, no one involved in custom draperies would ever feel more compelled!

We are responsible for measuring and estimating, for fabricating and installing, and ultimately for the satisfaction of the client. We are asked to solve insoluble problems and to work with impossible fabrics. We are expected to install in ceilings where there is no support and to make draperies appear to hang evenly when there is nothing level about the situation. We stretch inadequate yardages, work around flaws, and devise means to sew together and hem fabrics that are nothing but a bunch of strings. We attempt to interpret specs that give such unusual instructions as to allow 250% fullness and pleat to budget fullness in one area and deluxe in another. We are asked to install a movable and practical drapery on a window in a slanted ceiling and to drape boats, trains, vans, planes, and any kind of house or building in existence.

We are the problem solvers for designers who deal with draperies. We often get on the job when it is too late to stop design or architectural errors, but we do our best to minimize them. It hurts us to install for a client something we know is wrong, whether from a fabric, design, or installation viewpoint, when no more money, and sometimes less, would produce better results and a more satisfied client.

We are often working for people who know nothing about the construction of draperies, the characteristics of various fabrics and linings, the mechanics of rods, traverse or stationary, or the existence of time. By some inner sense we are supposed to be able to produce any size job on the exact day it is needed—whether construction is early or delayed (regardless of how many delays there are), whether the fabric has reached us late (back orders, strikes, and forgetful designers do exist), whether the carpet has been installed, and even in some instances whether the windows have been put in.

All of these things contribute to a situation that makes a workroom a difficult operation at best. When the people feeding work to it do not have the proper background and knowledge, the situation is impossible. That is why I felt compelled to write this book.

In the book I attempt to provide for the teacher, student, designer, specifier, or workroom a basic knowledge of the various aspects of custom draperies that influence the finished product and to establish a common vocabulary and terminology to make for better communication among them.

CUSTOM DRAPERIES
IN INTERIOR DESIGN

FUNDAMENTALS OF DRAPERIES

In spite of its many problems, the drapery business has many compensations. We are creating something both useful and beautiful, and we always leave a place looking better than it did when we started, whether it be a home, hotel, hospital, or office, since any place looks better when its windows are dressed.

This is, of course, the first thing that draperies do—they decorate. The effects can vary from the casual to the formal, from the grotesque to the tasteful, depending on you, the designer. Draperies can be a background or a focal point. They can disguise architectural faults, create illusions, or just dress the windows.

Draperies also help to control temperature. In these days of excellent heating systems and central air-conditioning one might not consider this important, but these systems need to be given the chance to function efficiently. It is very difficult for a furnace to warm a room with large expanses of glass that are cold on the inside as well as on the outside without overheating the rest of the house. It is also unrealistic to expect an air-conditioner to cool a room well where the sun beats in through ordinary window glass. As it becomes more necessary to conserve energy, it is essential to know that the insulating property of any fabric, even a sheer, is amazing. The fabric creates an air pocket that traps the heat or cold between itself and the glass. New fabrics designed for insulating purposes live up to their claims if properly used, making a room warmer in winter and cooler in summer.

However, draperies do other things as well. They furnish privacy. This is more important in homes, such as those whose builder put a full-length window in the bathroom with the commode in full view, for apartment dwellers with a constant parade past their sliding glass door, for those who are afraid with uncovered windows. In offices privacy seems less important, but a phenomenon is occurring in the beautiful new mirrored glass buildings: they turn into fishbowls at night. The mirror effect is on the side where the light is; so in the daytime, no one can see in, but if your clients are working at night with the lights on, every move is visible to those outside the building. Since the glass is reflective, a glance toward the window might startle them with their own reflection.

Draperies have great accoustical value. Contrast the sound in an empty house with that in a furnished one. Compare the noise in your kitchen, where there is little drapery and usually no carpet, with that in your dining room, where it is usual to have both. Fabric helps to deaden sound, so your home or office will be quieter with draperies at the windows.

Everyone knows that draperies control light and glare. You can soften light with sheers and casements; you can darken a room with lined draperies; or you can black out all light.

Obviously, draperies are in many cases a necessity. Certainly, they have many uses. With this book as a reference you should be able to handle with confidence all aspects of custom draperies from sales to installation.

DRAPERY TERMS

ACCORDIA-FOLD® pleating system that allows drapery headings to look the same inside and outside and stacks into much smaller space than conventional draperies. Heading is a tape that snaps to slides in rod. Similar systems are made by several rod companies but called by other names.

ALLOWANCE amount in inches deducted for clearance at bottom (or top) of draperies. Also amount added for hems, headings, overlaps, and returns.

APRON wood facing below the sill on a double-hung window.

ARCHIFOLD® similar to Accordia-Fold®. Uses plastic devices instead of tape to create pleats. Several similar systems exist.

ARCHITECTURAL NETS very open-weave fabrics varying from very fine fishnet types to weaves so open they are virtually strings.

AUSTRIAN SHADE sheer fabric panel gathered on shirring tape approximately every 12 to 15 inches. Fullness is vertical rather than horizontal. Total effect is of gathered scallops.

BALLOON DRAPERIES draperies tied back twice with puffy effect.

BALLOON SHADE shade made of fabric, with either gathered or tailored heading. Controlled by tapes, it blouses or balloons when raised.

BAR-TACK method used to tack pleats, sewing back and forth closely through all thicknesses, by hand or machine.

BATON wandlike device in various lengths, usually of fiberglass, attached to the leading edge of draperies (center) to move them by hand. Two per pair needed.

BAY WINDOW three or more windows set at angles to each other, projecting outward from exterior wall.

BITE amount of fabric picked up by the needle on the blindstitch machine.

BOLT LOSS   fabric lost when cutting, owing to flaws or bolts running out without enough for a drapery cut at the end.

BORDER PRINT   printed fabric having a border, usually 4 to 6 inches wide, on one or both sides. This border is usually of a different print.

BOW WINDOW   curved or circular bay.

BOX PLEATS   pleats stitched in the usual manner, then flattened out and tacked. Usually meet each other and require triple fullness. Do not traverse.

BUCKRAM   usually called crinoline. Stiff fabric used at top of drapery to stiffen pleats, in widths from 2½ to 5 inches (standard is 4 inches). Should have permanent finish.

CAFE CURTAIN   curtain hung from a round decorative rod with rings, clips, or loops. They may have scalloped, pointed, or pleated headings.

CANTONNIERE   small lambrequin. A shallow cornice that frames the top and two sides of a window.

CARRIERS   plastic devices in a traverse rod to which draperies are hooked or snapped. Frequently called slides.

CARTRIDGE PLEATS   pleats stitched like other pleats but rounded out and stuffed with rolled crinoline. Provide nice formal effect but do not traverse well.

CASCADES   shaped, pleated ends for valances; hang in zigzag folds to a point. Used in other ways but usually with swags.

CASEMENT FABRIC   loosely woven fabric varying in density from very open to fairly close, designed to screen glare and to be decorative, not designed to be lined.

CASEMENT WINDOW   a cased or framed window that comes together vertically at the center and opens outward. Screens are on the inside.

CENTER DRAW   draperies that open from and close to the center of the window.

CENTER SUPPORT   bracket to support the center of a drapery rod. On long spans they are spaced at intervals along the rod to support the weight and prevent sagging.

CHAIN WEIGHTS   series of BB shot or small rectangular weights covered with fabric and put in the bottom of draperies for even weight in hem. Cause a bumpy appearance in hem.

CLERESTORY   series of small windows set near the ceiling, found most often with slanted ceilings.

CLUSTER PLEATS   pleats formed in conventional manner, either pinch or french, and grouped with three close together and a wide space between (as much as 12 inches).

CONE   type of jabot.

CONTINENTAL HEADING   where lining comes to top of drapery, as opposed to regular rolled top where fabric is rolled to the back.

CORNICE decorative top treatment usually constructed of plywood on a 6-inch dust cap, shaped, padded, and covered with fabric. Decorated in various ways.

CRINOLINE see **BUCKRAM**. Stiffening at top of drapery.

CUT LENGTH finished length of drapery plus allowances for hem, heading, and pattern repeat, if necessary.

CUT TO MEASURE drapery rods, usually stationary, cut to specific measurements. Most traverse rods are adjustable.

CUT YARDAGE yardage less than a full bolt. Costs approximately 10% more than piece or bolt price.

DECORATIVE ROD rod, traverse or stationary, made of wood or metal with various finishes such as pewter, chrome, brass, bronze, or wood-tone. Most often round, occasionally square. Finished at ends with finials. Usually having rings to hold pleats.

DEPTH length of valance, cornice, or dust skirt from top to bottom.

DORMER WINDOW small window in alcove projecting through the roof line.

DOUBLE HEM hem turned twice to eliminate shadows and raw edges.

DOUBLE-HUNG DRAPERIES two sets on the same window, usually sheer and over-drapery, that traverse separately.

DOUBLE-HUNG SHUTTERS two sets on same window, one above the other, operating independently.

DOUBLE-HUNG WINDOW cased or framed window that meets horizontally and moves up and down.

DRIFT amount that a pattern falls off the perpendicular across a piece of fabric. One-and-one-half inches considered allowable.

DROP depth of a valance. Also the number of divisions in Empire, Austrian, or Swag valances.

DROPPED PATTERN repeat pattern that does not match at points directly across from each other at selvages. One side matches at a different point on the other. **CALL YOUR WORKROOM.**

DUST CAP tops and sides of a cornice or valance board that help cover the tops of draperies and protect them from dust. They also help hold the valance in front of the traverse rod so the moving drapery does not drag the valance.

DYE LOT variation in intensity of color from one batch of fabric to the next. Can even appear to be a different color.

FACE FABRIC fabric that faces the room in lined drapery.

FEATURE STRIP band of fabric added to cornice or drapery to provide interest and contrast. Usually about 2 inches wide and often edged on either side by piping or welt cord.

FENESTRATION use of windows, their arrangement in wall areas.

FESTOON alternate name for swag valance. More commonly a one-piece valance swagged through loops at the top corners of windows.

FINIAL decorative end on cafe or any decorative rod. Also end at tops of posts on poster beds.

FINISHED LENGTH total length of drapery when ready to hang.

FINISHED WIDTH width of a pleated pair or panel of drapery after returns and overlaps are added.

FLAME-RESISTANT fabrics either treated or woven of fibers that will not flame up when exposed to fire. Now required in most public buildings.

FLAWS holes, heavy slubs, misweaves, or misprints in fabric.

FRENCH PLEAT pleat stitched in the regular fashion, divided into three equal sections, and tacked to hold all sections separately. Does not traverse as well as pinch pleat.

FRENCH SEAM seam sewn once with wrong sides together, then trimmed closely, pressed, and sewn again with right sides together, leaving no raw edges exposed.

FULLNESS amount of fabric in pleats in a drapery or gathered on a rod in a curtain.

HAND feel of a fabric or how it drapes.

HAND-DRAW draperies that must be opened and closed by hand or with a baton.

HEADING top of drapery, usually pleated and with stiffening. The part of a gathered drapery that projects above the rod.

HEMS finished sides and bottoms of draperies, usually double-turned.

HOLD-BACK wood, metal, or fabric device that holds a drapery, preventing it from hanging straight. Drapery can be gracefully swagged and does not traverse. See TIE-BACK.

HOOK see PIN.

INTERLINING flannel fabric placed between face fabric and regular lining to add richness and bulk to lightweight fabrics.

JABOT decorative cone or double cascade between sections of a valance.

JALOUSIE windows of narrow, overlapping horizontal strips of glass that pivot and can be cranked in and out. If strips are wide, it is an awning window.

LAMBREQUIN usually defined as a cornice that frames a window, sometimes going all the way to the floor at the sides.

LENGTH distance from top to bottom of window or drapery.

LIGHT STRIKE light that comes in around the edge or at the top or bottom of a shade or drapery. Most common in recessed installations.

LINING fabric used as backing for draperies. Can be of several different kinds for various purposes.

LINTEL   strong beam over doors and windows to support the wall above. Can be wood, metal, or concrete.

MASTER CARRIERS   arms that overlap in the center of a traverse rod to which the attached and that overlap in the center.

MILIUM   lining fabric coated on one side with aluminum for insulation.

MITERED CORNER   finished corner at the bottom of a drapery where the hems meet at a forty-five degree angle to assist in correct hanging.

MULTIDRAW   simultaneous opening of two or more draperies on one rod at the same time.

MUNTIN   metal or wood divisions in a window.

NEAT PLEAT®   like **ARCHIFOLD**®, uses plastic devices to form accordian folds.

OFF-CENTER   pair of draperies with unequal widths on each side to enable the pair to close to the center of the window.

ONE-WAY   draperies made as panels that move in only one direction to stack in specified areas, such as the stationary side of a sliding glass door.

OVERDRAPERY   heavier drapery, closer to the room, over another drapery (usually a sheer). May be traverse, side panel, or tie-back.

OVERLAP   center portion of a traverse drapery that rides on the master carrier and overlaps to make a neat closing.

PANEL   two or more widths of fabric sewn together. A pair has two panels.

PATTERN REPEAT   distance from one point on a pattern to the same point further up the length of the fabric.

PICTURE WINDOW   large window, usually having a stationary center glass with a smaller window on each side.

PILLOWCASE   method of attaching linings where lining and face fabric are stitched together with right sides facing, then turned.

PIN (HOOK)   metal hook, sharp on one end, that pins into heading of a drapery so that it can be hooked onto the rod. There are several kinds.

PINCH PLEAT   pleat stitched in the regular manner, divided into three sections, pinched, and tacked through all thicknesses at about ¾ inch from the bottom.

PIPING   small double band of fabric sewed to the edge of another piece to give an accent of color. Like a welt cord with no filler.

PLEAT   fold sewn into a drapery to create or control fullness.

PLEATER TAPE   flat heading sewn onto the tops of draperies with pockets into which hooks are slipped to form pleats. Good only for Do-it-yourself.

PROJECTION   jutting out from the wall. The part of the rod that returns to the wall from the main rod.

RAILROAD   to turn fabric and run lengthwise on cornice or valance.

RAT-TAIL   chain weight.

RETURN   part of the drapery that returns to the wall from the front of the rod. Covers the rod projections. Also the ends of a valance or cornice board.

RIPPLEFOLD®   rod system that controls fullness by allowing it to roll back and forth under the rod in a rippling fashion. Has no pleats. Similar systems come from other sources.

ROD POCKET   hem at top of drapery through which a rod is inserted for shirred heading. Used frequently top and bottom on doors.

ROLLED HEADING   where fabric is rolled over crinoline to the back so that raw edges are concealed. Must be turned twice on sheers.

ROLL PLEAT®   like RIPPLEFOLD®. Even flow of fabric, front and back of rod. No pleats.

ROMAN SHADE   shade formed of flat piece of fabric, controlled by tapes to move up and down accordian fashion. Can also be made to remain pleated when down.

SASH   window framework that holds the panes in place.

SASH WINDOW   window whose bottom and top work independently. Can be wood or metal (double-hung window).

SELVAGE   edge of fabric formed on the loom when the fabric is woven. Frequently tighter than fabric body. Should be removed in draperies.

SERGED SEAM   seam formed by a special machine that cuts off selvages, sews widths together, and overcasts the edge.

SHEER   see-through fabric for glass curtains. Filters light and controls glare. Often shirred on rod.

SHIRR   another name for gather. Rod-to-rod curtains are shirred on the rod.

SIDE PANELS   decorative panels of draperies that hang on each side of a window. Do not meet in center. Can be tied back.

SINGLE HEM   single fold of fabric turned up with a small half-inch edge turned under. Can be used on heavier fabrics to conserve fabric.

SLIDES   see CARRIERS.

SLUB   lump of extra thread accidently woven into smooth textured fabric, appearing as a flaw. Some fabrics are woven purposely with slubs at random to give a textured appearance.

SMOCKED PLEATS   extra long pleats having triple fullness and tacked together to look like smocking.

SPACE   flat area between pleats. Must be equal in size. Smaller in full draperies.

STACK   area required for draperies when open.

STACK PLEAT®   knife-edge pleats riding below the rod and stacking in a minimum amount of space, like ACCORDIA-FOLD®.

SWAGS draped valance, pleated in scalloped effect, usually overlapped. Very formal.

TABLING process in workroom where drapery is stretched flat, length determined, and heading is put in.

TENSION PULLEY device to place tension on continuous traverse cord. Keeps cords organized and makes drapery operate smoothly.

TIE-BACK device used to hold back draperies. See HOLDBACK.

TIER curtain layers arranged so that one overlaps the other (usually 4 inches). Top tier must project further than the bottom.

TOP TREATMENT valance or cornice to add decoration and conceal rods.

TRAVERSE ROD drapery rod with a pulley mechanism that allows it to open and close with a cord.

UNDERDRAPERIES usually unlined sheers or casements that hang under heavier draperies to control light. May be a liner under a sheer or casement to give privacy or black out light.

VALANCE horizontal top treatment to conceal rod and give a finished appearance to window.

VELCRO® TAPE nylon tape having two parts, loop and pile. Used to hold valances on boards, panels to Paneltrac®, and for various other fastening needs.

WEIGHTS chain and lead (lead weights are usually one ounce, square or round and covered, sewn in hems at seams and in corners to insure straight hanging). See CHAIN WEIGHTS.

WELT CORD covered piece of cotton cord ranging in size from ¼ to 1 inch used to finish seams in bedspreads and slipcovers, edges of cornices and tableskirts, and in various other ways. Usually covered with a bias piece of fabric.

WIDTH measured distance from one side of window to other.

WIDTH single width of fabric of the cut length required to make a drapery. One or more widths are sewn together to make a panel.

BACKGROUND INFORMATION NEEDED TO DESIGN DRAPERIES

FACTS ON FABRICS

Fabrics That Should Not Be Lined

    Sheers
    Casements
    Architectural Nets
    Laces

Specialty Fabrics

    Hand-woven and Hand-printed Fabrics
    Crewels
    Silk
    Upholstery Fabrics

Problems with Fabrics

    Stability
    Dye Lots
    Odors
    Bad Weaves and Flaws
    Other Problems

Fabric Weight and Printed Fabrics

Flame-proofed or Flame-resistant Fabrics

    Inherently Flame-resistant Fabrics
        Fiberglass
        Verel®
    Fabrics Processed for Flame-resistance

Fabric Bargains

Sheets as Draperies

WINDOW TERMINOLOGY

Types of Windows

SELECTING THE TREATMENT

Shirred Curtains

Pleated Draperies

Tie-back Draperies

Cafe Curtains

Shades

Snap-on Rod Systems

Paneltrac®

Tools for Selling

CONSERVING ENERGY WITH WINDOW TREATMENTS

FACTS ON FABRICS

This is not a book on textiles. Therefore, there is no need to describe the infinite variety of wonderful fabrics available. The choice of blends of fibers, finishing processes, textures, colors, and designs is almost bewildering. Your client is probably concerned only with color, pattern, and texture. You, however, must be able to advise whether the fabric is suitable for its use, whether the drapery should be lined, and what type of lining to use.

From the workroom standpoint there are many pitfalls to avoid. In describing these we are not trying to scare you into confining yourself to a few "safe" fabrics, nor do we intend to be derogatory concerning any fabric. We are only trying to assist you in making wise selections.

Fabrics That Should Not Be Lined

Certain fabrics are not designed to be lined. This is true of all sheers and casements including architectural nets and laces.

Sheers. A sheer is a fabric with threads so fine and light that even though it is closely woven, light comes through, and you can see through it when there is light on the other side. Clients often ask for the sheer that you can see through in only one direction. There is no such sheer. There are only those that, like mirrored glass, screen the view to those on the lighted side. Those on the dark side can see through the sheer.

Sheers usually consist of 100% of the same fiber such as polyester, cotton, silk, and the like, although there are some blends. They may have a very smooth appearance such as chiffon or ninon, or they can look more opaque as does batiste. Some have a slightly slubbed appearance and others may have woven designs such as stripes. The look of silk gauze is also popular. Many sheers are now being woven on wide looms and can be turned, width for length (railroaded). This alters the effect, changing a horizontal weave to a vertical look.

Casements. A casement is usually a rather open weave. The threads are heavier than in a sheer, often quite rough in texture. There is frequently a woven design. Threads of different fiber contents are often combined to add interest to the fabric, thus causing some of the problems in working with casements since these fibers may not all react the same to moisture or stretch the same amount.

Almost all casement fabrics stretch with the exception of the "Stable Loc®" or "Solar-Loc®" type, which are woven with a special process, and some of the malimo weaves. When casements stretch vertically it is almost impossible to assure that the pattern will follow the top and bottom hemline of the drapery. This distortion usually happens at the top and is often unsightly and unacceptable. The only solution is a drapery pocket that disguises the problem. When a casement stretches horizontally, no workroom can guarantee an even hemline. This happens most often with fishnet-type fabrics.

Casements should not be used to cover cornices. Since no light can come through, the character of the fabric is lost. More important, fabric on cornices must be stretched tight and fastened, so, because casements usually stretch, sometimes in both directions, the pattern or weave would be distorted.

Often designers or their clients choose a sheer or casement and request that it be lined. In the first place this counteracts the reason for using these fabrics that are designed to screen the glare and soften the light. Second, if these fabrics are lined, you will almost certainly run into trouble. The lining is heavier than the face fabric and of totally different weave and fiber content. Consequently it will cause a problem where lining and face fabric are joined at the sides. It is best to suggest that a separate liner be used. This requires two rods but is the most satisfactory way to handle the problem. Usually, with a little effort, a fabric of similar effect can be found that can be correctly lined if the use of two rods is not acceptable. If the client insists, discuss fabrication with your workroom, explain to your client what will be done, and decline to guarantee the results.

Architectural Nets. The fishnet look is included in this group. Some have very small, square holes while the holes in others are much larger. There are many variations of openness and pattern, some being virtually nothing but strings.

Laces. Lace is made in many weights and designs. It can tend toward the sheer look or be much heavier and more open, thus being more like nets.

Specialty Fabrics

When choosing a fabric, a high cost or unique look does not always mean that the fabric is better than others. Many of these fabrics have characteristics that make them less practical than those with a lower cost or less distinctive look.

Hand-woven and Hand-printed Fabrics. Very expensive hand-woven and hand-printed fabrics can be beautiful and effective. Unfortunately, they have some disadvantages that are seldom mentioned. Hand-woven fabrics are often not as stable as those woven on a machine loom. Sometimes they are not uniform, one side being more tightly woven than the other, causing the looser side to sag when hanging. The density of the warp can vary, resulting in a look almost like a horizontal stripe. If the fabric has a woven design, the repeat may vary in size, making it impossible to match the design when joining widths. Hand-printed fabrics often have flaws that are entirely characteristic of the process but that may be unacceptable to the client. The printing can be out of register because of improper placing of the screens, or the background color can show through if dye is not applied heavily enough.

Crewels. Crewel embroideries show a lot of variation in both color and repeat. This is because the work is actually done by hand in the home by family groups. The wools are hand-dyed, and though the colors are close, they do sometimes vary. The stenciling is also done by hand, accounting for size variation in patterns from one repeat to the next. This variation is seldom noticeable in the finished drapery or upholstered piece and is considered characteristic in any case.

Silk. Silk is probably the all-time luxury fabric in the decorating business. It is a strong natural protein fiber, but as such, is subject to deterioration in sunlight. It must be lined to be lasting and is one of the more difficult fabrics to line correctly. It takes dyes in a beautiful way that no other fiber can duplicate. Irregularity of sheerness and weight in silk gauzes or satins is characteristic, and bands or shadings are normal. Black specks are also characteristic of dupioni silks and are not considered defects.

Upholstery Fabrics. Upholstery fabrics are beautiful, having excellent texture and design, but they are not designed for draperies and bedspreads. Some are light enough in weight to be acceptable, but most are so heavy that seams can be unpleasantly bulky. Most upholstery fabrics are not treated for stability. This is not necessary because they are ordinarily stretched tight and held this way. When made into draperies, it is not at all unusual for them to shrink while hanging. Also, upholstery fabrics are not inspected carefully for flaws that show when light is behind the fabric. Certain weaves can show up badly when hanging. A vertical-striped fabric can have a definite horizontal stripe on the back that will show through when light is behind it. Many tapestries also have stripes on the back. Some upholstery fabrics have backings on them that keep them from draping at all, and most are so heavy that they do not drape well.

Problems with Fabrics

Stability. Many designers are not aware that most fabrics are not truly stable and that many conditions affect them. Some fabrics will stretch from their own weight alone. This is most often true of casements but can be true of others as well. There is no way to predict accurately the amount of stretch as it is affected by so many things—weight, humidity, expertise of workmanship, and so on.

Perhaps the worst problem of the drapery business is humidity, whether natural or through air-conditioning systems. Most natural fibers shrink when they absorb moisture. Unfortunately, some fibers stretch under the same conditions. If the weather changes or if the conditions where the drapery is hung are different from where it was fabricated, then problems may develop. Most air-conditioning systems remove moisture in the summer and add it in the winter, and if a fabric is very sensitive to moisture, it will react to this change in humidity.

Many new buildings are designed so that draperies hang directly above the convectors that dispense air. This makes the conditions even worse. The only reasonable advice to offer is to use fabric that is close to 100% of the same fiber so that it will all react the same. A stable verel combined with an unstable rayon will give a seersucker effect when exposed to moisture. Glass, verel, modacrylic fabrics, and polyester are the only ones considered stable. Since they do not fill all needs, you must work with the limitations of the others.

Dye Lots. A very real problem, particularly where large yardages are involved, is variation in dye lots. Fabrics dyed at different times will vary in shade. If windows are in different rooms or areas, this is not too bad since colors will appear different in different lights, but all fabric in the same pair of draperies must be from the same dye lot.

Most fabric distributors will advise you if there is going to be a problem with your order. Do not expect to be shipped the exact shade of the sample. The fabric you receive is often quite different, sometimes as much as to seem to be another color. If you must have an exact match, request a cutting of the current dye lot before ordering and reserve the necessary amount of yardage.

Odors. Another complaint about fabrics is that they have an unpleasant odor. This is the result of heat or moisture on certain special finishes used on fabrics. The odor is not generally lasting, and room fresheners will help until it is dispelled. Some fabrics, particularly those with loose or rough weaves, absorb odors and smoke and retain them indefinitely.

Bad Weaves and Flaws. Fabrics that have a tight and loose weave combined in vertical stripes can have a tendency to ripple. This is especially true if the fiber content is different in the two stripes. A fabric of this type might look perfectly all right on the bolt or cutting table, but when exposed to heat or moisture, or even from the weight of hanging, it could have a puckered effect.

There is almost no such thing as a perfect bolt of fabric. A certain number of flaws per bolt is considered permissible to the trade, and many others will slip through inspections. There are many kinds to watch for and your workroom will do its best not to let them slip through.

HOLES are hard to spot on the cutting table but will show up when light comes through the fabric.

HEAVY SLUBS occur, usually when threads are joined in weaving. They are considered flaws only when they are so heavy as to show as dark spots when the drapery is hung.

FUGITIVE YARNS are caused by lint or threads of a different color caught in the loom during weaving. Occasionally they can be removed without damage to the fabric, but more often than not you will have a worse flaw if you try to remove them.

BAR MARKS are caused when fabric is woven more tightly or loosely at various points or where interruptions in the dyeing process have caused a color change.

All of these are major flaws.

Other Problems. The chapter on Cutting Draperies in the second section discusses certain other fabric problems that are of more concern to the workroom but that have a definite influence on the satisfactory completion of a job. It would be wise to familiarize yourself with this aspect to help in communicating with the workroom.

Fabric Weight and Printed Fabrics

A very long drapery should be made from the lightest possible fabric for the use it is to have. This will keep the weight down and help to eliminate some of the problems that develop with traverse draperies on high installations. A bulky fabric does not stack well and has a tendency to blouse at the bottom. This is aggravated when a bulky or heavy fabric is lined. There are several rod systems that help to control bulk and let draperies stack in the smallest possible area.

They do not eliminate the disadvantages of bulky fabric; they just control it better.

When using printed fabrics, remember that matching printed colors with a solid color can be very difficult, even impossible, if the print is on a colored ground. The colors become a mixture and seldom match dyed colors.

Flame-proofed or Flame-resistant Fabrics

Many specifications now call for flame-proofed or flame-resistant fabrics. This becomes more important to you as fire restrictions are tightened. It is essential that designers, especially those who specify fabrics for commercial installations, understand the facts about flame-proofing and the problems involved.

Inherently Flame-resistant Fabrics. *Fiberglass.* Fiberglass is the first of the inherently flame-resistant fabrics. Unfortunately, most workrooms prefer not to work on it. Most people are mildly allergic to it and others are violently so. Flecks of glass break off while it is being cut and sewn and these flecks irritate the skin. They also irritate the respiratory system and the eyes. Those who wear contact lenses should avoid it.

The fabrication of fiberglass is difficult because mistakes cannot be corrected, it cannot be pressed well, and it is extremely subject to abrasion. The advantages still remain. It is totally flame-retardant, can be washed and hung back up immediately, and is completely stable.

Verel®. Verel® is a trade name that has come into general use to describe a whole series of inherently flame-resistant fabrics. It is very satisfactory to use, easy to fabricate, and has none of the disadvantages of fiberglass. It comes in a wide range of weave, pattern, and color. In most cases it is stable unless too high a percentage of other fibers is combined with it. It can be washed and dry-cleaned (with a special solution). It can be pressed, and it drapes well.

Fabrics Processed for Flame-resistance. A large group of fabrics (mostly 100% cotton) is now being processed for flame-resistance at the time of manufacture, and the process is guaranteed for the life of the fabric. These fabrics are usually very beautiful since natural fibers dye better than most synthetics, and they handle well. There have been some problems with these fabrics becoming wrinkled and shrinking under high moisture conditions. This is caused by the fact that any treatment to make a fabric flame-resistant gives it the property of retaining any moisture in the air so it cannot flame up. The fabric will feel damp and smell musty. Metal surfaces that touch it such as pins and hooks may rust. The colors eventually fade and the fabric rots.

Most fabrics can be treated to be flame-resistant. Some processes are better than others. Be sure the treatment is done by a reputable firm that specializes in this process. Spray-on finishes are not permanent and do not adhere to the standards set by most states.

Fabric Bargains

For the small, independent decorator, shopping at textile outlets and mill end stores may seem to be rewarding costwise, but it has definite hazards. Because these stores frequently sell first-quality goods that are overruns from large buyers, they can sometimes sell the fabrics at costs equal to or below the wholesale cost from your source. You have the advantage of getting the merchandise with no waiting. However, you would not be able to mark it up, as your client might see it on sale at the lower price.

In buying fabrics at textile outlets you may also run into the problem of inadequate supply. The store may be able to obtain more, but there may be a long delay and dye lot problems by the time the fabric is delivered. Often the fabrics are closeouts and no more is available.

Some stores that buy and sell seconds do not always advertise them as such. Unless you carefully inspect the fabric as it is unrolled and measured, you may end up with any number of flaws that will make your fabric unusable. Even if you do inspect it, you may have to buy many more yards than you really need to get what you must have. This is a dubious saving.

Some stores are very conscientious in both advertising and selling, but it may not be worth the decorator's time to shop this way. If clients want to do it, be sure they know how much fabric they need, the cut lengths, how many they need, and how to work with pattern repeats.

Sheets as Draperies

The housewife has discovered sheets for draperies, and now designers are doing it too. Nearly every decorating magazine you pick up devotes some space to this subject, but it is best not to succumb to the trend.

You cannot make a fine custom drapery from sheets without a lot of problems. The sizes may not be adequate since the size given on the package is usually the size before hemming. The hems should be taken out and redone because they are single hems and machine stitched. Even if this were no drawback, part of the hem must be taken out if the sheets must be sewed together. The biggest drawback is that if you buy six sheets, the chance that the pattern will match on any of them is almost nonexistent. It is probable that because of the finished length of the drapery they cannot be juggled to make them match, and the result will be a drapery that is much more trouble to make and that does not look as well as one made from drapery fabric.

Sheet manufacturers have done an incredibly nice job with color, pattern, and design, and the cost is modest for what you get, but it would be much better to leave draperies made from sheets to the do-it-yourself homemaker.

Finally, now that you know what to watch for in fabrics, you will be able to give proper information to your clients or to specify fabrics that are more suitable for commercial installations. The more you learn about fabrics and their characteristics, the better your drapery jobs will be.

WINDOW TERMINOLOGY

There is no such thing as a "standard" window. There are so many different styles that the term means nothing. However, if one style might be considered standard, it would be the double-hung window. It is the most common type in homes, and the names of its components can be applied to components of most windows.

DOUBLE-HUNG WINDOW

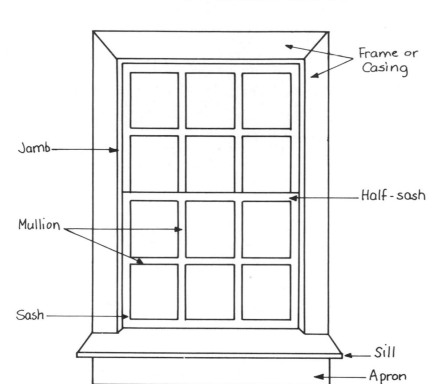

Everyone dealing with draperies should use the same terminology to avoid confusion. These are the parts of a double-hung window.

FRAME or **CASING**   frame around the window, usually of wood and flat against the wall.

JAMB   inner frame of the opening forming the recess of the opening into which the sash fits.

SASH   frame that holds the glass panes.

HALF-SASH   point where top and bottom sash meet, or meeting rail.

MULLION   division between panes of glass.

SILL   ledge at bottom of window.

APRON   flat wood trim just below sill.

DOUBLE WINDOW

Two double-hung windows set side by side with a common frame between and a common sill are called a double window. Measurements should be from the outside of one frame to the outside of the other as a unit. The unit should not be spoken of as two windows.

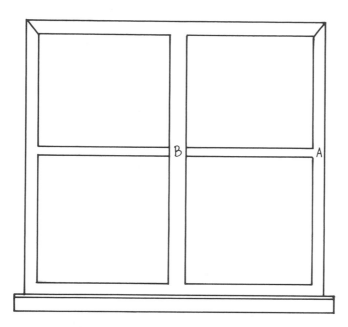

In addition to measurements shown for single windows, it is a good idea to give the width of the facing, A, and center mull, B.

Types of Windows

PICTURE WINDOW has one large fixed pane of glass, usually with a smaller sash window on each side for ventilation. Sometimes there are small windows under the large pane that can be opened. Not a practical window for ventilation as the drapery often covers part of the side windows.

DOUBLE-HUNG WINDOW most common type of window. It can be opened either from top or bottom, making it versatile for ventilation. These windows vary in that some have small panes in both top and bottom sections, some have small panes at top and a large pane at the bottom, and others have large panes in both sections.

CORNER WINDOW two windows of any style that meet at the corner of a room.

RANCH WINDOW wide, short windows high in the wall. They often have sliding sashes. Because furniture is frequently placed under them, they are hard to drape.

SLIDING GLASS DOORS doors that slide open and closed. They come in various sizes and combinations, the most common consisting of two sections set in separate tracks, with one stationary and the other sliding. Sometimes there are three sections with the center one opening.

BAY WINDOW three or more windows of any type set at angles to each other and projecting outward from exterior wall. Usually double-hung, often with a stationary window in the center. Require special treatments and rods.

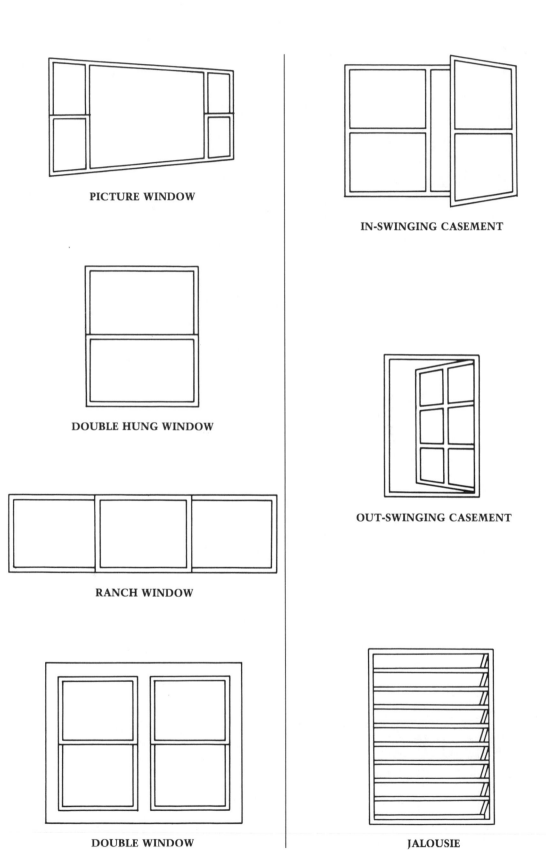

PICTURE WINDOW

IN-SWINGING CASEMENT

DOUBLE HUNG WINDOW

OUT-SWINGING CASEMENT

RANCH WINDOW

DOUBLE WINDOW

JALOUSIE

AWNING WINDOW

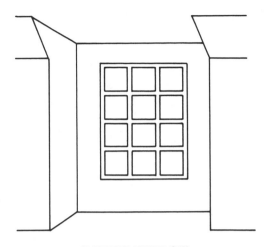

DORMER WINDOW

ARCHED or CURVED WINDOW

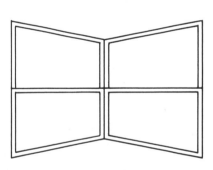

CORNER WINDOW

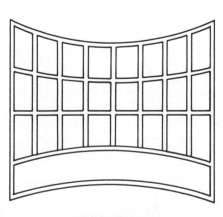

BOW WINDOW

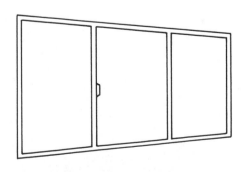

SLIDING GLASS DOOR

22

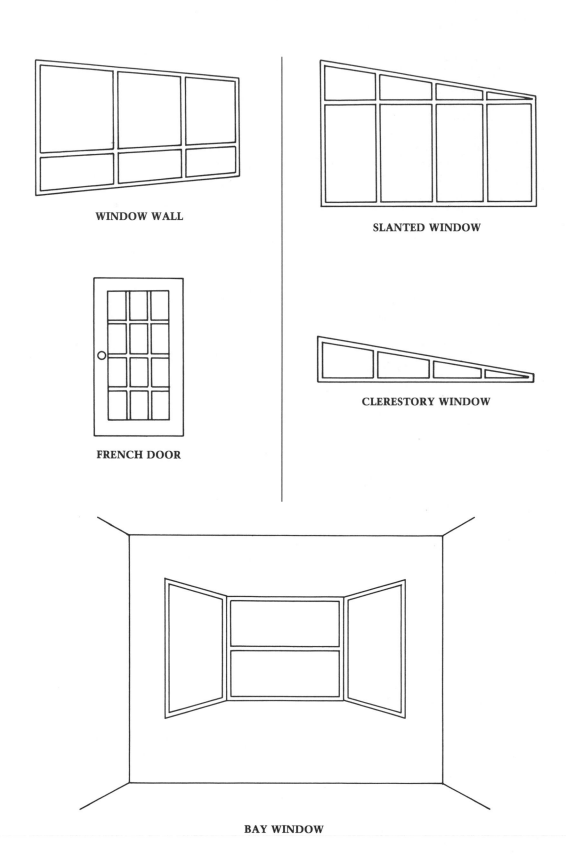

WINDOW WALL

SLANTED WINDOW

FRENCH DOOR

CLERESTORY WINDOW

BAY WINDOW

BOW WINDOW curved window similar to a bay. Most often stationary, providing no ventilation.

GLASS WALL series of windows, usually stationary, that form a wall. A sliding glass door may be part of this wall. Commonly found in contemporary homes and commercial buildings.

FRENCH DOORS doors made up in pairs with panes of glass framed by a casing. Can be a problem to drape if they open inward.

DORMER WINDOW small window projecting in an alcovelike extension through the roof line.

OUT-SWINGING CASEMENT window that opens by swinging out from the wall. Control of air is difficult as whole window moves.

IN-SWINGING CASEMENT window that opens into room, creating problems for any kind of drapery treatment.

JALOUSIE window, often recessed, constructed of narrow, horizontal strips of glass that open at an angle by means of a crank. Good air control, but may be a source of heat loss if not sealed well.

AWNING WINDOW similar to jalousie but has fewer wide, horizontal sections. Operates in the same way.

SLANTED WINDOW follows the slanting line of a cathedral roof and often takes up the whole wall. Usually has a mull across the window at the low point of the slant and can be draped there, leaving the upper section open. Upper windows are stationary. Lower section frequently has a sliding door.

CLERESTORY WINDOW small window set near the ceiling, often slanted. Not intended to be opened or draped.

ARCHED WINDOW any window curved at the top, often seen in banks, churches, and stairwells of residences.

SELECTING THE TREATMENT

The success of a drapery treatment is determined by whether it is correct for the type of window and the use for which it is intended. This must be your decision because clients usually do not know what they want or what would be best.

Determining the correct length for the drapery, the fullness desired, whether or not it should be lined, and how far to extend on the sides are discussed in the section on How to Estimate Yardage in the chapter on Measuring and Estimating.

In selecting the treatment, you will need to find out what the client expects. If the purpose of the treatment is merely to decorate with no particular need for ventilation or light control, stationary side panels and a top treatment can be used to frame the window and give color and interest. Stationary sheers or casements can be used with or without the decorative panels. If light control is important, a traverse liner can be used under the stationary drapery or a lined overdrapery can be traversed over it.

A double treatment is more versatile if both under- and overdrapery traverse. This allows complete control of light and offers the added convenience of being able to move draperies out of the way for ventilation and cleaning.

Top treatments serve two important purposes. They frame the window, tying the whole treatment together, and they hide the rods used for the draperies. They can make a treatment more tailored or more dressy, more casual or more formal. They can be used to disguise the shape of a window and to alter the apparent dimensions. The chapter on top treatments gives more complete information on how to use and estimate them.

The type of rod needed is usually dictated by the kind of drapery you are using. It is seldom necessary to discuss rods at length with your client. All clients really care is that the best rod for the situation be used, and you should be able to count on your workroom for this. Basically wall mount or ceiling mount is the most necessary information. Decorative rods are an exception, and you should be equipped with pictures or special information to show if you feel these would be indicated. Commercial installations can be a little more complicated since there are frequently built-in pockets, special conditions, or specifications calling for certain makes or types of rods. In almost all cases your workroom or installer is your best guide in selecting rods. If you feel that there will be a problem, ask either of them to measure and look over the job before you discuss the treatment with your client.

The same thing is true when deciding where to install the drapery. You will become more at ease with this question as you work with draperies, but unless a certain place is specified by the client, it is best to let your workroom be your guide. More information on where to place the rod is found in the chapter on Measuring and Estimating.

Since this is not a book on decorating, only simple basic treatments are illustrated. Variations of these types will be found in monthly decorating periodicals, idea books by trimming manufacturers, excellent publications by the rod people, and decorating books of all kinds.

There are very few original window treatments—just original uses and variations of the old tried-and-true ones.

Shirred Curtains

The simplest and least expensive type of window treatment is shirred or gathered on the rod. An ordinary curtain rod is run through the top hem of the curtain, which gathers up and hangs full on the rod. It has the disadvantage of being attached completely to the rod so that in order to take it down the rod must be taken down also. To open or close the curtains, the gathers must be pushed one way or the other at the point where the rod is inserted. This is difficult or impossible to reach, and nothing is gained by trying to move the bottom of the curtain. For this reason shirred curtains are considered to be stationary and screen light and view at all times. If windows are opened, they also collect dirt and billow in the breeze.

Another type of shirred curtain is the rod-to-rod curtain often used on doors since it is controlled top and bottom. These curtains are gathered on the rod top and bottom, but a smaller rod with less projection is used. They may be tied back either as a pair or in an hourglass effect in the center. They are also

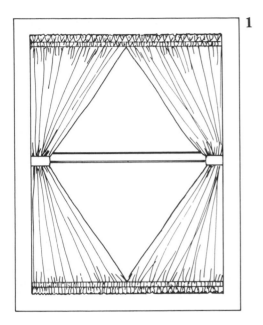

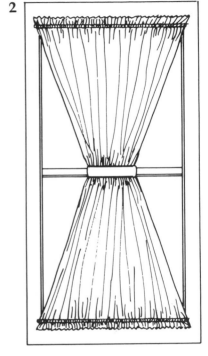

Figure 1. Rod-to-rod sheers—as a pair tied back to the sides.

Figure 2. Rod-to-rod sheers—tied back as a panel with hour-glass effect.

Figure 3. Drapery gathered on wood pole—tied back with sheers underneath.

Figure 4. Tie-back drapery with half cafe for privacy.

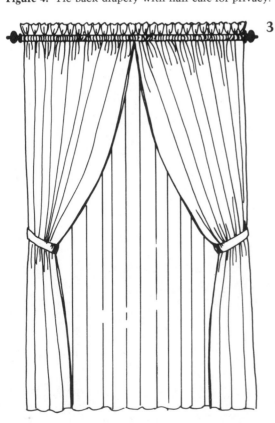

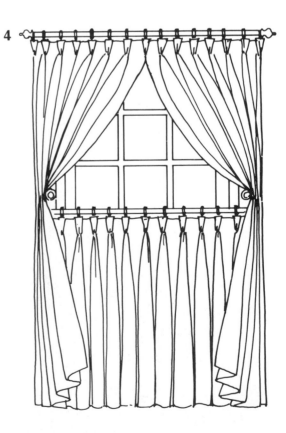

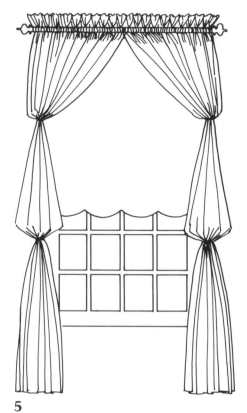

Figure 5. Balloon drapery or drapery tied back twice.

Figure 6. Balloon draperies in a series on bay window.

Figure 7. Fold-back or flat tie-back drapery.

7

5

6

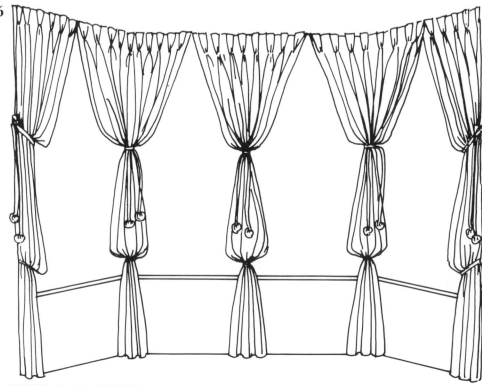

used on side lights beside doors and in the recess or narrow "slit" windows often seen in contemporary buildings and residences. With imagination they can be effectively combined with other draperies to give unusual treatments. Don't forget that a very beautiful and unusual casement or sheer can be made rod-to-rod and stretched flat to show the design.

Do not be limited to the ordinary use of sheer curtains. Use them long, short, tied-back, or trimmed. Use them on regular rods, or wood poles. Use colors, combinations of colors, laces, or prints. They will still be less expensive and easier to use than almost any other kind of window treatment. Do remember that colored sheers, laces, and prints will have a definite effect on the outside appearance of the house.

Pleated Draperies

The pleated drapery, whether traverse or stationary, is standard. This is the most versatile type that can be used. The kind of pleat can be varied, the fullness can be changed, it can be either lined or unlined, and it can be used on many types of rods. This is the basic drapery used in most window treatments and is well known to both decorators and their clients.

Tie-back Draperies

Tie-back draperies are a graceful way to decorate a window very simply. If the panels meet in the center of the window and tie back, there is no need for a top treatment as the rod is covered at all times, and the heading forms its own decoration. This same treatment can be used to good advantage with a decorative rod that is exposed and adds an additional special touch. This type of treatment is most often used with sheer curtains since part of the window is exposed at all times and sheers control light and give privacy. A variation can be done with a half cafe or one that comes further up the window. This cafe can be lined to give more privacy and can be moved back and forth as needed. A traverse underdrape could also be used if complete privacy or light control is a consideration.

The point at which a drapery ties back is never arbitrary, though many use 30 inches from the floor if in doubt. The point can be determined by some physical aspect of the window such as sill or sash height, by the point at which a chair rail intersects the window, by positioning it where the rod for a half curtain comes, or by allowing the eye to tell you what is most agreeable to you. The length of the tie-back itself also influences the height. A short tie-back is attached to the wall lower than a long one. The length of the tie-back also determines how the drapery swags or drapes when tied back. Draperies can be tied back twice for an unusual effect, the top tie-back always being longer than the bottom one.

A point to remember is that a tied-back drapery, meeting in the center, always covers one-half to two-thirds of the window at all times. This limits the light and air and must be considered.

The tie-back itself can be made of fabric, straight or contoured, plain or trimmed, gathered or pleated. It can be chain or rope, with or without tassels. It should be hooked to the wall with two separate hooks to allow room for the bulk of the drapery. If the return is deep or an absolutely correct hang is desired, a plastic arm (devised for this purpose) should be used to form a return in the tie-back. Additional length must be allowed in the tie-back to compensate for this.

A hold-back is a wooden knob or shaped metal arm. These are usually attached on the frame of the window, controlling the drapery only at that point.

It is never practical to plan, as some people do, to use a drapery tied back in the daytime and dropped for privacy at night. A properly adjusted tied-back drapery is gently set into graceful draping folds. It will be slightly crushed at this point and will look wrinkled when it is released. Conversely, if this drapery is released, it must then be rearranged when it is tied back. Most people do not know how to do this or won't take the time, so the drapery never looks right. Plan your treatment one way or the other.

A variation of the tie-back drapery is the fold-back panel. It can be made perfectly flat or gathered on the rod. It resembles a tie-back in concept, but instead of using a rope or piece of fabric to tie it back, you simply make a loop on the front edge and lay it to the back side of the drapery where the loop fastens to a hook. This is more tailored and controlled than the usual tie-back drapery.

Cafe Curtains

Cafe curtains are short curtains that cover the lower portion of a window giving privacy, while the upper part remains uncovered to admit light. Sometimes they are used in tiers, one overlapping the other so the window can be completely covered if desired. They are usually hung on decorative rods with rings and moved by hand, though the upper tier may often traverse for convenience.

Most often thought of as cafes by the client is the flat piece of fabric with scallops cut out between the points where rings are attached. Cafe curtains can be scalloped and pleated, just pleated, or even gathered. They all serve the same purpose and can be attractively combined with tie-back draperies, shades, shutters, or valances. They can be made of almost any fabric, depending on the intended use.

The main point to remember is that if cafe curtains are used in tiers, the upper tier should overlap the lower by the amount of the scallop or heading and, correctly, the upper tier should project further to eliminate drag when they are moved.

Shades

Window shades are useful, versatile, and beautiful.

The ordinary window shade, as we used to know it, is still around. It rolls up and down, screens light, and gives privacy. It can also black out light, giving complete control of the lighting in a room, or it can screen the glare and let you see out. It can have different colors on its two sides. It can have different textures such as linen, moire, boucle, burlap, or just plain shiny vinyl. It can have fabric laminated to it. It can have scalloped edges with trimming and a valance at the top. It can be plain and straight so it will disappear when you roll it up. It can even move from bottom to top of the window.

Woven wood shades are coming into their own. Formerly considered just a commercial product, they are now being used at almost any type of window for almost any purpose. They can be the match-stick bamboo that many people visualize when you say woven wood. They can be the plain wood look in many variations of slat size and finish, or they can be the very decorative type that combines wood and various decorative threads to give almost any look or color desired. They can even be woven to your color specifications. They will fit standard windows, arched windows, or slanted windows. They can roll up, fold up, or even traverse like draperies. Try them alone or in combination with draperies.

The Roman shade has become the darling of the design field. Ideally it should do just what everyone expects, but it often doesn't. This shade is discussed later in the book (see the section Decorative Shades in the chapter on Special Window Treatments). Just be aware that it has limitations that do not show in the illustrations you see in decorating magazines. These must be explained before suggesting them to a client.

Austrian shades and balloon shades are also discussed at length in the same section as Roman shades. They are very decorative and have special uses.

Snap-on Rod Systems

The several types of snap-on draperies all use essentially the same type of rod with different carriers and different types of headings. They all have the advantage that the draperies may be unsnapped from the rod to be cleaned and in most cases will open flat when cleaned.

One type snaps to the rod and is pleated with knife pleats between the snaps. These pleats are pleated alternately front and back so the draperies look the same on both sides. Since this type is controlled so well, it stacks back in the smallest possible space. The fullness specified determines the stack, and the stack can be determined in advance. Obviously, these draperies must hang below the rod so the rod is exposed at all times. A pocket is usually indicated.

A similar type is the Ripplefold® or beauty pleat where the drapery has no pleats but rolls from front to back, also giving a uniform appearance front and back. The rod is also exposed when this is used.

Other draperies of this same type are controlled at the top with plastic devices sewn to the heading of the drapery and then snapped onto the rod. These give a very sharp accordian fold and stack back well. Many variations of this exist. Technical information is essential before specifying them.

The Safe Snap® system was devised for mental hospitals and can be used ceiling mount, wall mount, or hand or regular traverse. This system has the advantage of covering the rod if necessary. Pleats are formed by snapping two snaps on a double-snap carrier. Safe Snap® can also be used in an economy fashion without the pleats. This system is excellent for places where draperies must be laundered frequently. The slides move easily on the rod so the effort to move the drapery is not great. If great strain is put on it, the drapery comes unsnapped and is not torn.

Paneltrac®

Paneltrac® is a rod system that allows draperies to move like shoji screens. Flat panels of fabric are attached with velcro tape to sliding panels in the rod. The panels are weighted at the bottom. They can be used for the same purpose as traverse draperies, either center-draw or one-way. They can be used to divide a room or to create an illusion. The rod is fairly prominent and should be recessed or concealed in some way.

Tools for Selling

A very important tool that can be used in selecting the treatment is one that you can make for yourself—a scrapbook. By collecting pictures from various publications such as home decorating and interior design magazines, and from publications by hardware and trim manufacturers, you can eventually show pictures of almost any treatment you might want to use. You can also include pictures of your own installations.

Kits are available to show different top treatments and how each might look on the same window. If you are one of the unfortunate people who can't sketch well, any visual aid you have will be a help in your work.

Always attempt to see as many different types of window treatments as possible in actual installations. That way you can judge the final effect and describe it much better. Be observant everywhere you go and you will be surprised at how much you can learn.

CONSERVING ENERGY WITH WINDOW TREATMENTS

Ideally a house built to conserve energy would have no windows. Unfortunately, people want and need to see out. Even if there is not a view to enjoy, windows provide a means of remaining in contact with the outside world and certainly provide much pleasure from the sun while conserving energy with natural light.

But unless a window is sealed so that it cannot be opened, it may leak air around the edges. In any case it is sure to be a source of heat loss. Window glass that is very cold will attract the warm air in a room and cool it. This is the reason most radiators and registers are placed under windows (to the consternation of decorators). The air at its warmest rises in front of the windows and helps to warm the air around the cold glass. This warm air is also cooled by its contact with the cold glass and some of its effectiveness is lost. Shades, blinds, or draperies at the windows keep the contact to a minimum so the heated air can be more effective in the room. Even a sheer alone can create a dead air space that helps to insulate the window. A blind or shade heightens the effect.

If a lined overdrapery is closed over the sheers and blinds, a very effective seal is created and the warm air in the room is preserved. This acts in the same way as layering clothing for bodily warmth. Be sure that these layers of window treatment can be opened, for on a bright sunny day the heat of the sun coming through the window can do much to warm the room. Don't forget to extend the draperies on the walls for maximum exposure.

All treatments used for their insulating value should be placed on the outside of the window opening and extend past it in all directions if possible so that all edges of the glass are sealed. From a practical standpoint, however, the shade or blind might need to be mounted on the inside to allow the others to traverse more freely. If the expense of layered treatments becomes too great, a plain traverse drapery with a good insulating lining will achieve good results.

In reverse the same process helps to keep hot air out in summer. If draperies are closed while the house is still cool from the night and before the hot sun hits the windows, hot air will not enter the room through the glass. An insulating lining or blind that is light on the outside will reflect the sun away and reduce the build-up of heat. Be careful not to use dark colors in linings or blinds since they absorb the heat and may cause a build-up that will cause the windows to pop out. Sometimes draperies on large expanses of thermal glass must have air space at the top and bottom to allow the circulation of air to prevent this excessive heat build-up.

MEASURING
AND ESTIMATING

HOW TO MEASURE FOR DRAPERIES

Measuring for draperies is simple if you do not try to make all necessary allowances as you go. This is one way to make errors without realizing it.

A steel tape must be used for all measurements. A 12-foot tape is good, 16 is better, and it is advisable on large, commercial installations to have a 20-foot tape. Any time you have to add two measurements, there is a good chance for error. Yardsticks or cloth tapes are much too inaccurate for good measurement. Measure in inches—multiplying feet and adding inches can be dangerous. Inches is what your workroom and installation person use.

General Procedure

Make a sketch of the window or wall and note all measurements on it as actual measurements. Note whether carpet or tile is down, and if not, give actual to-the-floor measurements so that all allowances can be made. Each person eventually develops his or her own shortcuts to this method, but it is still the best since it eliminates the need to wonder how many inches between windows or to the wall or molding. Your sketch will allow you to change your treatment without remeasuring since all necessary measurements will be there. See illustration, p. 36.

Any particular feature must be noted, such as a crown mold at the ceiling; woodwork with extra deep projection; radiators or convectors present. In the latter case a sketch is particularly useful since these are not always exactly centered under the window area. Never assume that all windows in a room are the same size. Measure! It is not uncommon for windows on the sides of houses to be a different width from those on the front or for those on the back to vary also. Never assume that all window mulls on commercial jobs are the same size. They frequently vary at the ends of sections of window walls and are often different on the sides of buildings.

On doors, if a drapery is rod-to-rod, the position of the handle in relation to the glass must be noted and how far above and below and to the side of the glass a drapery could go. It is also essential to know whether there is a door closer and where it is located.

If possible it is good to know the type of wall or ceiling involved. Draperies can be installed in a brick wall or a dropped ceiling, but it takes a different kind of drill or fastener from those used in other types of installations. You must know what is under a dropped ceiling and whether there is a metal grid for support.

If the measurement is ceiling to floor, it should be taken in three or more places—each side and in the center and, on very wide spans, at intermediate points. In homes, if measurement is ceiling to floor, it should be taken in several places also. If there is considerable variation, this should be pointed out to the client before the draperies are made. In older homes it is not unusual for windows to be set crooked in the walls or to vary in height. This should be checked and perhaps a valance should be used to disguise the fact.

Reusing Existing Rods

If rods are in place but must be removed, this must be noted since it involves an extra charge. If rods are up and are to be reused, the type of installation must be noted (wall-ceiling, for example). The width measurement is the face of the rod from one end to the other. Be sure to specify that this is rod width so the workroom will know returns and overlaps must be added. The length is from the top of the bracket that holds the rod to the appropriate length on regular traverse rods and from the bottom of the ring on decorative rods.

If you measure the drapery itself, you must first be sure that it is the right size. If it is a pleated drapery, you must have a measurement across the top where the pleats are. You must also indicate if this is the measurement for one-half pair. If you also measure across the bottom at the hem, the number of widths used in the existing drapery can be calculated. Don't forget the length; measure down the side hem. It would be helpful if the workroom could see at least one panel of the drapery to judge the quality of workmanship.

Unusual Windows

In all unusual installations accuracy is absolutely necessary. A corner window must be shown as such and preferably an illustration drawn. An allowance for rods must be made in the corner so it must be noted if one way is more desirable than another. See illustration, p. 37.

The measurements for a cathedral or sloped-top window are vital. A variation of one inch can make the whole drapery hang completely wrong. The distance from top to bottom must be shown on each side and in the exact center. The exact width must be shown. If at all possible a template of the slope should be taken. If not, very accurate measurements will allow the workroom to make one since this is essential for checking the finished drapery. See the section on Slanted-Top Draperies in the chapter on Problem Windows.

The same thing is true of a curved-top window. Most such windows are made with an exact half circle at the top, but this is not always true. Therefore, a template or exact measurements must be given. These include the length at the high point or center, the length where the circle breaks, the distance from this point to the high point, and a template if the distance from the break to the top is not equal to one-half the width at that point. See the section on Curved-Top Draperies in the chapter on Problem Windows.

A bay window must have exact measurements. They must be from the exact break in the wall, and window sizes in relation to wall space must be shown. Measurements must include length, of course, whether long or short. Each wing of the bay must be measured separately as wings are not always alike. The center or back portion must be a separate measurement. The width across the opening of the bay must be given and the distance from this point to the back center of the window is necessary. If you have a protractor for measuring angles, it is wise to use it. See illustration, p. 38.

A bow window needs the measurement around the arc, and from the arc to the opening at specific points. See illustration, p. 38.

Above all, accuracy and diagrams are the important things to remember when measuring. These can make the difference between success and disaster. If your measurements are wrong, the drapery will be wrong. On large or difficult installations it is a good idea to send two people at different times to measure as a check to reduce errors.

Covering Contingencies

At this point in a job, it is most important to discuss with your client exactly how the drapery is to be treated so there will be no surprises. If the client wants something that is not best, it is wise to explain this and why. If the client insists, you have covered yourself.

In all dealings, everyone must know exactly what is expected so the workroom will not be left holding the bag. However, if you are a workroom measuring for a designer, do not suggest changes to a client unless you have been asked to do so. Take all measurements, note what would be best, and discuss it with the designer, who will then contact the client.

The proper measurement taken in the proper way is the first step to a successful drapery installation.

GUIDE FOR MEASURING

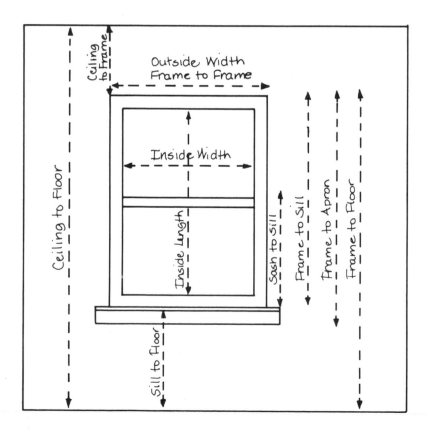

If the window is close to a wall or some feature such as a fireplace or bookshelf, this distance should be measured. If there is a crown mold, indicate this, and give measurement from below the crown mold to the top of the frame and to the floor. If the frame projects more than one-half inch from the wall, this should be noted. Show the position of radiators, vents, and light switches.

WINDOWS MEETING IN CORNER

Treated with two one-way panels.

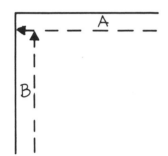

One panel all the way to corner.

One panel to meet other rod. Deduct for projection of rod.

A—measure from where you want drapery to start on wall to other window wall. Deduct 1 inch for clearance. Designate right panel.

B—measure from where you want drapery to start on wall into corner. Deduct 4 inches for projection of other rod plus 1 inch for clearance. Designate left panel.

WINDOWS OF UNEQUAL SIZE MEETING IN CORNER

If one window is considerably larger than the other, a pair and a panel can be used.

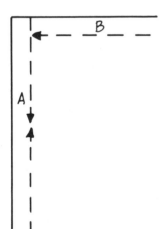

A—measure from where drapery starts on wall to other window wall. Deduct 1 inch for clearance. Designate one pair.

B—measure from where drapery starts on wall to other window wall. Deduct 4 inches for rod projection and 1 inch for clearance. Designate right panel.

CORNER WINDOWS WITH WALL SPACE IN CORNER

Treat with three panels. Extend on side to equal wall space so draperies will draw to center of window. Set up with two traverse rods with cords on opposite sides.

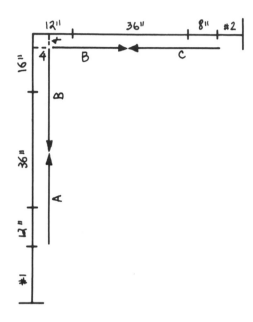

Rods project 4 inches in each direction in corner. Deduct from wall space to determine extension on other side of window.

#1—16 inches − 4 inches = 12 inches
Extension on left.

#2—12 inches − 4 inches = 8 inches
Extension on right.

Panel A—12 inches + 18 inches = 30 inches
Wall plus ½ window.

Panel B—18 inches + 12 inches + 8 inches + 18 inches = 56 inches
½ two windows plus two wall spaces less 4 inches each.

Panel C—18 inches + 8 inches = 26 inches
Wall plus ½ window.

BAY WINDOW

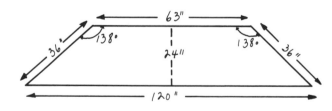

1. Measure the flat surface of the wall.
2. Actual dimensions of window with amount of wall space between can also be shown.
3. Do not assume that both sides are alike. They frequently are not.
4. Angle is not essential if all other measurements are correct.

BOW WINDOW

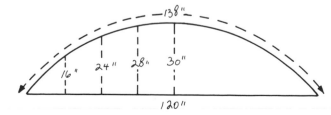

1. Bow windows are seldom half circles.
2. Measurements at four points allows the workroom to calculate the arc.
3. A template of half the bow insures perfect fit.

HOW TO INTERPRET MEASUREMENTS FOR THE WORKROOM

When measuring, write down actual measurements in all cases. This is for your own reference and should be kept with your own file on the job.

When transmitting your figures to the workroom, you must give them the finished drapery sizes you desire and indicate how draperies are to be installed.

For instance, you have measured a window that is 40 inches wide frame to frame and 82 inches long frame to carpet, with plenty of room at sides and top.

> To allow for extension with 2½ fullness
> Divide measurement by 5 (8 inches)
> Add this extension to each side (2 × 8)
>
> 40 inches window and trim
> 16 inches extension
> ‾‾‾‾‾‾
> 56 inches rod width

Many workrooms are accustomed to working with rod widths and adding for returns and overlaps. If you prefer to give finished width, figure as follows:

> 56 inches rod width
> 8 inches returns (4 inches each side for single traverse)
> 4 inches overlaps (standard on all traverse draperies)
> ‾‾‾‾‾‾
> 68 inches total finished width

Returns and Overlaps

You must have a full understanding of returns and overlaps before you can interpret your own measurements properly for the workroom.

The RETURN of a drapery is the part that covers the space from the end of the rod back to the wall. The OVERLAP is the part that rides on the master carrier and closes over the other side. The amount added to the width of the drapery to compensate for this is explained below.

Most traverse rods overlap a total of 4 inches at the center. This means that each half of the drapery must have 2 inches added to compensate. The projection or return of the average rod is 3½ inches to 4 inches, so this amount must be added to each half of the drapery to allow for this. Consequently, when figuring the finished, pleated width of a pair of draperies, 12 inches must be added to the pair. This is designated as FINISHED width as opposed to ROD width or window width.

When using double traverse draperies, it is not necessary to add returns to the underdrapery. An allowance of only 4 inches for overlaps is made. However, the returns on the overdrapery must be increased to 6 inches on each side to allow for the projection of the double brackets. Therefore, the allowance for returns and overlaps on an overdrapery for double traverse would be 6 inches + 6 inches + 4 inches, or a total of 16 inches. Allowances for one-way panels would be half this amount.

> Regular traverse add 12 inches per pair
> Under traverse add 4 inches per pair
> Over traverse add 16 inches per pair

One-way traverse add 6 inches per panel
One-way under traverse add 2 inches per panel
One-way over traverse add 8 inches per panel

There must always be at least 2 inches between underdrapery and overdrapery or between drapery and valance to eliminate drag when traversing.

On this same window you want your drapery to mount on the wall 4 inches above the frame to hide heading and hardware from the outside.

The finished length of the drapery would be 86 inches.

If you specify 86-inch-long wall mount, pins would be set 2 inches from the top of the heading, thus causing the top of the drapery to be ½ inch above the rod and clear the floor by ½ inch.

If a decorative rod is used, we do not recommend going above the top of the frame because it creates too many horizontal lines.

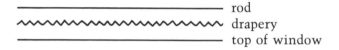

It is best to have finished length the distance from the frame to the floor (less ½ inch for clearance). Thus drapery and window frame are at the same height and the rod is just above.

Types of Draperies

Over- and Underdraperies. The underdrapery is always made ½ inch shorter so there is no chance that it will show under the bottom of the over-drapery. Also if it is a traverse drapery, you should specify that no returns are needed.

When a valance is used over a double traverse drapery, an additional 1½ inches should be deducted from the underdrapery and the pins should be set at ½ inch. This allows the underdrapery to traverse under the rod, thus giving additional clearance between the two draperies.

Wall-to-Wall. If a return is desired for this kind of drapery, the rod width must be 1½ inches less than the wall-to-wall measure to allow for returns to be made.

Ceiling-to-Floor. Allow 1 inch clearance (½ inch each, top and bottom) from your shortest measurement. (All ceiling-to-floor measurements should be taken in at least three places since ceilings and floors are rarely parallel for the entire distance.) For wall mounting, set pins at 2 inches. For ceiling mounting, set them at 1½ inches.

Recess. A drapery hung in a recess is treated as a ceiling mount and is measured the same way. However, in a recessed installation or one hanging to a convector, deduct only ¼ inch for length allowance if the fabric is stable. The drapery should hang as close as possible to the sill or convector since the illusion created by light coming under it makes it appear both short and uneven.

Off-center Pair. If a drapery is an off-center pair, it is specified as such, but the measurement of each panel should be given and indicate whether it is left or right. A sketch would be helpful. See illustration p. 41. Remember that an off-center pair will open back only as far as the smaller panel can open unless the pair is installed on two one-way rods.

Multiple-draw. This means that by drawing one cord, two or more draperies may be opened or closed at once. To be effective all window sizes should be the same, although distances between do not have to be equal. A sketch is an absolute necessity for fabrication of the rod. Window sizes and wall spaces must be clearly noted and an overall measurement given as in off-center pairs. See illustration p. 42.

OFF-CENTER PAIR

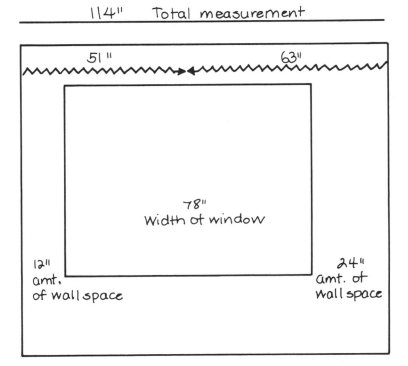

Left panel

½ width of window plus amount of wall space—

39 inches + 12 = 51 inches

Right panel

½ width of window plus amount of wall space—

39 inches + 24 inches = 63 inches

Total width of pair
63 inches + 51 inches = 114 inches

To equalize spaces between pleats, the left panel would have three widths. The right panel would have 3¾ widths.

MULTIPLE-DRAW

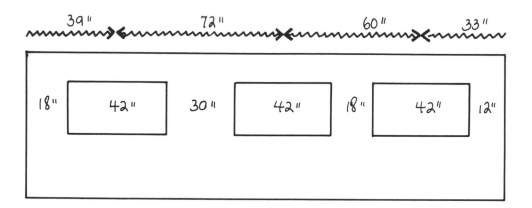

Left panel 2½ widths
Left center panel 4 widths
Right center panel 3½ widths
Right panel 2 widths

Returns and overlaps (6 inches) would be added to the left and right panels. Two overlaps (4 inches) would be added to each of the other panels.

If a drapery is a single panel, the *direction of draw* should be specified. This is indicated by the side on which the drapery stacks when open or where the cord is located. A left draw closes to the right and stacks on the left when open. A right draw closes to the left and stacks on the right when open. This is usually indicated on a plan or drawing by a squiggly line ending in an arrow that points in the direction that the panel closes. For a pair, draw two lines with two arrows meeting in the center.

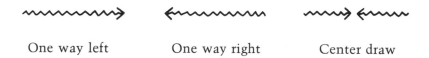

One way left   One way right   Center draw

Any special window—slanted, curved, bay, or bow—should have sketches included, and all measurements indicated.

Long and Short Windows. If there are long and short windows in the same room where the draperies will be made at different lengths, you must tell your workroom how they are placed in relation to each other. This is more important when you are using a print and want the pattern to be in line as the eye travels from one window to the other. Details such as this make all the difference in a fine custom drapery.

Door Curtains. When specifying door curtains, go above and below the glass at least far enough to conceal hems and headings. Three inches at top and bottom is usually enough. One inch on each side of the glass is sufficient and probably as far as you can go to avoid door knobs and the like. When giving the workroom information, be sure to specify that this length includes 1-inch headings (or whatever size headings you want).

Headings on Shirred Curtains. All shirred curtains look better with headings if they are exposed at the top. The heading is the part that projects above the rod at the top. One inch is traditional, but a drapery made from a fabric heavier than a sheer can have up to 4 inches. In this case the rod pocket should be as small as possible to let the rod slide through. If there is too much slack in it, the heading will sag. Shirr-on-rod draperies "take up" when gathered. A one-half inch allowance on sheers is usually sufficient, but heavier fabrics may take up as much as one inch.

Pleats

Pleats control the fullness of a drapery at the top so that the fullness is evenly spaced across the width of the window. Pleats also control how the drapery will hang and traverse. When giving your instructions to the workroom, specify the type of pleat.

Customary workroom procedure is to put five pleats in each width of 45-inch to 54-inch fabric. This means that the pleats will be spaced from 2½ inches to 5 inches apart depending on the fullness used. The amount of fabric in each pleat would vary from 4 inches to 7 inches. The method for arriving at these figures is given under workroom procedure, but since charts are available, it is unnecessary to perform these calculations each time.

Most pleats are formed in essentially the same way. The excess fabric not actually needed to cover the rod is divided by the number of pleats to be used. This amount is stitched to form a pleat and is then finished according to the type of pleat desired. There are several different kinds of pleats. They all serve the same purpose—to control fullness—but they are used for different reasons other than personal preference.

Pinch Pleat. This pleat is used most often because it traverses best. The pleat is stitched and divided into three equal sections. It is pinched together at the bottom and tacked through all thicknesses at about ½ inch from the bottom of the crinoline.

French Pleat. A french pleat is formed in the same way as a pinch pleat, stitched and divided into three sections. However, these sections are stitched or tacked in such a way as to separate them for the entire length of the pleat, forming three fingerlike projections. These pleats are attractive and hang well, perhaps best of all kinds of pleats, but when traversed, they meet too quickly and do not stack well. There is no point in specifying french pleats if the drapery goes under a valance or in a pocket. They will not be seen and a pinch pleat will traverse better.

Cartridge Pleat. This pleat is stitched and rounded into a cylinder by rolling extra crinoline and inserting it into the pleat. It frequently is used with wider crinoline (up to 6 inches) and looks especially good on long draperies. The pleats are somewhat heavy to traverse well.

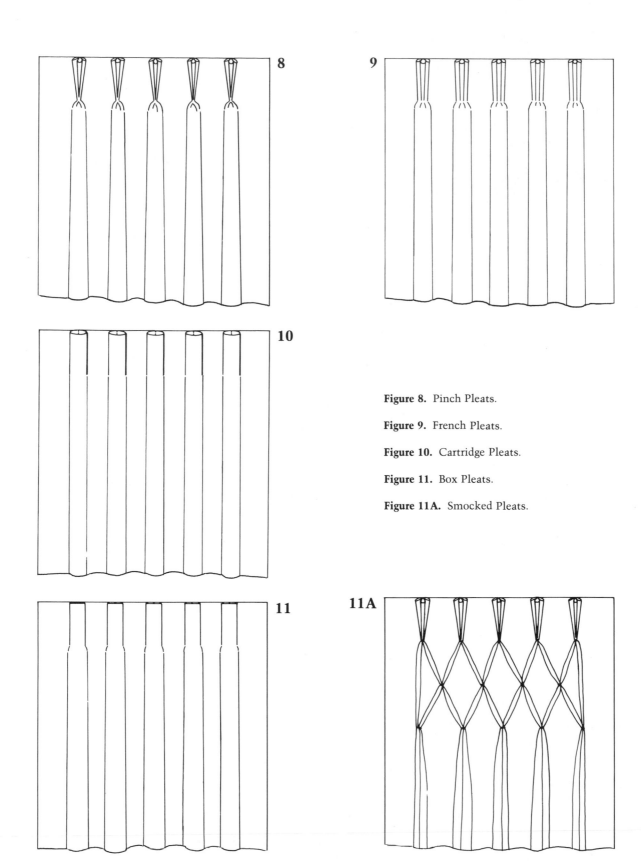

Figure 8. Pinch Pleats.

Figure 9. French Pleats.

Figure 10. Cartridge Pleats.

Figure 11. Box Pleats.

Figure 11A. Smocked Pleats.

Box Pleat. The box pleat is stitched, flattened, and tacked. It should never be expected to traverse. It could be used for stationary tie-back draperies or for side draperies that remain stationary.

Smocked Pleats. These are another variation. They also do not traverse. They require slightly more than triple fullness and look best with 6-inch crinoline. The pleats are formed like box pleats, then tacked to each other top and bottom and pulled together between to give a smocked or diamond effect. These are very effective on stationary sheers where the heading will be exposed.

Pleats to Coincide with a Pattern. A drapery can be pleated to coincide with a pattern provided the pattern is compatible with the fullness used. This is most often done with a striped pattern of some kind. Stripes do not naturally fall into pleats or spaces and will vary from one to the other across the heading.

The drapery systems that do not have pleats or that have knife pleats are discussed under a separate heading because they are seldom used except under special commercial conditions and the methods of calculation and fabrication are quite different from conventional draperies.

HOW TO ESTIMATE YARDAGE

Estimating yardage is as simple as taking the finished length of the drapery in inches, adding the allowance for hems and headings, multiplying by the number of widths in a pair, and dividing by 36 inches to get the number of yards, rounding out to the next full figure.

Before trying this simple process, read this entire chapter so you will know that in order to estimate properly, certain things must be established:

1. The length and width of the space to be covered.
2. Whether or not to extend on the side of the window opening and how much.
3. The fullness desired.
4. Whether the drapery will be lined.
5. Size of hems and headings.
6. The width of the fabric.
7. Whether the fabric is solid or printed.
8. If printed, the size of the repeat.
9. Whether there will be a top treatment.

Length and Width

The length and width must be measured before the fabrication of the drapery is done. However, for estimating purposes, these dimensions can be taken from a properly scaled plan.

A. There are only three correct stopping places for the bottom length of a drapery.
   a. To the sill or convector. This is the least desirable since this length is at eye level when you are seated and light coming under the hem will

be distorted by the folds and make the hem appear uneven, although it
may be absolutely straight.
    b. To the apron, the wood, or the metal trim at the bottom of cased win-
dows. Be sure the drapery is at least ½ inch longer so there will be no
chance the apron will show under it.
    c. To the floor with proper allowance. (Underdraperies should always be
½ inch shorter.)
B. At the top draperies can be installed:
    a. Within the window recess (not recommended because there will pos-
sibly be light-strike (light coming in around the edges) at the top and
sides and almost certainly at the bottom, causing an uneven appearance).
    b. On the wood or metal trim (not recommended because the heading
and hardware may show from the outside or the wood facing may be
split by the installation).
    c. Two to 4 inches above the frame or casing.
    d. To the ceiling or crown molding.
    e. At special heights for installing under top treatments or on decorative
rods.

Extending the Drapery

It is frequently desirable to extend the draperies beyond the actual window
dimension.

A. When draperies are opened, they do not disappear. They must stack
somewhere and, if not extended, will cover a certain amount of glass
area. Extending allows a maximum of light and ventilation.
B. Extending also eliminates the problem of light-strike.
C. In certain cases, in order to keep all fullness the same, some windows
will be extended more than others.

When stacked back to the furthest possible point, a panel will cover approximately one inch for each pleat plus the amount of overlap. All you need to
remember to be sure to clear the glass area is that the following formula works:

For double fullness, divide width of glass area by 6.
For two-and-one-half fullness, divide by 5.
For triple fullness, divide by 4.

Add this amount to each side of the window measurement and calculate the
correct number of widths according to the fullness desired. If the draperies
come very close to the wall on each side, extend them to cover the area wall-
to-wall. Or if an uneven amount of wall makes it look awkward, compensate
by extending uneven amounts and making an off-center pair.

Fullness

Fullness in a drapery is the excess fabric in width over the amount needed to
cover the rod. This is the amount included in the pleats or gathered on the rod.
Fullness determines how the drapery looks. If it is too full, making the spaces

too close together, and the pleats too large, it cannot stack back well when traversed. If it is too skimpy, it has a tendency to duck under between pleats. Short draperies can get by with less fullness than long ones. Gathered or shirred curtains can use less than those that are pleated (unless they are very sheer). Very long draperies will look very skimpy with double fullness, while short ones will not look bad at all.

Terminology of Fullness. There is a certain amount of confusion over the correct terminology for fullness. Figures of 50%, 100%, and 250% have come to mean nothing since these percentages are used so differently by so many people. Forget percentages and refer to fullness as double, two-and-one-half, or triple (or other multiples, if you desire). This means that the amount of fabric used is equivalent to that multiple of the rod width plus the allowance for returns, overlaps, and hems.

When calculated in this way, double fullness will have pleats spaced about 4 inches apart; for two-and-one-half, they will be spaced about 3½ inches, and for triple, approximately 3 inches. All will have 4 to 6 inches in each pleat, depending on the fullness used.

1. *Double Fullness* is adequate for most commercial installations (other than very elegant offices, clubs, and the like). Your good judgment should be used, depending on the weight of the fabric, whether or not the drapery is lined, and if it is not lined, whether glare will be a problem. The fuller an unlined drapery is made, the more light control it has.

2. *Two-and-one-half Fullness* is the most practical and has the best appearance for lined, custom, traverse draperies. There is enough fullness to look good and the pleats are spaced far enough apart to traverse well.

When figuring side panels, a spacing of 3½ inches between pleats, or two-and-one-half fullness, is good, allowing nice full pleats. The chart on side panels shows how much space each panel will cover if pleated this way. Of course, if a specified amount must be covered that differs from this, then the number of widths to be used must be figured according to the regular chart.

3. *Triple Fullness* should be used only on lightweight fabrics since pleats are large and spaced very close together. It is best to use them for stationary draperies as they do not traverse well and take up a lot of room for stacking.

How to Figure Fullness. A chart included on p. 50 gives the number of widths needed for different fullnesses in 36-inch, 48-inch, and 54-inch fabrics. Having ascertained how full you want the drapery and how much space you want to cover, find the rod size on the chart to see how many widths of fabric you need.

1. *Easy calculation without the chart.* If you do not have the chart available, an approximation can be reached for 45-inch to 54-inch fabrics in the following way:

> For double fullness, divide rod width by 22 inches.
> For two-and-one-half fullness, divide rod width by 18 inches.
> For triple fullness, divide rod width by 15 inches.

Always go to the next figure if there is a remainder. See the actual charts for the number of widths on different sizes of fabric.

2. *Regular method to figure fullness.* A drapery that is to have two-and-one-half fullness on a 48-inch rod is figured as follows:

```
      48 inches
×      2½
     120 inches
+     12 inches  for returns and overlaps
     132 inches
+     12 inches  for side hems per pair
     144 inches  total fabric needed
```

Divide this amount by 48 inches and it would require three widths of 48-inch fabric. You would also use three widths of 45-inch or 54-inch fabric since the difference is so small.

To figure triple fullness with 48-inch fabric on a rod that measures 78 inches:

```
      78 inches
×      3
     234 inches
+     12 inches  for returns and overlaps
     246 inches
+     12         for side hems per pair
     258 inches  total fabric needed
```

Divide by 48 inches and you have 5.3. You will use five widths, dropping the remainder if it is under ½, adding one width if it is over.

On a much larger window the number of widths of fabric to be used with various widths of material might be varied, though this is not usually done since the only difference is in the amount of fullness in the pleats when using 45 inches, 48 inches, and 54 inches. The spacing remains the same for all three. (For further explanation see the section Pleating for the Workroom in the chapter on Fullness and Pleating.) If having the draperies look full is the most important consideration, keeping the spaces small is the deciding factor. If cost is most important, cutting back the number of widths is the best solution.

If it is necessary to figure widths on 60-inch, 72-inch, or 118-inch fabric, the procedure is exactly like the one just described.

Assume that the rod is 84 inches wide and you want two-and-one-half fullness:

```
      84 inches
×      2½
     210 inches
+     12 inches  for returns and overlaps
     222 inches
+     12 inches  for side hems per pair
     234 inches  total fabric needed
```

Divide this amount by 60 inches to get 3.9 or 4 widths per pair.
Divide this amount by 72 inches to get 3.25 or 3 widths per pair.
Divide this amount by 118 inches to get 1.9 or 2 widths per pair.
(Always go to the next full width if the remainder is over ½. Drop back one if it is under ½)
If the remainder is exactly ½, go to the next full width.

Fabric of 118 inches can be railroaded or used with its width as the length of the drapery if the drapery does not finish longer than 100 inches. The advantage to this is that there will be no vertical seams in the panels. To figure yardage in this case, multiply the rod size times the fullness needed, add allowances, and divide by yards.

$$
\begin{array}{rl}
84 & \text{inches} \\
\times \quad 2\tfrac{1}{2} & \\
\hline
210 & \text{inches} \\
+ \quad 12 & \text{inches} \quad \text{returns and overlaps} \\
\hline
222 & \text{inches} \\
+ \quad 12 & \text{inches} \quad \text{side hems per pair} \\
\hline
234 & \text{inches} \quad \text{amount of fabric needed} \\
\div \quad 36 & \text{inches} \quad \text{inches in a yard} \\
\hline
6.5 & \quad \text{yards needed—order 7 yards}
\end{array}
$$

Always remember, if you plan to railroad a fabric, that the fabric width must be equal to the finished length of the drapery plus allowances for hems and headings (or equal to the cut length).

Balancing Fullness. There are times when you have two windows in a room where they will appear not to have balanced fullness if the table is strictly adhered to. Balanced fullness simply means that the spacing between the pleats is the same on both pairs.

1. In the same room you have two windows, one 54 inches wide and the other 97 inches wide.
2. The table calls for three widths for the 54-inch window and six widths for the 97-inch window.
3. Divide 54 inches by three and you will see that each pleated width will cover 18 inches.
4. Now, if you divide 97 inches by six, the number of widths called for in the table, you will see that each width will cover 16.1 inches. The pleats would be closer together and the 97-inch drapery would appear to be fuller.
5. To compensate for this, multiply six widths times 18 inches to equal 108 inches. Extend the 97-inch window 5½ inches more on each side and the pleats will be spaced exactly the same.

This would be necessary only if the windows are placed so the eye can easily see both at once and compare them. At opposite ends of a room or under valances this is not necessary.

FULLNESS CHART

# Widths	36-inch Fabric			48-inch Fabric			54-inch Fabric			
	Double	2½	Triple	Double	2½	Triple	Double	2½	Triple	
2	28–32	24–28	20–24	30–44	30–36	28–32	to 48	to 40	to 34	2
3	33–48	29–42	25–36	45–66	37–54	33–48	49–70	41–60	35–51	3
4	49–64	43–56	37–48	67–88	54–72	49–64	71–100	61–80	52–68	4
4	49–64	43–56	37–48	67–88	54–72	49–64	71–100	61–80	52–68	4
5	65–80	57–70	49–60	89–110	73–90	65–80	101–125	81–100	69–85	5
6	81–96	71–84	61–72	110–132	91–108	81–96	126–150	101–120	86–102	6
7	97–112	85–98	73–84	133–154	109–126	97–112	151–175	121–140	103–119	7
8	113–128	99–112	85–96	155–176	127–144	113–128	176–200	141–160	120–136	8
9	129–144	113–126	97–108	177–198	145–162	129–144	201–225	161–180	137–153	9
10	145–160	127–140	109–120	199–220	163–180	145–160	226–250	181–200	154–170	10
11	161–176	141–154	121–132	221–242	181–198	161–176	251–275	201–220	171–187	11
12	177–192	155–168	133–144	243–264	199–216	177–192	276–300	221–240	188–204	12
13	193–208	169–182	145–156	265–286	217–234	193–208	301–325	241–260	205–221	13
14	209–224	183–196	157–168	287–308	235–252	209–224	326–350	261–280	222–238	14
15	225–240	197–210	169–180	309–330	253–270	225–240	351–375	281–300	239–255	15

Lining the Drapery

Whether the drapery is to be lined or unlined is influenced by several things discussed in those chapters. Yardages may be calculated differently but can all be figures on an unlined basis. Do not forget to add lining yardages (same as face fabric in most cases). Reasons and methods for figuring separately are outlined on p. 65. A discussion of linings is on p. 64.

Hems and Headings

The size of the hems and headings determines the cut length of the drapery. To arrive at the cut length, add the amount you need for a double hem of the size you specify (always use double hems except under special conditions) and whatever is needed for headings. Under ordinary conditions with double 4-inch hems and headings, adding 18 inches for cut lengths will be safe for solid fabrics, either lined or unlined. (Further information on this is in the chart on p. 57.) Just remember that if hems and headings vary from the standard, cut lengths will vary.

Width of the Fabric

The width of the fabric in inches determines how many widths of fabric must be used in a pair of draperies. A width of fabric is one piece of fabric the proper cut length for making the drapery. It could conceivably be called a length, but it would be a little strange to speak of a 5-length pair. It might also be called a panel, but since a pair has two panels and a one-way draw has one panel, we would not want to speak of a 5-panel panel. Therefore drapery workrooms speak of widths regardless of whether the fabric is 36 inches, 45 inches, 48 inches, 54 inches, 60 inches, or 118 inches wide. The tables included cover fabric widths of 36 inches, 45 inches, 48 inches, and 54 inches, which are standard. Other widths, such as 60 inches, 72 inches, and 118 inches, must be calculated according to instructions in the section on Fullness of this chapter.

Solid and Printed Fabrics

The instructions above hold true for solid fabrics. Your cut length will vary according to the pattern repeat of a printed fabric.

Pattern Repeats. If the fabric being used has a pattern repeat, this must be taken into consideration when figuring yardage. The repeat of a pattern is the vertical distance between one point on a pattern and the same point where the pattern reoccurs vertically.

Figure 12. Pattern repeat—dotted lines show three possible reference points.

The reason for figuring this is so patterns will line up or match when widths are sewed together.

If this were not done, the following situation would exist.

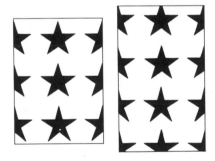

Since most prints match at the selvages, it is essential to allow for repeats.

To figure yardage with a pattern repeat,

1. First determine the cut length: Assume it is 98 inches.
2. Divide by pattern repeat—25¼ inches.

$$
\begin{array}{r}
3.8 \\
25.25 \overline{)98.00000} \\
75.75 \\
\overline{22.250} \\
20.200 \\
\overline{2.050}
\end{array}
$$

3. If the pattern repeat does not divide evenly into the cut length, you must go to the next number of repeats for your cut lengths. In this case, use 4

pattern repeats

$$25.25$$
$$\times \quad 4$$
$$\overline{101.00}\text{—cut length}$$

3 inches will be lost in cutting.

There are times when 18 to 20 inches or more will be lost with each cut. If you have a great many widths, much yardage can be lost. If cost is a factor, it might be wise to consider another fabric with a repeat more compatible to cut length.

Designers or architects are inclined to say if you ask the repeat, "Oh, figure an average repeat" (there is none), or "It doesn't make any difference; it's a big repeat," or some such remark. These must be ignored. A big repeat can work this way.

Take a cut length of 101 inches with a 36-inch repeat.
Divide cut length by repeat.
$36 \sqrt{101}$ 2+ or 3 repeats will be needed.
Multiply number of repeats by repeat in inches:
$36 \times 3 = 108$ inches—there will be a cutting loss of only 7 inches.
However, if the cut length is 115 inches, see what happens:
$36 \sqrt{115}$ 3+ or 4 repeats needed,
$36 \times 4 = 144$ inches $-$ 115 inches—29 inches will be wasted. ⅔ yds.

In the latter case if the pattern repeat had been smaller, or only 20 inches, the loss would be have been minimal.

$20 \sqrt{115}$ 5+ or 6 repeated needed.
$20 \times 6 = 120$ inches—5 inches only would be wasted.

It is obvious that pattern repeats must be considered when figuring yardage.

Dropped Pattern. There is such a thing as a dropped pattern. This means that the pattern does not match itself directly across the fabric, but matches at a point further down the edge, usually about halfway between the repeats on the opposite edge. Unfortunately, this is usually not mentioned on samples or in price books and may cause a lack of fabric when cutting takes place. If you know that it is a drop match, the only safe thing to do is to add one extra pattern repeat for every other cut.

Patterns That do not Match. Some patterns do not match at all because some of the design has been left out when it was printed. This happens when a print designed for a 48-inch fabric is printed on 45-inch goods, or when one designed for 54-inch fabric is printed on 48-inch goods, and so on. In some cases it can be matched by moving farther over into the fabric, thus losing some of the fullness, but in most cases you would be losing far too much to make it feasible. In most cases the best that can be done is to line up the design so that it occurs in the same place in each width. Properly made draperies have their seams at the back of the pleats, and the lack of match is not too obvious if there is sufficient fullness in the drapery.

There are other patterns that may not match that, oddly enough, frequently occur in very expensive material. Crewel embroidery is one. Since this work is done by hand, not only will the actual size of the design vary, but even the colors may be slightly different where it should match. This would be especially obvious on a cornice. It is wise to be sure the client is aware of this. Hand-printed or silk screen prints may have the same problem owing to the placing of the blocks or screens and the amount of dye used. These are not considered to be flaws, but are characteristic of such fabrics.

Ordering Fabrics with Repeats. A word of caution is necessary when ordering fabrics with pattern repeats.

1. Be sure to order enough since nonmatching dye lots are particularly noticeable in printed fabrics.
2. Be sure to specify cut lengths, because if you do not, it is fairly standard to assume that they would be approximately three yards each. As previously shown, this could wreck your yardage figures.
3. It is particularly necessary to order all yardage needed at the same time in printed fabrics since not only dye lots but also pattern repeats can vary from one bolt to another. The reasons for this are known to manufacturers, but all you really need to know is that it *can* happen. This is why pattern repeats are given as approximate and, once again, why you should never figure down to the inch when ordering fabrics.

Border Prints

A very special kind of yardage requirement is encountered with border prints. Some very beautiful and exciting prints of this type exist, but to make effective draperies, certain cautions must be observed.

If the border is on only one side of the fabric, the fabric panels must be reversed to make the border appear in the center on each side of a pair. Be sure to check the pattern to see whether it can be turned upside down. If not, the only way this could be done is to cut the border off of one side of the width and sew it back on the other side, sometimes slightly distorting the pattern where the seam occurs.

If there is a border on both sides of the fabric, you must decide whether you want the border on the return and, in multiple-width draperies, whether you want double borders showing where the widths are seamed. One or both borders can be cut out, but remember that this reduces the amount of fullness in your drapery and additional widths must be allowed. These borders that are cut out can be used to continue the border across the bottom of the drapery or as trim on cornices, valances, or other draperies made from plain fabrics.

In using borders as trim, remember there must be some left for a seam when you cut them off.

Top Treatments

If there is to be a top treatment, yardages must be calculated separately and will be discussed in that section on p. 80.

NOW YOU ARE READY TO ESTIMATE YARDAGE

Take the amount of space you have decided to cover, including extensions, if desired. (The chart compensates for returns and overlaps.)

Find the size on your table to determine the
    number of widths per pair or panel.   _____

Determine finished length of drapery
    (add for hems and headings, allow
    for pattern repeat if applicable).   _____

Multiply by number of widths per pair   × _____

Amount needed in inches.   _____

Divide by 36 inches.   ÷ _____

Amount needed in yards (round out figure).   _____

When ordering fabrics, never order the exact number of inches needed. If the fabric is stretched when it is rolled and measured (as sometimes happens when it is done by machine), you will be lacking some inches when it is cut.

If the fabric comes from out of town or has a dye lot to be matched (as most do), it may be impossible to get more as soon as you need it. Cut lengths should be specified when ordering to help the inspector estimate yardage needed when filling your order.

Unless extra fabric has been allowed when figuring, it is best to inspect the fabric for flaws before cutting it. If this is done, a good cutter can frequently work flaws into hems or headings and save ordering more fabric. Manufacturers will not accept cut goods for return.

When figuring large jobs of 50 yards or more, you must figure a cutting loss of 10% unless lengths are quite short. In that case 5% will do. This will take care of losses at ends of bolts and flaws that may exist. The reason you get a better price on full bolts is because they are not reinspected by the distributor. They are shipped just as they are received from the mill (often drop-shipped), and since a certain number of flaws per bolt is considered acceptable, this is what you will receive. Therefore, you must make allowance for this situation.

The constant discussion of flaws may be upsetting to you, but they *do* exist, and four major flaws per bolt are now considered permissible in a fabric shipped as first rate goods. Try to understand the relationship of flaws to excess fabric needed when ordering, but do not let it be a major worry to you otherwise.

Designers often feel that workrooms should unroll their fabrics as soon as they come in and inspect for flaws, dye lots, and so forth. Actually this should be the responsibility of the person who purchases the fabric. Can you imagine how long it would take a workroom to unroll, inspect, and reroll hundreds of yards of fabric daily? Extra space and personnel would be required and the labor price would have to be adjusted accordingly.

SUMMARY FOR ESTIMATING YARDAGES

Determine size of window.

Determine extension, if any.

Decide on fullness and determine number of widths.

Determine cut lengths in inches. (Don't forget pattern repeats).

Multiply by number of widths.

Divide by 36 inches—proceed to next even number.

This is correct number of yards (plus 10% allowance if necessary).

Specify yards, number of widths, and cut lengths when ordering.

HELPFUL CHARTS

DETERMINING FINISHED WIDTH OF DRAPERY

Single traverse	Rod size plus 12 inches
Under traverse	Rod size plus 4 inches
Over traverse	Rod size plus 16 inches
Single one-way	Rod size plus 6 inches
Under one-way	Rod size plus 2 inches
Over one-way	Rod size plus 8 inches

RETURNS

Single traverse or tie-back drapery	4 inches
Underdrapery	none
Overdrapery	6 inches
Valance over single drapery	6 inches
Valance over double drapery	8 inches
Drapery over blind or shade not in recess	6 inches
Austrian shade on board	2½ inches
Valance over Austrian shade	6 inches
Valance over stationary Austrian shade	4 inches

Valance returns may be 4 inches in the following instances:

1. Over any treatment set in recessed windows where the valance is on the outside of the recess.
2. Over shirr-on-rod curtains if there is no overdrape.
3. Over tie-back draperies on a narrow-projection rod.

Valance return must always be 2 inches deeper than the deepest return to go under it.

There should be a clearance of 2 inches to 2½ inches between each item hung at the window—shades, sheers, draperies, valances.

EXTENSION NEEDED TO CLEAR WINDOW

Double fullness—Divide window size by 6—add to each side

2½ fullness—Divide window size by 5—add to each side

Triple fullness—Divide window size by 4—add to each side

TO DETERMINE NUMBER OF WIDTHS NEEDED WITH NO CHART

Divide rod size by number indicated and go to next even number

36-inch fabric	Double fullness—pleats each width to 16 inches 2½ fullness—pleats each width to 13 inches Triple fullness—pleats each width to 11 inches
45-inch fabric	Double fullness—pleats each width to 20 inches 2½ fullness—pleats each width to 16 inches Triple fullness—pleats each width to 14 inches
48-inch fabric	Double fullness—pleats each width to 22 inches 2½ fullness—pleats each width to 18 inches Triple fullness—pleats each width to 14 inches
54-inch fabric	Double fullness—pleats each width to 25 inches 2½ fullness—pleats each width to 20 inches Triple fullness—pleats each width to 16 inches

FINISHED SIZE FOR TIE-BACK DRAPERIES OR SIDE PANELS USING 2½ FULLNESS

Widths Pairs	Pleats each side to	Covers each side	Length of Tie-back
2	22 inches	17 inches	21 inches
3	29 inches	24 inches	24 inches
4	39 inches	34 inches	27 inches
5	46 inches	41 inches	30 inches
6	57 inches	52 inches	33 inches
7	64 inches	59 inches	36 inches
8	74 inches	69 inches	39 inches

PIN SETTINGS

Decorative rods	½ inch from top of drapery
Wall mount	2 inches from top of drapery
Ceiling mount	1½ inches from top of drapery

CUTTING ALLOWANCES

Unlined sheers and casements
Twice the hem + twice the heading + 2 inches
4-inch hem × 2 + 4-inch head × 2 + 2 inches = *18 inches*

Opaque unlined draperies
Twice the hem + twice the heading
4-inch hem × 2 + 4-inch head × 2 = *16 inches*

Lined draperies with rolled heading
Twice the hem + twice the heading
4-inch hem × 2 + 4-inch head × 2 = *16 inches*

Lined draperies with continental heading
Twice the hem plus depth of heading
4-inch hem × 2 + 4-inch head = *12 inches*

Sheers with rod pocket at top
   Twice the hem + size of top hem + 1 inch
   4-inch hem × 2 + 3-inch hem + 1 inch = *12 inches*

Rod-to-rod curtains
   Twice the desired hem + 2 inches
   3-inch hem × 2 + 2 inches = *8 inches*

Sheers and rod-to-rod curtains may have double hems at top or top and bottom, but it is not necessary since the hem does not show when gathered. Double hems add considerable bulk.

TO FIND AMOUNT OF TRIM NEEDED FOR ROUND TABLE COVER

Multiply the diameter of the cloth in inches times 3.2. Divide by 36 to find number of yards.

BASIC DRAPERY CONSTRUCTION

UNLINED DRAPERIES

Seams

Hems

Weights

Casements and Architectural Nets

Heavier Fabrics Unlined

LINED DRAPERIES

Seams

Hems

Lining Construction

Replacing Linings

Interlining

Self-lined Draperies

LINING

Cotton Sateen
Taffeta
Rayon Challis
Milium
Blackout Lining
Roc-lon®
Thermal Suede™
Flame-resistant Linings

Liners

Figuring Lining Yardage

UNLINED DRAPERIES

An unlined drapery is constructed of one or more widths of fabric sewn together to create panels, one for each side of the window in most cases, one for the entire window in others. Naturally, since the seams are exposed, they must be finished in some way.

Seams

For many years a french seam (or double seam) was used almost exclusively in making draperies. It is still used by people who do not have the equipment to do otherwise or who do not care to try new methods. The advantage of this seam is that it leaves no raw edges exposed. The drawback is that for every row of stitching there is a possibility of puckering or take-up in one or the other widths (usually the one on the bottom), and with two rows in a french seam, the chances are doubled. The seam is also often bulky, especially in casement fabrics. French seams are described in the chapter on Drapery Construction Techniques under the section Joining Widths.

A better and more favored method in large workrooms now is the serged or overcast seam. The machine that does this is usually a four-thread machine. It cuts off the selvage edge, sews the two pieces together, and overcasts the edges while also providing a safety or lock stitch. If thread color is closely matched to the fabric, the resulting seam is invisible and not bulky. A skilled operator can virtually eliminate the puckering factor. Some architectural nets require other methods such as the use of the zigzag machine.

Hems

After being sewn together, the drapery panel is hemmed, by hand on very expensive draperies, with the blind-stitch machine if available, or with the straight or lock-stitch machine as a last resort or in certain special cases.

Hems put in with a lock-stitch machine show a fine line of stitching across the top of the hem. Even with closely matching thread, the line is quite obvious. These hems are easy to pucker and difficult to remove, often leaving a noticeable mark if it is necessary to do so. Naturally, there are exceptions. Some loosely woven casement fabrics must be hemmed this way since the blind-stitch machine will not pick them up and hold them. Also a very neatly stitched hem in sheers is not objectionable where both sides are equally exposed and the blind-stitch loops might be objectionable on the wrong side. The blind-stitched hem is least obvious and, when properly done, resembles a hand hem on the right side. It is very fast to do and consequently much less expensive than hems done by hand.

Sides are hemmed first, then bottoms, a double 1½-inch side hem and double 4-inch bottom hem being standard. On very sheer fabrics extreme accuracy is necessary since all hemming is visible. Deep hems in sheers are decorative.

Weights

Any weights used in sheers must be covered in self-fabric, doubled or tripled to conceal the weight. Even these will show as a dark shadow in the hems, so where possible, we suggest using none with the exception of the leading edges, where they help the drapery to hang straight and can be more easily concealed. Some people prefer to have chain weights (or rat-tails) in sheers—a continuous weighted tape that gives added weight across the entire bottom for graceful hanging and to prevent billowing, especially in situations where the drapery hangs over air-conditioning or heating vents. This chain weight will show in the bottom of the hem as a series of bumps about the size of a BB shot. Any weights, except those used in the leading edges of unlined draperies, where they are inserted and stabilized by the side hem, must be tacked to the seams to prevent shifting.

After hems are done and weights inserted, the drapery is tabled to the desired length, the pleats are marked and stitched, tacked and finished. These procedures are discussed in fabrication of draperies in Section Two—Drapery Construction Techniques—Tabling and Pleating.

Casements and Architectural Nets

Casement fabrics should always be unlined and are handled in much the same way as other unlined draperies except for special problems. Weights must be an individual decision. Since casements have a tendency to stretch, weights in leading edges frequently make the drapery too long at this point. However, sometimes weights are quite necessary at the seams to keep them from pulling up because the fabric is held more tightly at that point. Once again, the weights must be covered in self-fabric. A competent workroom will do what seems best according to their experience, but do not expect loosely woven fabric to hang perfectly.

Many people think that one way to get a nearly perfect hang in a casement is to baste the hem, allow it to hang for two to four weeks, and then rehem on the job while hanging—a very expensive and often futile operation, since even this will not guarantee that the drapery will continue to hang straight. This is because most decorative casements are composed of more than one fiber and these will react differently to moisture and heat while hanging. Therefore, most workrooms finish the drapery and adjust later where necessary. It is not fair to expect the workroom to absorb this cost if they were not consulted about the fabric, since they know there will be trouble but have no control over it.

Open-weave architectural nets are very effective. However, their limitations are much greater than the average architect or designer realizes. Very few workrooms will accept the responsibility of guaranteeing draperies from these fabrics. The stretch factor, the unevenness of pattern repeat, the built-in problems mean that, for the effect, other things must be sacrificed. It is almost certain that they will stretch, there may be problems with seams, and the design will not follow the line of the pattern when tabled. These problems should be thoroughly discussed by everyone in advance of fabrication.

Unlined sheer or casement draperies are used basically to screen glare and to decorate. This is the purpose for which they were designed and, as previously stated, it is usually a mistake to line either. Only when a special effect is needed that can be created no other way or when a client absolutely insists and is willing to accept the responsibility for the problems involved should it be considered.

Heavier Fabrics Unlined

Heavier fabrics can also be used unlined. This works very well and is an economical measure when color and texture are the chief considerations. Most fabrics not in the casement category cause very few problems when used unlined. Cottons, linens, solids, woven designs, or prints are usually rather stable and make very nice manageable draperies. If sun fading is no problem or if the more luxurious look of a lined drapery is not desired, it is both practical and economical to use them unlined. Heavy velvet stage draperies are seldom lined. If a drapery covers a wall, lining would be superfluous.

Finally, if cost is a factor, unlined draperies can save money and are quite decorative for temporary dwellings such as some apartments.

LINED DRAPERIES

Draperies are lined for several reasons. The foremost is to protect the face fabric from the sun and dirt coming through the windows. Sun causes fabrics to deteriorate and will also burn, scorch, or fade them. Dirt is almost as destructive as sunlight. Appearance is another reason, giving added body and helping them to hang more gracefully. Appearance from the outside is improved if all draperies are lined in the same color. Linings help to insulate and to black out light.

Lined draperies are constructed of a face fabric, plain or printed, and a lining attached to the face fabric at the sides, pleated with it at the top, and tacked loosely to it at the bottom.

Seams

The widths of fabric are sewn together with a regular seam. It is desirable to make this seam wide enough so the selvages can be trimmed off before the seam is pressed open. Selvages must not be clipped to release the tight edge because this shows through the finished drapery and is not considered acceptable. If the fabric has a pattern, this pattern must be matched very carefully as the seam is stitched.

Hems

After the appropriate number of widths have been sewn together, selvages trimmed, and seams pressed open, the desired bottom hem (usually double 4 inches) is pressed in and weights attached at the seams. If the fabric is a print, the hem must be pressed to coincide with the line of the pattern across the bottom. The panel would be hemmed as in unlined draperies, leaving off the side hem.

Lining Construction

After the face fabric is hemmed, the lining is constructed in a similar manner, preferably from lining the same width as the fabric. If this is not done, lining seams will not fall behind the face fabric seams and will add additional vertical lines when the drapery is hung. Since it is expensive to stock many sizes of lining, some workrooms do not do this, so if it is important to have the seams match, you must specify it. The bottom hem in the lining is usually 2 inches wide and is often stitched on the lock-stitch machine. The lining is set up 1½ inches from the bottom of the drapery to prevent it from sagging below the hem. Linings in tie-back draperies should be set up at least 3 inches.

When the face fabric and lining have been prepared, it is time to attach them together. This is done by a process called *tabling,* discussed under workroom procedure in Section Two—Drapery Construction Techniques. Tabling is a process where the drapery is squared, lining attached, length determined, stiffening inserted in the heading, and pleats marked. Once off the table the drapery is pleated, tacked, pins inserted, pressed, and folded.

Replacing Linings

Since the lining protects the face fabric, it may become stained or even sunrotted. It can be replaced with excellent results in many instances, but it is foolish to do so unless the original fabric is very valuable or in excellent condition. Great care must be taken in removing the old lining, the drapery must be taken almost completely apart, and most workrooms will charge double labor to reline any drapery.

Interlining

Some draperies are interlined. They have an extra lining of flannel between the face fabric and the regular lining. This interlining gives a more luxurious look, reduces the light, and is considered by many decorators to be the only way to make draperies. Interlining adds a lot of weight to lightweight fabrics such as silk, but it can be bulky and heavy in many other fabrics as well. Interlined draperies must be hand-made and require special handling. Consequently they are considerably more expensive than simple lined or unlined draperies.

Self-Lined Draperies

Self-lined draperies are exactly that—a fabric lined with the same fabric as itself. This is necessary only where both sides are equally exposed as in a room divider or in a show window seen from both sides. The only difference in construction from regular lined draperies is that the side used for the lining is not set up from the bottom but is even with the hem of the face fabric.

Properly constructed lined draperies will last for years. They hold up well when cleaned and are certainly worth the extra cost.

LINING

The lining picture is changing so rapidly that what is written now may be out of date in a matter of months. This is the situation at the present time.

There are many types of linings. We list some below.

Cotton Sateen. This is an excellent lining for almost any job and will probably remain a standard material for this purpose. Certain variations with polyester are becoming popular because of the no-wrinkle factor.

Taffeta. Another old familiar lining is rayon taffeta. It has a luxurious look and is commonly used only with very dressy fabrics or if someone insists on lining a sheer. It does not cling well to the face cloth but can be tacked to compensate.

Rayon Challis. A fairly recent addition to the lining family is rayon challis, which is wrinkle-free and stain-resistant. It has a lustrous look and is cheaper than cotton. Its chief drawback is that it does not cling well to the face fabric, causing a blousing effect that is a problem when working with multiple widths and tie-backs.

Milium. The first of the insulating linings. It was originally sateen on one side and aluminum-coated on the other. Now it can be made white on both sides. It is very satisfactory for insulating purposes and helps to control light but not to black it out. It is stiffer than other linings, and thus does not hang as softly.

Blackout Lining. True blackout lining has a vinyl or foam backing. It will black out a room if it completely covers and extends past the window opening in all directions. The vinyl-backed material is quite stiff, and any pinholes or line of stitching will show when there is light behind it. The foam-backed material is much easier to work with and hangs more softly but will still show pinholes.

Roc-lon®. Another insulated lining, Roc-lon® (there are also some new similar ones), has a special finish impregnated in the fabric. It resembles sateen except that it has no sheen. It is probably the most used of the insulating linings at this time. It is available flame-retardant and comes in a wide range of colors.

Thermal Suede™. The newest of the insulating linings, Thermal Suede™, looks like any other lining on one side but has a napped, foam backing on the other. It is easy to use, clings well to the face fabric, insulates well, and is competitive costwise, although all insulating linings are more expensive than regular linings.

Flame-resistant Linings. Though frequently specified, these are available from most manufacturers only as a treated lining. At this time there are no inherently flame-resistant linings on the market. Some inherently flame-resistant fabrics can be used as linings.

Interlining. This flannel fabric comes in white, natural, or gray. It is used between the face fabric and the regular lining to give a more luxurious look to draperies and requires special handling.

Milium, Roc-lon®, and blackout finishes can be laminated to a fabric to save the cost of an extra lining. This is not usually done except on large orders, as the mills will not run small quantities. Some distributors stock some fabrics with laminated finishes.

Liners

Liners may be added to unlined draperies very easily and without the addition of a second rod. A flat piece of lining is made up and hemmed to be the width of the drapery at the top (finished width including return and overlap), and 3 inches shorter than the finished length. The top hem should be 1½ inches double and reinforced with crinoline if it is not a fairly stiff lining. At ½ inch from the top a grommet is placed to coincide with the placement of each pin in the drapery. These are then slipped over the drapery pins and the whole thing hung as a unit, the liner remaining flat behind the pleated drapery.

A liner used in this way has the advantage of providing insulation in summer or winter and can be removed when not needed. It remains with the drapery at all times whether open or closed, while a separate liner on its own rod can be opened or closed under the drapery as desired. If a separate liner is used, it is wise to have only minimum fullness to eliminate as much bulk as possible when stacking.

Figuring Lining Yardage

It is less complicated to figure the same amount of lining as face fabric when you are estimating yardages. There are some instances when you should figure them separately.

If the fabric has a pattern repeat and there will be considerable loss between cuts, you can save a little on lining by figuring as if it were a solid fabric. It is necessary only to add 6 inches to the finished length for lining so the lining is figured at the finished length plus 6 inches. Multiply this by the number of widths used and estimate yards. Do not forget valance yardages.

If you are using 48-inch lining for a 54-inch fabric, you will need additional lining if pairs are over three widths. A four-width pair would take an additional one-half width. A full width would be needed for anything up to eight widths, and two full widths for anything over eight widths up to sixteen. It is much better to use 54-inch lining. Most wholesale houses now stock this width.

When figuring anything that has cascades, the amount of yardage allowed for cascades can be deducted from the lining yardage, as the cascades are self-lined.

PROBLEM WINDOWS

Conventional windows nicely placed are a joy to the designer. Unfortunately, not all windows are like this and means must be devised to make them look the best they can for the use they must have.

When you have a problem window, try to visualize the best way it could look, then try to create that look. A window can be disguised to make it look wider, longer, shorter, arched, and even moved (a little).

WINDOW DIMENSIONS THAT APPEAR TO BE CHANGED

The Too Narrow Window

It is easy to make a window appear wider. All that is necessary is to extend the treatment on the sides. The window appears wider and the proportions better. If this is not practical, use horizontal stripes for your fabric or perhaps a trim used horizontally about 6 inches below the pleats to lead the eye from side to side (several rows can be effective). For a narrow, slit window, sometimes the best thing to do is to shutter it and paint it to match the wall, thus causing it to "disappear." Rod-to-rod sheers to match the wall have much the same effect.

The Too Tall Window

A very tall window that needs to be shortened can be treated with tie-backs and a half curtain to give a horizontal division. It can also be treated with a cornice or valance set down to the top of the window frame and allowed to come lower than normal over the window. Tiers of curtains or cafe curtains combined with shutters also visually lower the too tall window. Use any possible horizontal line such as rows of trim or decorative rods. And, obviously, if draperies are extended on the sides of the window, its proportions change and it looks less tall.

The Too Small Window

The too small window is completely different in proportion from the "average" window. It is frequently square and almost always badly placed. It sometimes occurs in a room with other more conventional windows. If this is true, the best solution is to blank it out by matching the treatment to the wall, using shutters or sheers. This is usually the best treatment for the small windows often found in older homes over bookcases and beside fireplaces.

If the small window is the only source of light in the room, it is sometimes best to frame it with a small swag and cascades or with a cantonniere. A shade can be used for privacy if necessary.

A small window can be deliberately extended on the sides to make it look wider, like a ranch window, but this would look good only if there were something under it to give it a base, such as a bed, bench, or table.

Perhaps the best way to disguise and reproportion a short window completely would be to hang a curtain from the sill to the floor with full-length tie-backs from the top of the window. In most cases the simplest and least obtrusive treatment is best for the small window.

The Too Short Window

In very rare cases you will find windows that are set too low in the wall. These are very difficult to treat. The most practical thing is to use a cornice or valance that extends above the window and just barely comes to the top. The head casing, if any (these windows are frequently recessed), would be covered with a fairly dense or very full sheer. An arched cornice would achieve a whole new look.

The other solution is to use sheers and a tie-back drapery with the top of the tie-backs set at a more normal height and tacked together at the top of the window so no wall is exposed.

The Dormer Window

These windows often have the same problem as the small window. Since they are confined, some of the usual solutions to problem windows are not available.

It is best to use the simplest possible treatment and to match the drapery and wall color. If these are the only windows in a room, you must be sure to allow for maximum light and ventilation.

Dramatize these windows only if the room is large enough to take such a treatment and if there are other sources of light.

The Corner Window

The corner window is not usually considered a problem window, but certain things must be considered in treating it. You may want to treat it as a unit, but bear in mind that light will come into the two sides differently, especially as the sun moves during the day. One side may have a pleasant view and the other may overlook an eyesore. Thus it is a good idea to control the two sides independently. Two panels or two pairs may be used, and if there is wall space in the corner, you may want to combine either with a stationary panel in the corner.

DOORS

Single, double, or sliding glass doors are big problems for decorating wherever they occur. Often a single door is located in such a way that the light coming through it is important for illumination in the room. Since the window in the door needs to be covered for privacy, a shade of some type can be the best solution. Laminated shades or woven wood shades are excellent for this purpose since they expose the entire glass when raised. Shirr-on-the-rod curtains can be used and are best done rod-to-rod so they will not flap around when the door is used. This excludes a considerable amount of light, but they can be tied back—either to the sides or with an hourglass effect in the center. If this is done, the sides must be slightly longer so the curtain will have enough "give" to cover the rod without sliding back when tied.

French or double doors that open outward can be treated quite easily by extending the treatment high and to the sides enough to allow for passage through the doors. It is not necessary to clear the entire opening in this situation. However, more often the doors open in for safety reasons so the hinge cannot be tampered with. In this case a treatment mounted on the door is the best solution. This calls for a rod-to-rod treatment that many clients do not like because it blocks out light and cannot be moved. Various kinds of shades can be considered—laminated, woven wood, or roman, any of which can be mounted on doors. If there is wall space, there is no problem. Extend the treatment to clear the doors and treat as you wish.

A cornice can be used above doors as long as it comes no lower than the top of the door itself. This is a situation where a cornice that is straight at the bottom and shaped at the top is interesting and appears to heighten the opening.

Sliding glass doors are no problem if they are part of a window wall and only the center part opens. It is more usual for the door to be 6 to 8 feet wide with only one side opening. Once again, if there is plenty of wall space, there is no problem. The treatment can be extended. If wall space is a problem, the obvious solution is to make a one-way panel that stacks on the stationary side. This has an awkward look when the drapery is open. Sometimes if the door is wide enough and there is a little extra wall space on the opening side, a single stationary side panel can be hung to help balance the look when open. Another idea is to use woven wood or roman shades extended above the window so the opening will be clear when they are raised.

TWO WINDOWS TREATED AS ONE UNIT

Conventional Rods

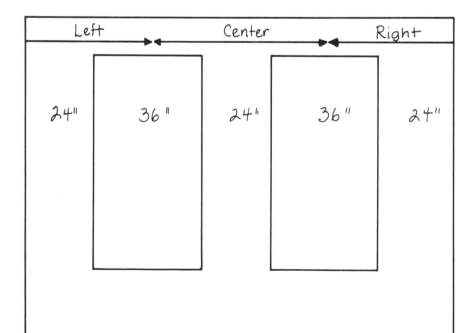

Treat with 3 panels:

    Left panel—24 inches + 18 inches—wall + ½ of window

    Center panel—24 inches + 18 inches + 18 inches—wall + ½ of 2 windows

    Right panel—24 inches + 18 inches—wall + ½ of window

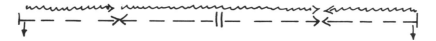

Rods butted together at center. Cords on opposite sides.

Center panel hooks from one bracket to the other.

SPECIAL TREATMENTS

A Window Can Appear To Be Moved

A window crowded into a corner can be visually moved by starting the treatment exactly at the edge of the window nearest the corner and extending out on the other side to expose as much glass as possible.

This might not seem wise unless the window has no muntins. However, even then, if sheers are used, this is feasible. Remember, there will be an uneven look on the outside unless there are sheers, but the inside will be vastly improved.

Figure 13. Window set in wall close to corner.

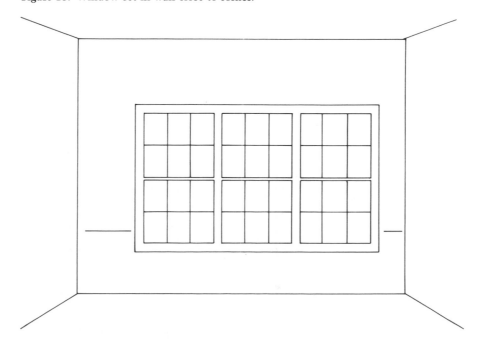

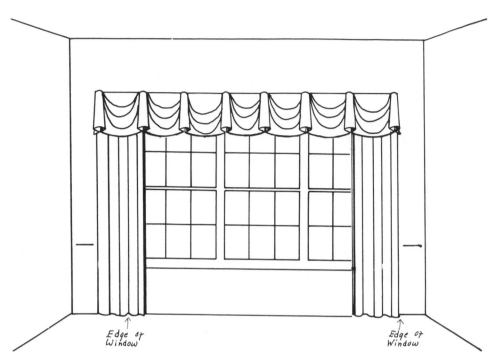

Figure 13A. Window draped with right side of drapery panel at right edge of window frame. Right side of left panel at edge of window and drapery covering wall. Window appears to have been moved to left and is now centered in wall.

Figure 14. Sheers used to disguise uneven appearance of panes and mulls.

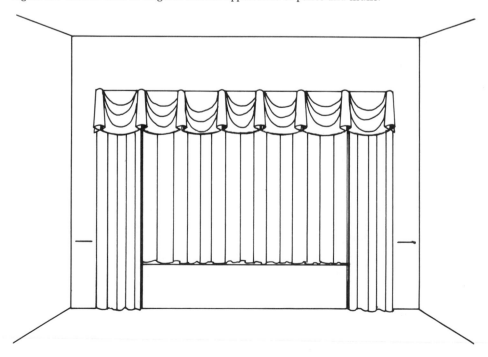

Figure 15. Window and door in same wall with tops at unequal heights.

Awkwardly Placed Windows

Two or three windows set awkwardly in the same wall can be disguised to appear to better advantage. Visualize the way they would look best and use drapery to achieve that look.

Off-center Windows

Occasionally, a window or wall and window combination calls for an off-center drapery. This means that the two halves of the pair are unequal in size.

Figure 16. Continuous valance with drapery panels placed to disguise uneven height and unify the look. Sheers could be used with the panels to make the illusion better.

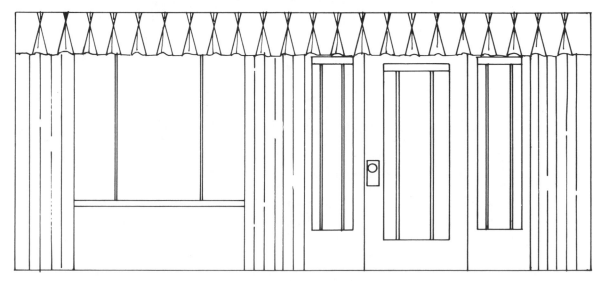

Let us assume that an office with a window wall has been set up so that the walls intersect the window mulls at uneven distances. The half-way point is not in the middle of a section of glass. When the drapery is closed, this would make no difference, but if a pair of draperies with equal panels were drawn back, the window would appear to be off-center. Therefore, the correct thing to do would be to make a pair of draperies that meets in the middle of the center section. Then when the drapery is open, the glass areas and mulls will be centered between the open panels. An unequal number of widths will be used on each side, and these must be calculated so pleats will be spaced the same on both sides.

The same thing is true for a window placed off-center in a whole wall that is to be covered.

Always remember that in off-center draperies controlled by one cord on one rod the treatment will open back on both sides only as far as the small panel opens. If for any reason the large panel needs to be able to be opened back further, the two sides must be controlled independently, either by using two rods or by special rigging of one rod.

Window Air-Conditioner Units

Air-conditioner units present a problem that cannot be beautifully solved. If the unit is located centrally in the window, the drapery can be cut out around it so the unit is exposed when the drapery is closed. The drawback to this is that when the drapery is opened, the leading edge is bobtailed. A short stationary panel can be used over the unit and the draperies can be closed to the edge of the unit. The advantage to this arrangement is that in winter a long panel could replace the short one, making the treatment appear uniform. There is no ideal solution. Discuss the various solutions with your client and do what seems best for the situation.

All problem windows require imagination and ingenuity. Be sure that everyone involved understands what you are doing and why you are doing it. The result will be pleasing to all concerned.

SLANTED-TOP DRAPERIES

Many contemporary homes have windows that slant at the top, and sometimes at the bottom also.

Generally the purpose of the architect in using these windows is to allow maximum light, emphasize a view, or blend the interior with the outdoors. Ideally these windows would not be draped. However, for reasons of privacy and energy conservation it is often necessary to have some type of drapery, preferably an unlined casement that is in keeping with the contemporary look.

If a workable traverse drapery is desired, it is best to drape the window at the mull below the slant and leave the upper portion exposed. In this way you retain the view of the sky and trees and still achieve the privacy and light control where it matters. The drapery can traverse one way or from the center. It is possible to add a valance at the top that remains stationary but gives the illusion of a full-length drapery when the traverse portion is closed. Much of the impact of the window is lost if this is done because the upper part of the window is closed off at all times.

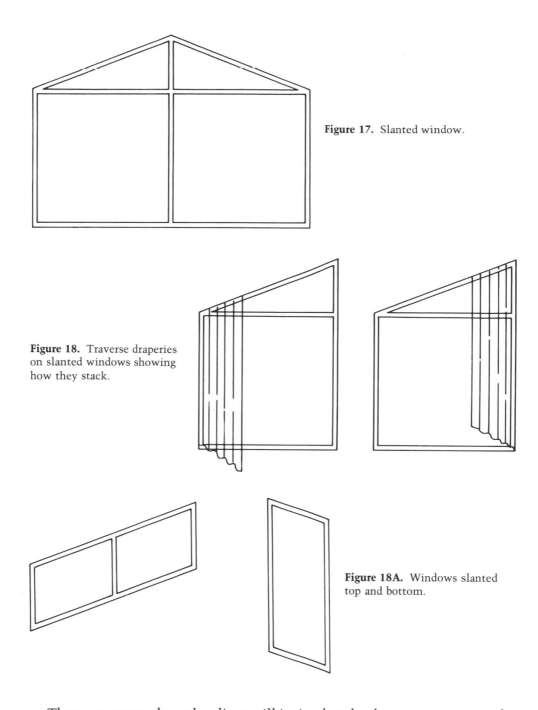

Figure 17. Slanted window.

Figure 18. Traverse draperies on slanted windows showing how they stack.

Figure 18A. Windows slanted top and bottom.

There are cases where the client will insist that the drapery traverse on the slant. It is obvious that it must traverse from the low point to the high point; otherwise the drapery would lie all over the floor when open. Conversely, it will be short and bobtailed when opened to the high point, but this is still the best solution.

Draperies can be tied back on these windows with good effect, and this is probably the only situation where we would suggest tying back by day and releasing at night.

When windows are slanted top and bottom, it is best to take draperies to the floor if they must traverse. If the shape of the window is important, follow the contour of the window top and bottom and let the drapery remain stationary.

Measurements for all slanted windows must be precise. If not, the effect will be a disaster. It would be extremely helpful to make a template of the slanted portion.

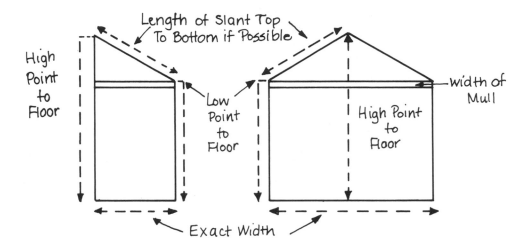

Be sure to note whether the drapery will go on the window frame, wall, or ceiling. Specify whether or not a return will be needed and if so, how much. Note any other unusual details.

If the drapery is to be straight and go on the mull between top and bottom sections, specify the width of the mull and include it in the sketch.

If no other solution is acceptable, and the ceiling is not slanted, the drapery can be made straight at the high point and traverse like an ordinary drapery, thus losing the impact of the window.

CURVED-TOP DRAPERIES

Curved-top draperies are found in many locations, most frequently churches or commercial buildings such as banks and clubs. They are also favorites for stair landings.

These windows can be treated in many ways. The one thing that cannot be done is to traverse around the curve. As in slanted windows, they can be treated with a traverse drapery straight across the window at the break in the curve. They can also have straight traverse draperies mounted on the wall or ceiling above the arch, thus distorting the shape of the window.

Most often a drapery pleated around the circle is used to preserve the integrity of the shape. In these cases the drapery is usually tied back, the effect varying with the placement of the tie-backs.

A sheer curtain can be either shirred or pleated around the arch and can be allowed to hang straight since it does not shut out all light. In many cases these curtains can be mounted within the recess to reveal the frame if it is decorative.

Figure 19. Curved-top windows.

A combination of straight-hanging or curved drapery with cornice or valance can be used. A sunburst can be used at the top for a soft effect. These windows are quite adaptable to woven wood or minislat blinds, especially for commercial use or in paneled rooms.

There are times when it is desirable to create an arch where there is none. If a window is placed too low in a wall, a curved cornice set down just to the top of the window frame can be effective, giving apparent height to the window.

When figuring yardage for either slanted- or curved-top windows, confine yourself to the actual width of the window, allowing no side extensions except under special circumstances. Select your fullness and measure from the highest point as your finished length.

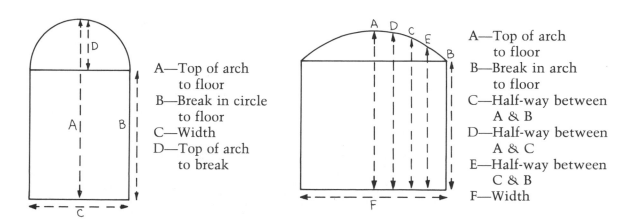

A—Top of arch
  to floor
B—Break in circle
  to floor
C—Width
D—Top of arch
  to break

A—Top of arch
  to floor
B—Break in arch
  to floor
C—Half-way between
  A & B
D—Half-way between
  A & C
E—Half-way between
  C & B
F—Width

Once again, measurements must be exact, and for curved tops a template is essential if the curve is not a half circle. For either slanted- or curved-tops a pattern must be made in the workroom for each particular window, and special handling is required. Be sure to check labor cost with your workroom.

TOP TREATMENTS

VALANCES
Gathered Valance
Gathered Swag Valance
Pleated Valance
Spaced-pleated Valance
Scalloped-pleated Valance
Box-pleated Valance
Kennedy Valance
Empire (or Flag) Valance
Austrian-pleated Valance
Austrian Pouff Valance
Swags
    Cascades
    Jabots
Valance Boards

CORNICES
Parts of a Cornice
Cornice Designs

FEATURE STRIPS AND TRIM

VALANCES

Valance is the term generally used for a decorative horizontal treatment at the top of a window. There are two basic types of top treatment—cornices and soft valances. Cornices are valances, but all valances are not cornices. Whether formal or casual, valances are pretty. They conceal the rod and finish the treatment by framing the window.

A valance can emphasize a window, change the proportion of a window, or visually raise or lower the ceiling height. It can make a window treatment appear more or less formal by the type you use. You can even use a valance over sheers alone to dress a window without overpowering it.

Care must be taken that the valance not be overpowering in itself. If it is too deep, it will seem to lean toward the room or look top-heavy. One-fifth to one-sixth the length of the overall treatment should be the maximum for the shallow point. The shallow point of the lower edge should always come at least 3 inches below the head casing of the window. All valances in the same room should be installed at the same height and be the same depth.

The terms used here in describing valances are those in most common use in workrooms. The treatments discussed here are the ones most often used; any others depend on the ability and versatility of your workroom and your ability to sketch or describe what you want.

Gathered Valance

The gathered valance can be made by anyone who sews, since it is a flat piece of material with a heading sewn in that is gathered or shirred on the rod. A variation of this can be done by sewing shirring tape to the back of the fabric and pulling the cords to form gathers. This spaces the gathers more evenly and holds them in place. This type, however, must go on a board or be attached to the rod with drapery pins. The gathered valance can have a little less fullness in heavy fabrics and still look good. In sheers it must have triple fullness. In heavy fabrics it frequently has a single hem to help it hang gracefully. In sheers the hem must be double.

To determine the fullness, find the number of widths from the chart on p. 50. Add 12 inches for cut lengths, and multiply by the number of widths and calculate yardage.

Gathered Swag Valance

The Gathered Swag Valance is more complicated than a plain gathered one and requires a special pattern that most workrooms do not have. If your workroom can make it, you need 3 yards of fabric and 4 yards of trim for a single window. Each drop added uses one additional yard of fabric and trim. This valance is very effective with ruffles. (See Figure 33 on p. 90).

Pleated Valance

The simplest and least expensive custom valance is the pinch-pleated or french-pleated valance, which is simply a duplicate of the top of a drapery. It is made in the same way, and the same allowances should be made for hems and

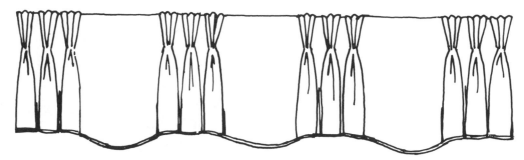

Figure 20. Space-pleated or Cluster-pleated valance.

headings. This type of valance should always have at least 2½ times fullness since a skimpy look achieves no decorative purpose.

Spaced-pleated Valance

A spaced-pleated valance is essentially the same thing as a pinch-pleated one except that the pleats are rearranged. Three pleats (either pinch or french) are spaced very close together, almost touching, then a wide space is left before the next group of pleats. This pattern is continued across the valance with a set of pleats at each end of the board. Returns of appropriate size must be added. The bottom of this valance can be scalloped to coincide with the sets of pleats and spaces, or it can be straight to emphasize a pattern in a fabric. Figure yardage the same way as you would for pinch-pleated valance, at two-and-one-half fullness.

Scalloped-pleated Valance

This valance is another variation of those discussed above. In this case the entire amount of material normally used for three pleats is made into one pleat, which is then broken into five to seven folds and tacked like a pinch pleat. A wide space of usually at least 12 inches is left before another pleat is formed. The last pleat at each end should be 3 to 4 inches from the end of the board. The bottom is always scalloped to coincide with pleats and spaces and is always finished with cord or trim. Extra labor must be charged if this type is

Figure 21. Scalloped-pleated valance.

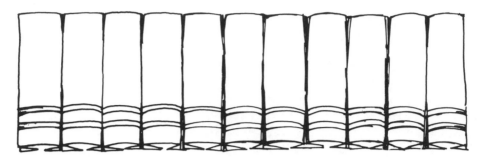

Figure 22. Box-pleated valance.

made unlined because an additional facing must be used. This valance is excellent to use when you want to show off a handsome pattern.

Figure yardage as you would for a pinch-pleated valance at two-and-one-half fullness. The amount of trim needed is determined by the number of widths used plus approximately an extra 2 inches for each scallop.

All of the pleated valances can be hung from rods by using drapery pins. Even for pleated valances it is best to put them on board to keep the heading from sagging and to allow sufficient projection to keep the draperies from dragging as they traverse. A 6-inch projection is needed for a valance with regular traverse draperies, an 8-inch one if a double traverse is used.

All other types of valances must be put on boards. Do not back down on this point with your client because in the long run you will both regret it. A discussion of valance boards follows later in this chapter.

Box-pleated Valance

This valance is often misunderstood and abused. At its best it can be used to emphasize a nice patterned fabric; at its worst it can look as if you had run out of ideas. However, used properly it is very effective. If it cannot be pleated exactly with the pattern, the pattern appears to change as it goes across the valance, giving a strange effect. It does not open up at each pleat showing little touches of color, as some people think. It is a pleasant change from pleated valances and though tailored has a softer effect than a cornice. An interesting change is to cover a 6-inch board and cord it, then drop box pleats below this.

To figure yardage, triple the length of the valance board plus returns.

Divide this amount by the width of the fabric to determine the number of widths required.

> Allow for hems plus 2 inches at the top
> Figure pattern repeats if any
> Multiply by the number of widths needed
> Convert to yards.

Kennedy Valance

The Kennedy valance, so called because the best picture we have of it was in President Kennedy's office in the White House, is perhaps the most tailored of the soft valances. This is a series of flat scallops with a cone sewed in at

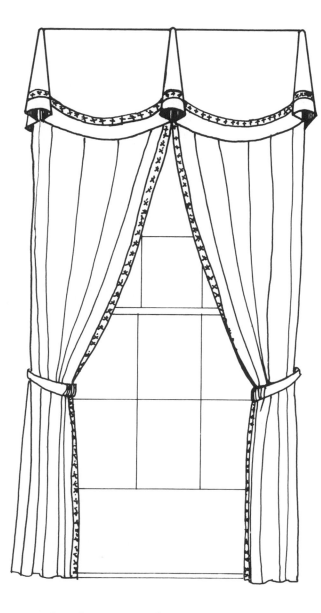

Figure 23. Kennedy valance with tie-back draperies. Ready-made band of trim.

intervals. The cone in this case is not separate, so the effect at the bottom is continuous. This valance looks good with a coordinating braid or band of trim at or near the bottom.

In solid fabrics it requires twice the face of the board plus 20 inches.
In printed fabrics it requires one width for each scallop and cone.
Add 10 inches to the finished depth and calculate as for other valances.
Don't forget to allow for repeat.

Empire (or Flag) Valance

These valances are more formal than the preceding. Their style can be varied in several ways according to the skill of the fabricator, but the best known is a series of gently swagged scallops with cones between, once again made from a

Figure 24. Empire valance with tie-back draperies and sheers. Band of trim fabricated from contrasting fabric.

continuous piece, and oddly enough, straight at the bottom. For this reason, they take well to flat bands of trim or braids.

Yardage required is the face of the board plus 14 inches for each cone plus 20 inches for returns. This works out to double the face of the board plus 20 inches for easy calculation.

It is best to allow the full width of the fabric for a solid fabric that can be railroaded. If the fabric cannot be turned, a full width must be allowed for each combination of scallop and cone, as in the Kennedy valance, so the seams may be juggled to fall behind the cones where they will not be noticeable.

The cut length for each width is the finished depth of the valance plus 14 inches. Be sure to calculate pattern repeats if necessary.

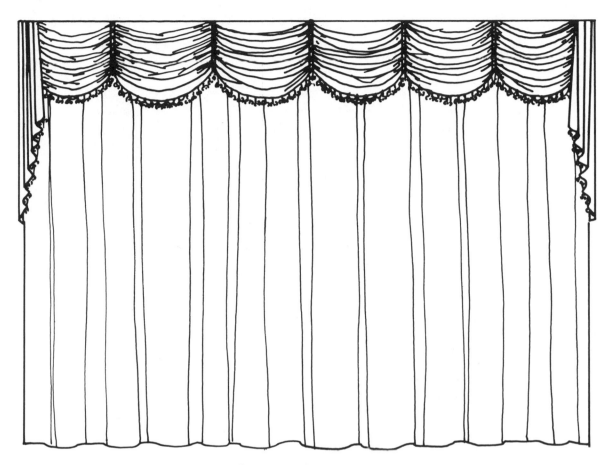

Figure 25. Austrian pouff valance with cascades.

You must consider the pattern carefully if you plan to use this type of valance, since it must coincide properly with cones and scallops. Bad design will look worse than no valance. When in doubt, use a solid fabric with a trim.

Trim yardage will be equal to twice the face of the board plus 20 inches.

Austrian Pouff Valance

This valance is actually a short Austrian shade and is fabricated the same way.

It requires ⅓ width of 48-inch fabric for each foot of board it covers plus ⅓ width for returns. These widths must be three times the length of the proposed valance depth. In some cases if the tapes are to be more than 12 inches apart, fabrics may have to be cut to accommodate the need for the seams to fall behind the tapes. Call your workroom for help. The amount allowed must always have 4 inches extra for each foot of board covered; otherwise the shirring will not "droop" but will pull straight across the space, forming horizontal pleats instead of soft scallops.

The trim yardage is equal to the number of widths used times the width of the fabric.

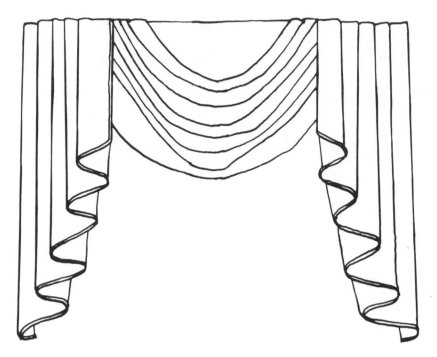

Figure 26. Traditional swag with piped edges on cascades

Austrian-pleated Valance

These have a similar effect to Empire Valances, but the pleats are more defined and the cones can be eliminated since on this valance they are separate. A flat band frequently replaces the cone. These valances are cut on the bias so the pleats will roll nicely.

One-and-one-half yards of fabric are required for each drop if they are spaced about 18 inches apart and are no deeper than 20 inches. If they are larger, a pattern must be made and yardage calculated.

The trim required is ⅔ yard for each drop and 18 inches for each cone if cones are used.

Empire and Austrian valances can be made with cascades at the ends. These vary slightly from the usual cascades, but yardages can be figured the same way. Always remember that they must be self-lined.

Swags

Swags are the most formal of the valance treatments. They are sometimes called "festoons," but since this term refers to several other things as well, the name swag has come to be preferred. Each individual swag is sometimes called a "drop." An uneven number of swags is properly used, but in some cases it is necessary to use an even number. In this case, they must all overlap in the same direction (see Figure 27). They can also just meet each other and have jabots between them.

Figure 27. Even number of swags. All must lap in same direction.

To find the correct number of drops for an average swag valance where each will cover approximately 44 inches, divide the overall width to be covered by 22 inches and subtract 1 from the result. The 22-inch figure can be varied down to 18 inches (for a 36-inch swag) and up to 24 inches or 26 inches (for swags up to 52 inches wide). The figure of 22 inches is based on multiples of a swag that would be used on a single window. Swags on all windows in a room should be as equal in width as possible. This can be achieved by extending some windows as in balancing drapery fullness.

The maximum and minimum depth should be specified, the maximum being the deep point at the center of the swag. The minimum is the point where the swags overlap. These points usually vary by about 8 inches.

Swags look better with some kind of trim on the bottom, even if only a piping. Fringe is best and adds to the formal look. They are also better looking if they are made on the bias, allowing the pleats to roll gently instead of breaking at the low point. This always requires at least one seam, but if the swag is no wider than 44 inches, this seam is usually covered by the overlaps of the other swags or cascades. Stripes and certain prints should not be turned. Pattern repeats must be considered.

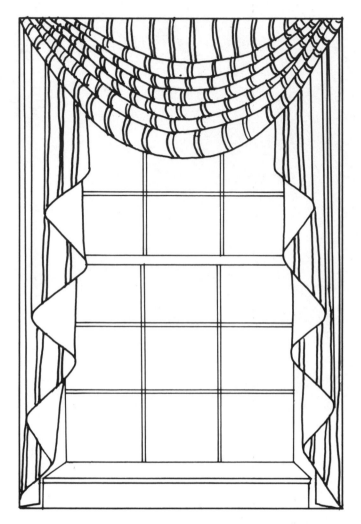

Figure 28. Traditional swag with cascades underneath acting as side panels.

To estimate yardage you will need the width of the swag plus 30 inches for each swag used. This is based on needs for an average swag dropping about 22 inches. A wider or deeper swag requires more fabric. To determine the amount needed, drape a piece of cord or string the width and depth needed. Then measure the string. This will be your running yardage. In depth you will need one-half width for each 11 inches of drop or fraction thereof. A 36-inch fabric requires ⅔ width for each 11 inches of drop.

The trim for swags is equal to the amount of fabric needed.

Cascades. Cascades should not come too far over the face of the board. They should cover only the pleated portion of the end swags, usually 7 to 10 inches. The front depth of the cascades should coincide with the depth of the swag where the two meet. The long depth of the cascade should never be exactly one-half the overall height. There is usually some physical point on the window that suggests where to stop.

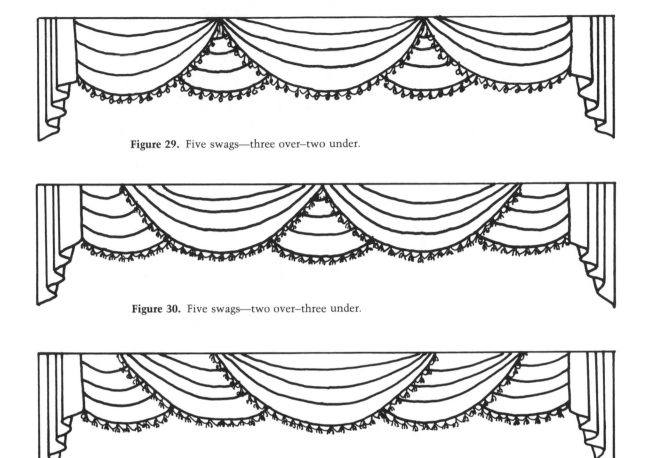

Figure 29. Five swags—three over–two under.

Figure 30. Five swags—two over–three under.

Figure 31. Five swags—center over–others lapping under to end.

Figure 32. Five swags—center under–others lapping over to end.

Cascades can come to the floor and replace side panels of drapery, but if they do this, the treatment should be scaled so they can be pleated wider at the top.

Cascades can be placed over or under the end swag.

Each self-lined cascade will take the depth of the cascade plus about 18 inches if the fabric is solid and has no nap. On cascades with a contrasting lining, divide the yardage in half to get the amount of contrast fabric needed and deduct this from the face yardage. If a print fabric or a fabric with nap is

Figure 33. Gathered swag valance.

used, each cascade will require twice the depth figured. Pattern repeats must be calculated so all cascades will look alike.

The trim for cascades will take the depth of the cascades plus 24 inches in most cases. For special cascades and jabots a pattern should be made and yardage calculated.

Jabots. Jabots are short double cascades used between the drops of swags when the swags do not overlap or when they meet in corners. They must be self-lined. Yardages are figured the same way as for cascades but have to be doubled.

Swags may be draped in several different ways.

Valance Boards

When installing valances on boards, the rods can be mounted in the boards, but it is best to mount them separately. Valances can then be adjusted in height if the overall effect is not quite what you planned.

Valance boards are made of 1-inch shelving, 6 inches wide for the average return. They are a horizontal board with returns dropping 6 inches or more on the sides. The width must be figured 2 inches wider on the inside than the draperies they cover, thus allowing for the draperies to return underneath. The depth must be 2 inches more than the maximum return of the underdraperies.

CORNICES

A cornice is a straight or shaped board attached to a dust cap. This board can be painted or padded, covered and embellished in many ways. Its depth can vary so long as it covers the top of the window frame and remains in scale with the overall treatment. It can be made longer on the sides than in the center or it can frame the window on three sides, in which case it is called a "lambrequin" or "cantonniere."

A cornice can be designed to enhance the pattern of any fabric, it can be perfectly straight, it can have shaped ends, or it can have a crown mold added at the top. It can be shaped at the top and straight at the bottom, or it can be shaped top and bottom. It can be draped with swags and jabots. It can also have holes cut in it with grills set in. It can have overlays or any kind of trim from double welt cord to elaborate fringe. In short, a cornice is what you make it.

The same rule for determining depth applies to cornices as to valances—one-fifth to one-sixth the distance of the overall window treatment.

One of the greatest mistakes in making cornices is choice of design for boards on different size windows in the same room. A design that looks really good on a 48-inch window will look like an entirely different board when scaled to go on a 84-inch window. Curves flatten out, points widen, and the whole effect is bad.

Some designs repeat themselves across the board. These can be readily adapted to different sizes. Other boards lend themselves to using the same end design and perhaps repeating a center design on a wide board.

Parts of a Cornice

Cornices are made of the lightest possible rigid material that can be easily stapled into. The parts of a cornice are as follows:

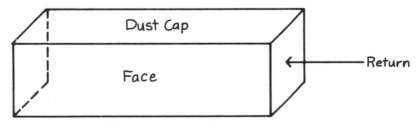

The dust cap does, in fact, help to keep dust off the drapery.

The face and returns are padded with various things such as quilt batting, foam, or a wood by-product called Tufflex. The batting is the most luxurious of paddings, though the others are quite adequate. After the board is padded, the chosen fabric is stretched very tightly across the face and returns and stapled on the backside. Welt cord is glued to the lower edges and any trim desired is applied—usually glued. The finishing touch is to line the backside of the board and dust cap for a finished look.

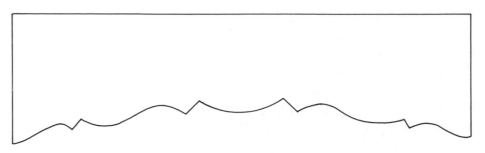

Figure 34. Cornice designed for wide board. Character is changed when scaled for small board.

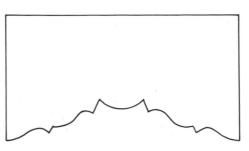

Figure 35. Cornice designed for small board. Design looks different when scaled for large board.

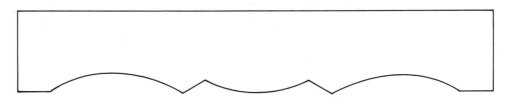

Figure 36. Small cornice with center scallop. Scallops can be repeated in center of large board.

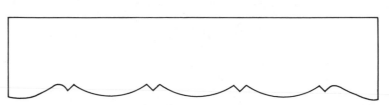

A beautifully upholstered cornice adds a very special touch to a window. It has the added advantage of being able to be recovered if the draperies are changed. Do not ask to have it reshaped or changed in size because in most cases there is more work involved than there would be in making a new one. If a cornice is to be recovered, it must be taken to the workroom and a charge must be made.

A cornice must always be at least 1 inch wider inside than the rod width. This must be stated as inside measure. The size of returns must be given—6 inches to go over a standard traverse, 8 inches over double treatments. Specify if the cornice is wall-to-wall and give exact outside measurement. This measurement must be taken at the height where the cornice is to be installed, since walls are seldom straight and the space might be narrower at the top than at floor level.

If a solid fabric is to be railroaded (run lengthwise) on a board, the yardage requirement is 30 inches more than the face of the board. Even though the grain of the fabric is slightly different when done this way, it is usually preferable to having seams on the face of the board because they are very prominent in solid fabrics. Some fabrics shade when turned, so it is wise to check this before specifying.

If the fabric must be seamed, add 30 inches to the face of the board and divide by the width of the fabric to see how many "cuts" will be needed, always going to the next full width. The cut length will be 4 inches more than the face depth. If there is a pattern repeat, this must also be calculated. Be sure to allow extra material for welt cord.

There are hundreds of cornice designs or sketches. Many are variations of some fairly standard ones. These designs have been passed around and copied so extensively that they are common property in the design field. If you want an original design, you must do it yourself, and the chances are that it will resemble one that has already been done. Several pages of designs follow to show the common variations used most often.

Cornice Designs

The following cornice designs are drawn to a scale of 1 inch equals 1 foot.

Numbers 1 through 56 are designed for single windows only. If they are rescaled for larger windows, the designs change. Curves become flat and points widen. A small board and a large one will not look alike.

Numbers 57 through 63 drop very deep on the sides. Be sure to remember that the shallow point of the board must cover the woodwork at the top of the window. If the board appears too deep, the sides may be adapted as shown, but not after the board is covered. If in doubt, make a paper pattern just like the board is planned and tape it to the window to get the effect.

Numbers 64 through 68 can be used for both large and small boards because the designs can be used once or twice for small boards and can be repeated several times for large ones. The designs will look alike even if there are two or more sizes of board in the same room.

Numbers 69 through 78 are suitable for boards 5 to 7 feet wide. They are scaled here for 6 feet.

Numbers 79 and 80 are lambrequins.

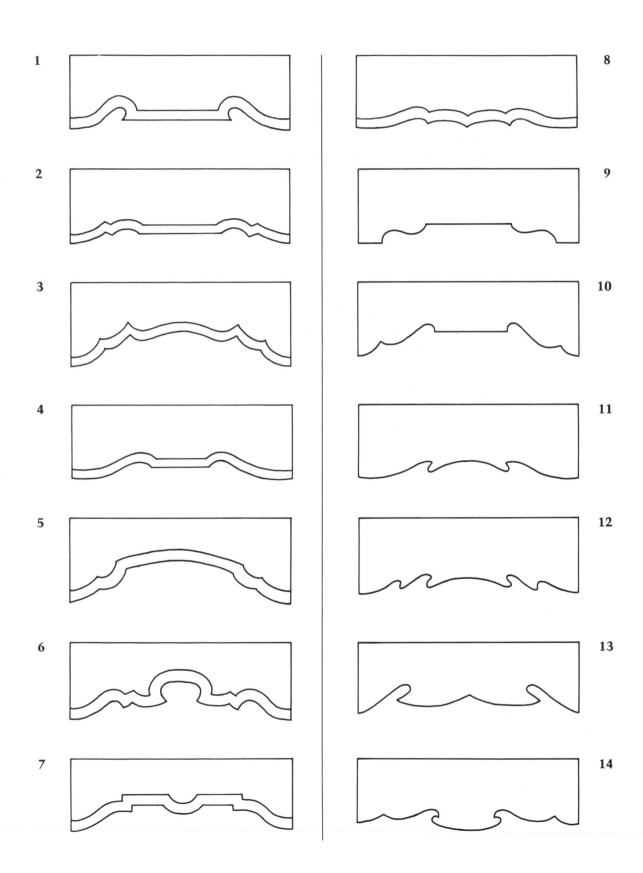

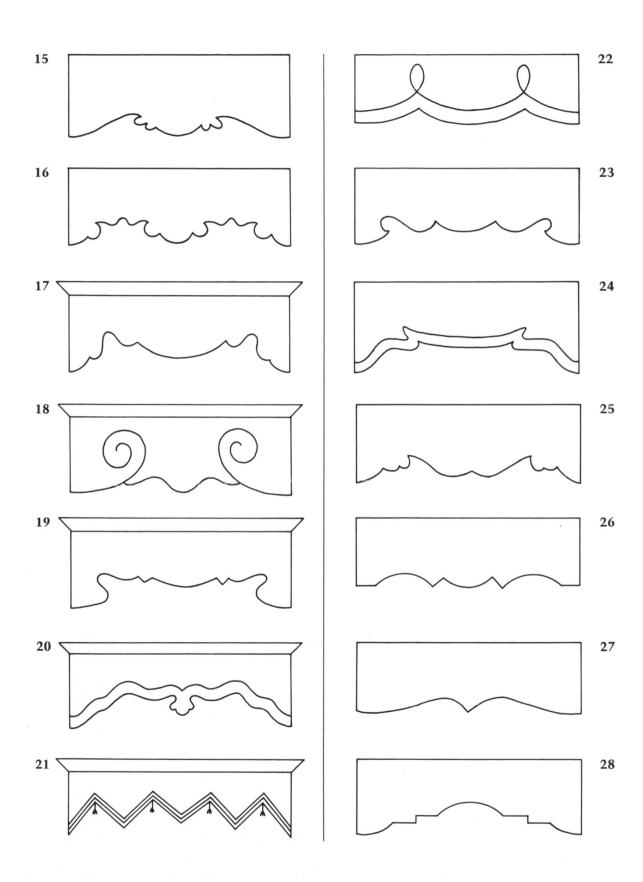

95

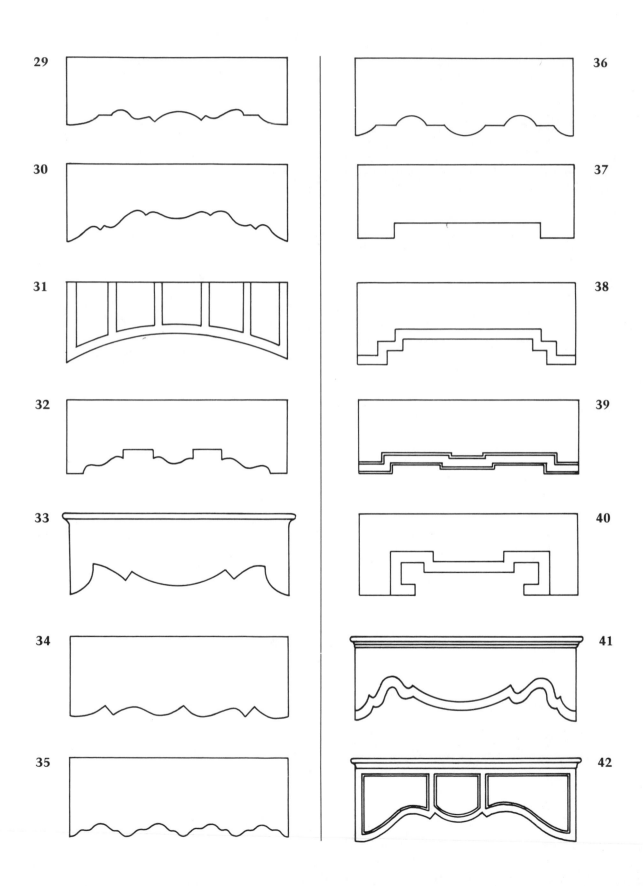

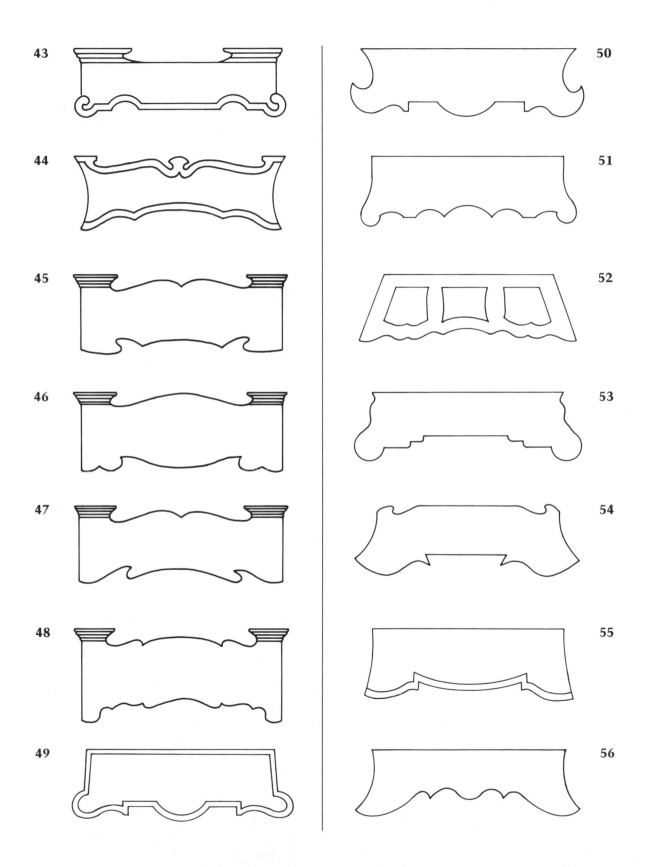

43

44

45

46

47

48

49

50

51

52

53

54

55

56

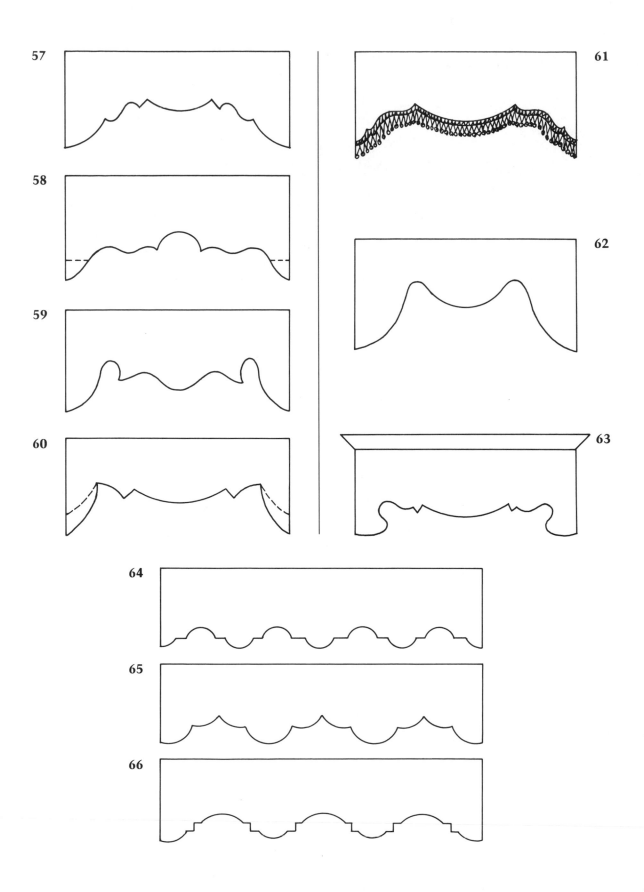

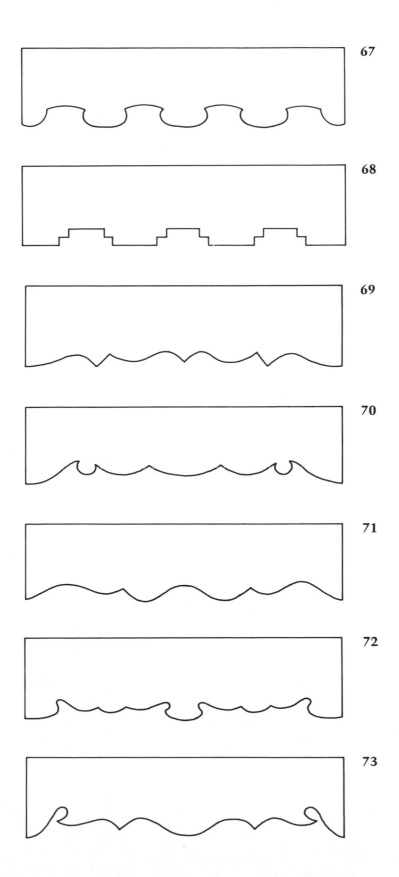

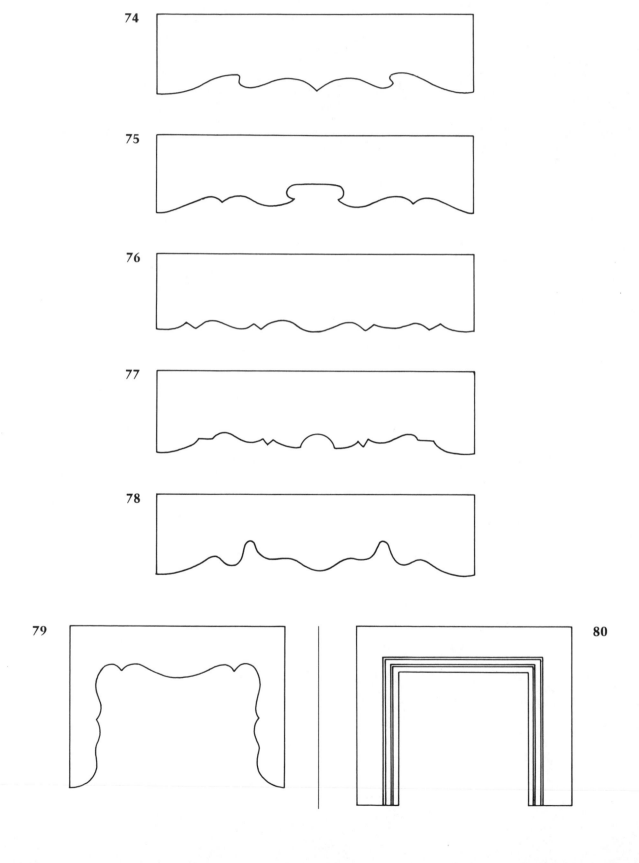

FEATURE STRIPS AND TRIM

Draperies with trim have become very popular, particularly those with bands of trim either ready-made or fabricated by the workroom. It is much easier to find one or two contrasting fabrics to use as a trim than it is to hunt endlessly and perhaps fruitlessly for just the right braid. Therefore many decorators design their own trim.

Most people do not understand the intricacies of sewing trim. It is a very time-consuming process and consequently expensive. Most trims can be sewed successfully on the machine if the operator is skilled. Extreme care must be taken to keep both fabric and trim from puckering. The best way to do this is to sew the trim on after the widths are joined and before they are hemmed or tabled. Many decorators think that trim is sewed on after the drapery is completed and do not understand that a delay in receiving the trim delays actual fabrication of the drapery.

The process of making bands of trim requires a meticulous worker. The fabric must be measured and cut to exact size and pressed carefully. It must be pinned on the drapery at an even distance from the edge and top-stitched in place down both sides. If this top-stitching is not done accurately, the effect is amateurish. The charge for this is by the yard and the charge is adjusted if two or more colors are used.

It is not wise to use very heavy trims on very lightweight fabrics, such as velvet on taffeta or silk. It is difficult to do, and often the drapery does not hang well.

To estimate yardage for ready-made trim, bands of trim, or borders, you must determine whether the trim is going down the front edges of the pair only or down the front and across the bottom. Do not forget tie-backs, cornices, or valances.

To go down the front edges only of one pair you will need twice the cut length of the drapery. If you are going across the bottom also, you will need twice the cut length plus the number of widths per pair times the width of the fabric. Thus a 5-width pair 86 inches long with trim down fronts only would take

$$
\begin{array}{ll}
86 \text{ inches} & \text{finished length} \\
+\ 12 \text{ inches} & \text{allowances for hems and headings} \\
\hline
98 \text{ inches} & \text{cut length} \\
\times\ 2 & \\
\hline
196 \text{ inches} & \\
\div\ 36 \text{ inches} & \text{inches per yard} \\
=\ 5\frac{1}{2} \text{ yards.} & \text{Allow 6 yards because trim often "takes up" when sewed.}
\end{array}
$$

For this same 5-width pair made of 48-inch fabric with trim down the front and across the bottom you would need

$$
\begin{array}{ll}
196 & \text{as above to go down fronts} \\
+\ 240 & \text{5 times 48 inches or widths times width of fabric.} \\
\hline
436 \text{ inches} & \\
\div\ 36 \text{ inches} & \text{In this case the amount lost in seaming and hemming} \\
=\ 12.1 \text{ yards.} & \text{fabric would allow for "take up" and} \\
& \text{12 yards would be enough.}
\end{array}
$$

Tie-backs use a lot more trim than you might think. A minimum size pair is 21 inches for each tie-back:

$$\begin{array}{r} 21 \text{ inches} \\ \times \ \underline{\ 2\ } \\ 42 \text{ inches} \end{array} \quad \text{or } 1\frac{1}{4} \text{ yards for one pair.}$$

Figure the length of each tie-back, multiply by 2 for a pair and then by the number of pairs needed, converting to yards.

Trims for cornices or valances are equal to the total number of running yards of fabric required to fabricate them.

If a band of trim is being made, the minimum yardage is the cut length of the drapery, as it must not be seamed down the front edge. Consequently even though you have only one pair to be trimmed, 86 inches long, you must have 86 inches plus 12 inches, or 98 inches of fabric for trim. If the trim is to be 2 inches wide, it requires a strip of fabric 4 inches wide to make it, as it must be completely double so seams will not show as light comes through. If the strips are to be cut to 4 inches, a piece of 48-inch fabric should yield 12 strips, but it is best to count on only 11 as selvages must be removed. So even though you need 98 inches of fabric to trim one single pair of draperies, this same 98 inches will give you 98 inches × 11, or 1078 inches of trim, or 29 yards for use to go down the fronts, across the bottom, or on tie-backs or valances. If the total number of yards needed is more than can be obtained from one cut length, then divide the amount needed by the number of strips you can get from each width and round out the yardage, being sure that there are enough strips equal to the cut length to go down the fronts of all pairs. If there are two colors, you must have the same yardage of both colors.

If ruffles are to be used as trim, the total yardage is figured the same way. Allow for double the width of the ruffle plus 1 inch for seams. A 2-inch ruffle must be cut to 5 inches. You must have twice as much running fabric for ruffles as for straight trim to allow for gathering. The charge for ruffles is by the yard after ruffling. Heavy fabrics cannot be easily ruffled. Chintz or polished cotton are good choices of fabric.

SPECIAL
WINDOW TREATMENTS

DECORATIVE SHADES
Roman Shades
Austrian Shades
Balloon Shades

SPECIAL TRACK SYSTEMS
Safe Snap®
Roll Pleat® or Ripplefold®
Accordia-Fold® or Stack Pleat®
Archifold® or Neat Pleat®
Paneltrac®

DECORATIVE SHADES

Roman, Austrian, and balloon shades are all related in that they are made and rigged in essentially the same way. Roman shades are tailored, Austrian shades are dressy, and balloon shades are somewhere in between.

Roman Shades

The roman shade in its simplest form is a flat piece of fabric, usually lined, with vertical tapes sewed on and rigged so that the shade can be raised. As it is raised, it forms accordian folds, stacking in a minimum amount of space. It can be made of solid or printed fabric, trimmed or plain. It can be shaped at the bottom and have a valance at the top. It can have decorative trim over the tapes or around the edges or both.

A more decorative version is often called tie-folded, prepleated, or other names that mean the shades remain accordian-folded when down. This eliminates the plain look and somewhat disguises the stitching lines of the tapes.

Many clients and decorators do not understand the nature of roman shades. They see them on windows in displays or in pictures, pulled partway up and very neatly arranged, and they do not realize that they do not achieve this effect just by pulling a cord and fastening it to a cleat. Usually the shades must

Figure 37. (left) Flat Roman shade. Partially open to show pleats.

Figure 38. (right) Prepleated Roman shade.

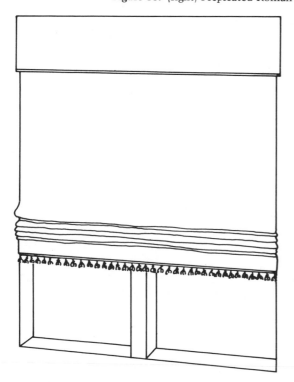

be straightened or arranged in folds each time they are moved. They pleat up from the bottom first when raised, the top remaining flat. This is quite acceptable to many clients but should be explained to those who might not understand.

Roman shades are better not very wide. The problems of rigging and the weight on wide shades can make them very difficult to handle. Unless the shade remains stationary at all times, it is best to make a series of smaller ones.

The tapes sewn on the back of roman shades vertically at 12- to 18-inch intervals have white bone rings on them spaced 5 inches apart. These are the rings through which a small traverse cord is strung to rig the shade. All of this shows on the outside of the window and cannot be concealed. If outside appearance is important, do not forget this feature.

If all of this sounds somewhat negative, it is to protect you and your client. The popular thing is not always the best thing in window coverings. However, roman shades have a definite place in the window covering scheme. They have several advantages that make them attractive. They can be fitted close to the window glass, thus aiding in insulation. This close-fitting characteristic is also an advantage when space is a problem. They do not interfere with furniture or plants set close to a window. Also, since they stack in a very small area when open, they give maximum light and air and take up no wall space. The small amount of fabric used is a desirable factor, though the labor cost is much greater than that to make a drapery.

The top of a roman shade is very plain. Many prefer to have a small flap or valance, which should not be deep, 6 inches being standard. It can be straight or shaped. If the bottom of the shade is shaped, the valance is often shaped to correspond. Trim can be added to both. A rod is inserted in the bottom of roman shades to make them rigid. This rod is inserted in a tuck set up about 4 to 5 inches from the bottom. In some cases the bottom is shaped in a Greek key design and a decorative brass rod is run through the bottom for interest and weight.

Yardage for a roman shade is very simple to calculate. Fabric must be 3 inches wider than the width desired and 10 inches longer for a flat roman shade. For a pleated one the fabric must be twice the length plus 10 inches. Since valances are self-lined, the amount needed is twice the depth of the valance plus 4 inches. For the shade an equal amount of lining is required. If the window is wider than the fabric, two full lengths must be allowed (or more for wide spans). Seams must fall behind the tapes, so you cannot count on adding just a few inches on one side. In other words, if you need more than one width, you must have two.

Another version of the roman shade is the roll-up shade, made flat just as the roman but with no tapes. It has a 1½ inch diameter wood pole in a pocket in the bottom and two sets of ties suspended from the top. These are made of flat pieces of fabric 2 to 3 inches wide, one suspended down the front and the other down the back of the shade. The ties must be a little longer than the shade so they can be tied when the shade is down. When the shade is raised, it is rolled around the pole and the ties are tied under the pole to hold it. This is obviously a two-person job since it would be impossible to roll, hold, and tie at the same time. This is the least expensive of the shades and can be used with good effect.

Figure 39. Austrian shade with swag.

Austrian Shades

The Austrian shade is elegant and very dressy (fussy, if you listen to some designers). They are similar to roman shades but are much softer since the fabric gathers instead of pleating. Generally you will find that people like or dislike them very definitely. In the dressiest or most elegant form, they are made of very sheer fabric with triple fullness and can be trimmed with fringe on the bottom. They can remain stationary on the window or be rigged to raise and lower. In the latter instance they often need adjustment when lowered as the folds are disarranged when moved. They can be used very effectively to screen a glass area where the view is not necessarily pleasant but it is desirable to admit light.

Austrian shades are not confined to sheer fabrics. They can be used as true shades to give privacy as long as the fabric used is soft enough to drape well. Some designers use them to give the blousy effect of a balloon shade. This is done by spacing the tapes farther apart so the folds are not so well controlled.

The Austrian shade becomes a valance or pouff simply by making it short, leaving off the rigging, and putting it on a board.

Always remember that everyone does not like this type of treatment and it is not safe to use it unless you know your clients well enough to know that this look will please them. This is a good time to be armed with pictures.

The Austrian shade is usually made unlined starting with a flat piece of fabric. Tapes are sewn on vertically, spaced from 15 to 24 inches apart as on romans. But these tapes are of double shirring tape with rings attached every 13 inches. After all the tapes are sewn on, the cords in the tape are pulled and the shade is gathered to triple fullness (or a little less in heavier fabrics). Traverse cord is then run through the rings as on roman shades and it is rigged to draw.

Fabric requirements are a lot different from roman shades. You must have the width of the space plus 4 extra inches for each foot to be covered. This allows for the folds to droop instead of pulling straight across. The length must be three times the finished length. Austrians look better with a bottom trim. This amount must be equal to the width of the fabric used to make the shade. A simple method of figuring is to allow one width of 48-inch fabric for each 36 inches to be covered in width. Multiply the finished length by three for sheer fabric and by two-and-one-half for heavier ones. Be sure to allow for pattern repeat if necessary.

> A window is 78 inches wide by 60 inches long.
> The fabric is 48 inches wide.
> To 78 inches add 24 inches (4 extra inches for each foot in width).
> 78 inches + 24 inches = 102 inches.
> 102 inches ÷ 48 inches = 2+ or 3 widths needed.
> 60 inches × 3 = 180 inches cut length needed.
> 180 inches × 3 widths = 540 inches amount needed.
> 540 ÷ 36 inches = 15 yards.

The trim needed is 102 inches or the total width of fabric needed. If the fabric has a 23-inch repeat, you would divide the cut length by the pattern repeat: 180 ÷ 23 inches = 7.8. Since it requires 7+ repeats, you would need 8 repeats or 8 × 23 inches = 184 inches for each cut length

> 184 inches × 3 = 552 inches, or 15½ yards. Order 16 yards.

Balloon Shades

Balloon shades are similar to both Austrian and roman shades, resembling one or the other according to the way they are made. They are more casual than either because the folds are not so rigidly controlled and therefore give a blousy

Figure 40. Balloon shade with wide spaces.

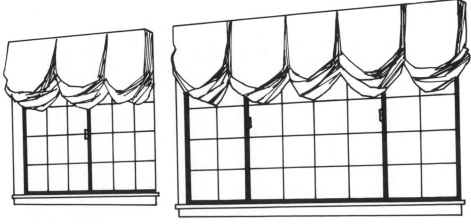

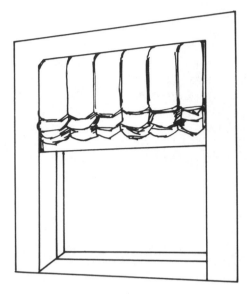

Figure 41. Balloon shade with narrow spaces.

effect. Once again, people react strongly to them and should see a sample or some very good pictures before choosing them.

When balloons are pleated at the top, they resemble a plain roman shade when they are down. As soon as they are raised, they blouse and the tailored effect is gone. They can, however, be dressed down to give the effect of a soft roman.

If balloons are shirred at the top, they should have three or four rows of shirring tape to give them a finished effect. The effect is of softly hanging

Figure 42. Balloon shade with shirred or gathered heading.

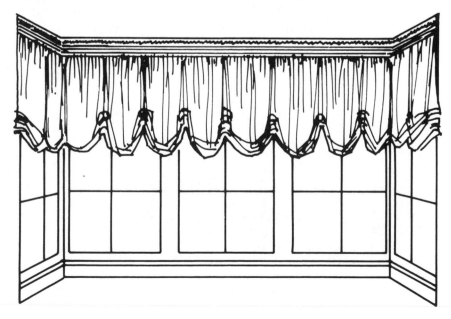

sheers until they are raised, when they have somewhat the effect of an Austrian shade at the bottom.

Yardage requirements are for double fullness across the window and the finished length plus 10 inches for the length.

The spacing for divisions or drops in Austrian or roman shades is fairly standard, but in balloon shades it makes a lot of difference in their look. If the tapes are close together, the shades are much more blousy, whereas a softer look comes from having the tapes farther apart.

Balloons are made like romans with tapes sewed on vertically at intervals, spaced much wider to allow inverted pleats to be laid in at each tape, and secured top and bottom. If the description for making these shades sounds simple, please remember that the flat piece of fabric must be prepared and measured very carefully. The stitching lines for tapes must be marked in parallel lines. The tapes must be sewed on both sides with rings carefully aligned and the shades must be rigged accurately. The process is very time-consuming and painstaking.

SPECIAL TRACK SYSTEMS

Several systems of draperies do not use conventional pleats. They have special uses, mostly in commercial installations, but in some cases they work well for residential use also.

All of these systems have special uses and you should study them well for their application to your window situation and familiarize yourself with all aspects before specifying them. They can be used with less fabric than the conventional, thus saving yards of fabric on a large installation. However, with the exception of Safe Snap®, the rods used are more expensive than the conventional rod, so costs must be carefully considered. The ease of maintenance may offset the rod costs, so this is a factor to consider.

Safe Snap®

This system was created primarily for use as a hand-traverse operation. It has no brackets, cords, pulleys, master carriers, or hooks. Therefore it is almost trouble-free and requires virtually no maintenance. The track is simple to install since it screws directly into the wall or ceiling. Although designed for hand-traverse, it can be adapted to a cord-traverse rod if desired.

The draperies are made as flat panels with a special heavy-duty snap tape sewed at the top. No crinoline is needed. This method can be used economically by hanging the panels flat when closed, giving a pleated effect when open. If a pleated look is desired at all times, a double snap allows fullness at each slide but does not do away with the simplicity of the installation.

This system is excellent for use in dormitories, hospital rooms, mental institutions, and any other place where many people may handle the draperies. If used too roughly, it simply comes unsnapped. Nothing tears or rips.

Maintenance is almost eliminated. The drapery unsnaps from the rod and becomes a flat panel. There are no hooks to be removed and reinserted. The panels can be machine-washed and run through a mangle or tumble-dried and rehung.

Roll Pleat® or Ripplefold®

This system is fabricated in a similar fashion to the snap pleat, but the rod is different and has a special rigging. Fullness can be controlled by using different spacing of the slides on the rod.

The drapery rides under the rod and rolls softly from front to back so that there appears to be no wrong side and the draperies look equally well from inside or outside. They stack back in less space than that required by conventional installations.

The draperies are made in flat panels and special nylon tape is sewed on. The exact hemmed size of the panel needed is given in a chart that also gives predetermined fullness and the number of snaps and carriers needed. The rods should be mounted on the ceiling.

A similar system has been adapted for residential use and is franchised throughout the country.

Accordia-Fold® or Stack Pleat®

This system has a more tailored look than the previous one. It works in a similar way, snapping to the rod and riding under it. However, it has knife-edge pleats, stitched alternately—front and back to form accordianlike folds. The depth of stack back is controlled by the tape that is used and the width of stack back is almost half that of conventional systems.

Charts are very precise, giving fullness and size of hemmed panel needed for each size of tape. Draperies are hemmed and tabled with crinoline as in conventional pleated draperies. Then snap tape is sewed across the top as in the other snap systems. However, the difference here is that single-fold pleats are formed alternately front and back on guide marks provided on the tape and the pleats stitched to a depth shown on the chart for the fullness desired.

Archifold® or Neat Pleat®

These two and several other systems are made with plastic devices about 1 inch by 3½ inches sewed across the top of the drapery and snapped to the rod. The general effect is the same as that of the other systems—more tailored than one, less tailored than others.

Paneltrac®

Paneltrac® is adaptable for many uses since it is flat and slides like oriental shoji screens. The panels are interlocked so that moving one panel moves them all. They can be used center-draw or one-way. They stack in a predetermined space.

There is no fullness, so a patterned fabric shows to its best advantage and less fabric is used. Fabrics can be easily changed so you could have a summer and winter installation. The panels are held to the track with VELCRO® Tape so they can easily be removed for cleaning.

Paneltrac® could be used as a liner under another drapery, as the only treatment at a window, or as a room divider since there is no track on the floor. It must be used as a ceiling mount, and for multiple panels the track is quite wide—up to 4 inches. It could be mounted below ceiling height if mounted in a cornice.

SPECIFICATIONS

Specifications must be specific to be of any use at all. They must spell out what is to be done, materials and hardware to be used, and anything else that is pertinent so that all bids will be on an equal basis. They can be wordy or simple, but they must be complete. Even if a job is not being bid but is going to your regular drapery contractor, it will save time and avoid misunderstanding to have everything clearly defined.

Several things are necessary to writing good specifications:

1. Time and place where bid must be submitted,
2. Instructions to bidders,
3. Indication of necessary insurance and bond,
4. General instructions,
5. Scope of work,
6. Workmanship and method of fabrication,
7. Fabric and hardware schedule.

If it is required that a job site be inspected prior to a bid, it is wise to ask that a form be signed by those who do so to protect the specifier, the bidder, and the client. It is also wise to provide for a formal inspection and approval after the installation is complete to be sure that specifications were followed. It is very upsetting when you are underbid on a job to find that the work is not in accordance with specifications and that nothing has been or will be done about it.

A sample bid is included at the end of this chapter to give you an idea of how the more technical bids are written.

Certain small things that are somewhat traditional in specifications are not really necessary.

1. Unless there is some special reason, it is unnecessary to specify size and kind of thread. Only stipulate that the thread match the fabric.
2. Whether weights are square or round matters little, but it is wise to specify covered weights since they are made of lead and rub off on the fabric if not covered. The number of a weight indicates its size.
3. Stitches per inch mean little since it is unlikely that anyone will ever count them, and if the workroom involved is reliable, they will use the best setting for the job.

If you want to include such small details, be sure the information is accurate.

COMMON MISTAKES

There are many mistakes made by those who specify that cause problems for workrooms and clients.

Bids Lacking Specifications

Jobs are put out to bid with no fabric, hardware, or fullness specified (e.g., draperies shall be unlined of a flame-resistant fabric. Hardware shall be heavy duty.). In this case bids would have no relation to each other at all. They would mean nothing and you would probably get what you deserved if you accepted the lowest bid—a cheap, skimpy, badly made drapery on an inadequate rod.

Fullness must be specified. In most cases it is either specified incorrectly or not specified at all. At no time should it ever be specified in percentages, and if it is not specified, bids will not be related. (See the section Fullness in the Chapter on Measuring and Estimating.)

The size of hems and headings and whether double should be stated.

Fabrics and hardware must be defined, sources given, and the acceptability of substitutes indicated. (Substitutes should not be allowed unless submitted for approval.)

Unless all of this is done and carefully checked on completion, the whole bid system is a farce.

Specifying Discontinued Fabrics

Many firms do not maintain up-to-date collections of samples. Once upon a time it was safe to expect samples and prices to remain current for a year. No longer! Fabrics come and go at an alarming rate and prices change even faster. Keep your samples current or do your selecting at showrooms where this is done for you. Always check with your fabric source to be sure of availability before specifying large jobs. It is always harder to find a suitable substitute than it was to find the original fabric. It also delays bids and tempts unauthorized substitutions if the bid goes out with incorrect information.

Using Fabrics Incorrectly

Casement fabrics should not be lined. Very long, heavy draperies should not be interlined. Heavy blackout lining should be used only when absolutely necessary. In most cases upholstery fabrics do not make satisfactory draperies. The section Facts on Fabrics in the chapter Background Knowledge clarifies these and other aspects of fabric.

Using Unrealistic Treatments

Three sets of traverse rods in a pocket designed for one is an example. Here are several more: Very heavy draperies to be installed on a ceiling where there is no adequate support. Long lined draperies hanging directly over air-conditioning convectors where the flow of air blows between the lining and fabric, causing them to billow. Huge cornices that cannot be taken up the stairs or elevators in a building. Basically what is needed is common sense and a little thought.

Taking Measurements from a Plan

Assuming that draperies can be made from measurements taken from a plan is a reckless fallacy. Ceiling heights may change, and even if they do not, in most cases they are not exactly what the plan states. Window locations are often changed and windows added or left out. Walls are frequently relocated and ceiling or pocket construction may differ from that specified in the plan.

Asking for Prices in Linear Feet

Asking for drapery prices in linear feet is unrealistic. In order to figure this you would have to take a specific size, such as 10 feet in width and 9 feet in height, determine the fullness, figure yardage, multiply by cost per yard, figure labor, rod, and installation, and then divide by 10. A difference in length would cause the whole figure to change because yardage would be different. If there were many small rods or several large ones, the price would change because the first 3 to 6 feet of a rod are the most costly. If pattern repeat or fullness changed or if the drapery were lined instead of unlined, the whole thing would change. So price per linear foot is an educated guess and not reliable except for specific instances.

Tinted or Thermal Glass

Not understanding the problems of tinted glass or thermal glass can lead to trouble. Find out from the glass dealers if they have standards for allowing for air flow and pass these on to the drapery makers. If proper allowances are not made for air flow, heat can build up behind the drapery and the glass will break.

Installation and Hardware

Probably the worst mistakes that are made concern installation and hardware.

1. Drapery pockets that are not large enough or are incorrectly designed for the rods to be used.
2. Dropped ceilings that create a pocket that is too narrow and too high for anyone to reach to install a rod (such as 2 feet deep and 8 inches wide).
3. Specifying rods to be hung at a point where there is no support in the ceiling.
4. Specifying off-brand rod systems with no information as to source. Some of these systems are quite good—just unusual—but your bidders may be unfamiliar with them. Sometimes the source may be hard for them to locate.
5. Specifying motorized rods that are inadequate for the job. A regular traverse would be better if the motor won't work.
6. Specifying drapery track by general contractor. In most cases this is a disaster because this is exactly what is done. The contractor usually knows little or nothing about draperies and traverse rods so he orders a certain number of feet of the rod number specified and puts it up without regard to where it is spliced, or whether it is bent or was damaged during installation. If it is put up with no parts, as is most often done, the installer has to take it down to rig it and put it back up, thus increasing the chances of damage. There is also an extra cost involved.

Three actual examples may illustrate the problem of specifying rods by general contractor. In one case hundreds of feet of rod were put up backward so that when it was rigged, the master carriers faced the outside of the building. In another case rods were put up throughout a building and spliced wherever they ran out of track. Consequently, slides and masters would not traverse properly and all rods had to be taken down, respliced, and rerigged. Another building had two floors of rods put up, this time with all parts. However, the drawing of the rods related only to the windows and not to the walls, causing no end of confusion, such as having to go into the next room to open or close your drapery.

From all of this it should be obvious that accurate specifications are very important and that a lot of thought should go into them before they are sent out to be bid.

SAMPLE BID

Instructions to Bidders

1. All bids to be submitted on enclosed bid form (or by letter). If duplicates are required, be sure to specify.
2. Bids must be received at NAME OF FIRM, ADDRESS OF FIRM, no later than DATE, TIME. No bids will be accepted after the scheduled closing time.
3. Bids will be by invitation and no security is required with bids.

OR

3. Bids will be by invitation and will be accompanied by a bid bond of $_____. Successful bidder will be required to submit certificate of insurance indicating coverage for Workmen's Compensation, Comprehensive General Liability, and Comprehensive Automobile Liability in limits approved by owner (or other).
4. Proposals shall remain firm for a period of _____ days after time and date set and may not be withdrawn for thirty days after that time.
5. Any bidder receiving an invitation to bid and who elects not to do so should notify the person sending the bid immediately.
6. Each bidder represents that his or her bid is based upon the items specified and that no substitutions will be used unless approved by those who issued the bid.
7. Before submitting the proposal, bidders should carefully examine all specifications and drawings. They should visit the site, if construction is nearing completion, to inform themselves of all conditions and limitations pertaining to the job. Any conditions that may prevent a first-class installation are to be stated in the proposal. Ignorance of conditions will not excuse deviation from the contract.
8. The right is reserved to reject any and all bids and to waive informalities and technicalities in proposals. The owner reserves the right to award the work as he or she deems best and is not obliged to accept the lowest bid.
9. All items shall be guaranteed for one year after official acceptance against defects in material and workmanship.
10. The drapery contractor shall supervise each phase of fabrication and installation and shall be responsible for all safety precautions. The contractor shall coordinate with the building management to determine unloading and parking facilities and use of elevators.
11. Specify whether progress payments will be made or if payment is made only when job is complete.
12. Specify damages and liabilities (if any) if all conditions of contract and specified delivery are not met.

General

1. Work includes all fabrics, labor, hardware, freight, and any other material or equipment required for a complete installation of the draperies as specified.
2. The drapery contractor shall be responsible for taking field measurements at the site and checking field conditions before proceeding with work. The project manager must be notified in writing of conditions that would hinder completion of work as specified.
3. Installation should not be completed until temperature and humidity in the building approximate the conditions that will exist when the building is occupied.

Scope of Work

1. Fabrication shall be performed by a reputable drapery contractor who is normally engaged in the business of making finest quality custom draperies.
2. This contractor shall guarantee his or her work against defects of fabric, workmanship, and installation for a period of one year. The contractor must also guarantee to make good any damages to building or contents created by installation.
3. The drapery contractor shall keep the premises free of the accumulation of waste material and rubbish and must leave the site clean and free of implements and surplus material at the end of each work day. All glass, hardware, fixtures, and wall surfaces must be left clean and undamaged.
4. The owner shall inspect the draperies after installation and any required adjustments such as soil marks, flaws, or defects in workmanship must be carried out by the contractor.
5. The drapery schedule indicates the scope of work. Sizes are approximate for bidding purposes and are not to be used for final measurements.
6. Names, numbers, and sources of materials listed are those desired, but samples of fabrics must be submitted tagged with manufacturers number and color and the name of the bidder. No substitutions will be accepted. (A certificate from the manufacturer stating that his fabric was used may be required.)
7. It is the responsibility of the contractor to inspect all materials before cutting and to report any defects immediately.
8. (Optional) The contractor shall make and install one complete drapery for approval. When approved this drapery shall serve as a quality standard for the entire installation.
9. Manufacture and installation must be done using appropriate union labor (if applicable).

Workmanship

1. All draperies shall be of the finest quality to withstand hard usage and dry cleaning. Methods of manufacture; cutting allowances for shrinking, tabling, and finishing; and pressing shall be of highest standards as followed in the best custom drapery manufacturing.

Fabrication

1. Fullness—All draperies are to be at least double fullness (or other). Under no circumstances is the fullness to be less, and nothing less than half-widths may be used. Total width of fabric to be used must be twice (or other) the length of the track plus necessary allowances for seams, side hems, returns, and overlaps. Each 48-inch width of fabric shall be pleated to budget fullness—21 to 24 inches (or other, such as 2½—18 to 21 inches). All pleats are to be evenly spaced.
2. Coverage—All draperies are to extend the full length of the rod and shall overlap by at least 4 inches in the center and return to the wall if necessary.
3. Each width of fabric must be cut exactly square, and allowances must be made for the pattern to match.
4. Each selvage shall be removed to insure correct hanging. All widths are to be joined with a french seam or with an overlock serging machine on unlined draperies or other approved methods on lined draperies.
5. All draperies are to be made with double 1½ inch side hems, blind-stitched if possible. If not, they shall be sewed not more than ⅛ inches from the fold. Side hems on unlined draperies shall be put in first.
6. Bottom hems are to be double 4 inches (or other) and blind-stitched as above. Covered weights of 1 inch are to be tacked inside all corners and at each seam. Open ends of hems are to be closed by hand or with a blind-stitch corner closer.
7. All thread shall match fabric as closely as possible.
8. All draperies will have a double heading of 3 to 4 inches to cover a top grade, permanently stiff crinoline.
9. Before crinoline is set, panels must be tabled to assure squareness and correct length.
10. Crinoline must extend the entire width of the panel in one continuous piece. At each side of the panel it must come to within ¼ inch of the edge and must be turned back at least 2 inches. The ends of the panel at the crinoline must be closed by machine or hand, as specified, and must be sewed across to the first pleat on each side.
11. All pleats (specify pinch or french) must be evenly spaced and stitched by machine or to the depth of the crinoline. Each pleat shall be tacked within ½ inch of the bottom and a second tacking used at the top if required for appearance.
12. Lined draperies must have all seams on face fabric and lining pressed open before the lining is attached.
13. Lining shall come to 1½ inches from the bottom of the drapery.
14. Bottom hems of both lining and face fabric are to be put in before they are attached.
15. When linings are put in, all lining seams must coincide with face fabric seams.
16. All linings are to be loosely tacked to face fabric at the top of the hems at each seam and each half-width.
17. All patterns are to be perfectly matched in order that the design will be identical at each window both horizontally and vertically.
18. Pins must be placed in heading as specified for the rod used—one ½ inch from each end of the drapery and one in the center of each pleat.

19. All draperies are to be pressed before installation and dressed down properly after installation.
20. All draperies must extend from ceiling to floor (or others as shown in drapery schedule).
21. Clearance from floor (convector or sill) must be no more than 1 inch (or other) from finished surface.
22. All draperies shall be removable from hardware for cleaning purposes. All metal permanently affixed to drapery shall be non-corrosive.

Fabric

If all fabric is the same for the entire job, specify

Manufacturer

Pattern name and/or number

Pattern color

Fiber content

Flame-proof requirements (if applicable)

Any other applicable information, such as width of fabric, pattern repeat, and special finishes.

If fabrics are different in different areas, provide a drapery schedule showing room numbers and fabrics, giving all of the above information.
Specify the type and color of lining with all necessary descriptions, as above.
See the sample of a drapery schedule at the end of the chapter.

Hardware

Hardware shall be

Manufacturer's name (or equivalent if desired)

Stock number of rod

Finish of rod

Specify if tension pulleys are required

Special parts, if any.

The direction of draw must be stated or clearly shown on the plan. Where drapery is to hang—in recess, on wall, on ceiling, or in pocket—must be specified.

Special Treatments

Cornices, valances, and the like must have separate specifications with clear sketches drawn to scale.

Fabrication and Hardware Specifications

Fabric A
    Source—Name and address
    Pattern name, number, and color
    Width of fabric—pattern repeat
    Fiber Content

Fabric B
    Same information.

Fabric C
    Same information.

Lining
    Same information.

Drapery Type D (Example)
    Pinch-pleated traverse
    2½ inch fullness—ceiling to floor
    Lined.

Drapery Type E (Example)
    Accordia-Fold® or equivalent
    100% Fullness—ceiling to convector
    Unlined.

Hardware #1
    Source—name and address
    Stock number—tension pulley.

Hardware #2
    Source—name and address
    Stock number—cord weights

FABRICATION AND HARDWARE SCHEDULE

Room number	Fabric	Drapery type	Window style	Hardware style	Direction of draw	Where mounted	Approximate size
234	A	D	T	#1	C–D	W	84w × 106L
235	B	E	S	#2	C–D	C	72w × 55L
236	C	E	S	#2	C–D	C	72w × 55L
237	B	E	S	#2	C–D	C	72w × 55L
238	C	E	S	#2	C–D	C	72w × 55L
239	A	D	T	#1	Rt	W	36w × 106L
240	A	D	T	#1	Lf	W	36w × 106L

Room number from plan; Window style obtained from plan; C—ceiling mount; W—wall mount; C–D—center draw; Rt—one-way right; Lf—one-way left.

SPECIFYING FOR APARTMENTS

Workrooms or factories that make draperies for apartment complexes try to provide you with the best possible product for the least amount of money. They can do this better if you specify with that thought in mind.

Standard size draperies are the least expensive kind. Workrooms are set up for these sizes and can produce them more easily and for the least amount of money. The basic standards are:

> Finished widths—50 inches, 72 inches, 96 inches, 120 inches, 144 inches
> Finished lengths—54 inches, 63 inches, 84 inches

If you stay within 2 inches of the frame at sides and top, the installer will usually hit wood.

Wall-to-wall draperies in rental units are not realistic. They probably add nothing to the decor since most of the fabrics used are very neutral. If the tenants need the wall space, they will likely take the drapery down, push it aside, or perhaps even cut it off. Ceiling to floor is also unnecessary. It only uses more fabric and adds to the installer's woes if the ceilings are not level, which is true more often than not.

Installing in a recessed window can be a mistake as well. Recesses are seldom exact in height and width, so mass-produced draperies may be too long for some, too short for others, and fit very few. Even if they fit, light will show around the edges and the drapery will appear uneven at the bottom. It is best to go at least 4 inches above, below, and to the sides of the opening.

This advice holds true if you are selling custom draperies to an apartment dweller. Many of them move fairly often, and standard size draperies will fit many different apartments. If the client will want to sell the draperies to the next tenant, simple style is best. Treat these clients right while they are in modest circumstances and they will come to you when they need custom draperies for their house.

TECHNIQUE

FOR THE WORKROOM OPERATOR

The decisions you make in the workroom will ultimately determine whether or not the draperies you produce will look and hang as well as they should and whether they will please the client. It is for you to decide whether or not to use a questionable fabric, if weights are advisable, if a single hem can be used to save fabric, and in short, to resolve all of the many questions that arise during a workday. Work constantly toward any system that will minimize mistakes in cutting, sewing, tabling, and finishing.

Always remember that mistakes are costly. They waste time. To remake the drapery will take more time than to make it originally, using time that should rightfully be devoted to make something else. New fabric may have to be bought, resulting in a loss to you. By the time it is ordered, dye lots or pattern repeats may have become a problem. Most important of all, when something goes wrong, a customer immediately becomes more critical and may never be completely satisfied.

Setting up your workroom is the important first step. The operator is responsible for this and all that follows. All workrooms vary somewhat in their techniques of making draperies. The methods described here are fairly standard and work well in a workroom designed to make large numbers of custom draperies. They are not necessarily the best methods for small workrooms, and they certainly do not apply in large commercial workrooms geared to turn out factory-type, machine-finished draperies.

We hope anyone who sets up a workroom has a basic knowledge of sewing and the machines to use. It would be helpful if someone in the shop could do minor repairs and adjustments on the machines. It is essential to know a good mechanic who will make major repairs in reasonable time so you will not lose the use of an essential machine indefinitely. All of the machines described here are expensive, and it is not feasible for most shops to have backup machines.

If you are the operator of a workroom, it is necessary that you know the facts in the preceding chapters, especially the chapter on Measuring and Estimating, but it is also important to know why these facts are true so when you are faced with comparable situations, you will know how to handle them. The following chapters should help to clarify many technical points.

THE WORKROOM

SETTING UP THE WORKROOM

DRAPERY ACCESSORIES
Thread
Weights
Pins (Hooks)
Crinoline
Tapes

WORKROOM ACCESSORIES
Shears
Pins
Push Pins
Rulers
Yardsticks
Steel Tape
Irons
Razor Blades
Needles
Water Bottles
Pencils

MACHINE ACCESSORIES
Bobbins
Needles
Screwdriver
Pins
Magnet
Ruler
Snips

SETTING UP THE WORKROOM

There is no definite plan for setting up a workroom because the amount and shape of the space varies so much. Ideally, the space should have no posts or columns to allow for the best positioning of machines and tables and to allow for freedom of movement around them.

A small one- or two-person workroom could get by with multiuse tables, but a larger workroom must keep separate tables for cutting and for pressing so that tabling can go on at all times. Some shops can get by with only one serger, blind-stitch, and lock-stitch machine, while others need at least two of each.

The main thing to remember is that the flow of work should be even to avoid wasted motion between steps in making the drapery. Storage should be close to the area where fabric is received. Storage bins should be close to the cutting table. There should be space next to the cutting table to stack cut draperies and linings.

Machines should be placed so that work progresses logically. The pleaters and tackers should be near the pressing table. Racks for hanging completed draperies should be near the pressing table with a supply of plastic wrapping tubing close by. Time spent walking across the room to get something is time wasted.

Small tables or shelves should be near each main table to hold pins, rulers, scissors, pencils, and other implements. The tables themselves should be kept clear so time is not wasted clearing them off for use. Each table should have a drop cord over it for plugging in an iron. It should be positioned so that when the iron is in use all parts of the table can be reached.

Storage bins for fabric must be at least 48 inches deep, preferably 54 inches. They should be divided into sections up and down and across to avoid stacking too many rolls on top of each other. Rolls on the bottom are very difficult to pull out, and if they are small, they can be lost under the larger rolls. The divisions from side to side keeps the rolls from rolling sideways when others are removed. It might seem simpler to store rolls on their ends in a stand-up bin, but this is a definite no-no for drapery fabrics. The fabric has a tendency to slide down the roll if stored for any length of time and ripples will form in the fabric that are almost impossible to press out. When fabrics are put in the bins, it is a good idea to write the client's name on the exposed end of the roll since other markings on the package cannot be seen.

The cutting table should be at least 60 inches wide and as long as practical. Eighteen feet is a good length since very few draperies are longer than 17 feet. The table should have a smooth finish with no splinters. Polished oak with a bar finish is a good choice. The side should be permanently marked in inches. Lines across the table at no less than two-inch intervals are helpful. A clamp to hold the fabric at the zero line is also of use. There should be a device for holding rolls of fabric at the other end of the table and a good light source along its entire length. Tables with lighted panels are helpful in detecting flaws, but most flaws can be seen without them.

Another table for stacking cut widths should be nearby, preferably close to the opposite end from the fabric holder. This is where one stands to fold fabric. This table should be 24 to 30 inches wide and 6 to 8 feet long. A small table in a convenient spot can hold scissors, pins, rulers, pencils, and tags for marking leftover fabric, and should have a space for cutting tickets. The cutting table must stay free of such items.

Each machine should have an aid table, which extends at least 2 feet to the left side, 2 feet to the front of the machine, and 2 to 3 feet to the back on the left side. This allows space for the fabric to lie while being sewn. A small space on the right to store pins, scissors, rulers, and so forth is also useful. It should have a 3- to 4-inch lip to keep things from falling off.

It is helpful to have one or more rolling racks with a 2-inch diameter bar at the top to lay draperies across as they are processed, joined, hemmed, tabled, and so on, but it is not an essential item and can take up a lot of vital space.

The pressing table must be padded and covered with canvas or some other durable fabric resistant to scorch. It is of no particular advantage to have the table more than 5 feet wide, but it should be at least 10 to 12 feet long.

A cabinet for supplies should be located in a central spot. Thread, crinoline, tapes, and other like items should be kept there. Neatness should be encouraged. Thread is much easier to locate if it is sorted by color and kept that way. It should not accumulate on the machines, nor should partially used cones be thrown helter-skelter into boxes, for they may never be used. Machines should be kept free of all but essential accessories and dusted daily. Many a drapery has been ruined by oil or dirty lint from machines.

The workroom supervisor needs a desk and a file for current and completed orders. Here is where the process begins, sewing tickets are made and distributed, pleats figured or bar markings noted, and phone calls relating to orders received. The desk should be placed so the supervisor has an overall view of the workroom while seated.

The planning for the workroom setup should be done very carefully. The room should be drawn off at a scale of 1 inch to 1 foot and templates of all machines, bins, racks, and tables made on the same scale. These can then be placed and rearranged until a satisfactory layout is reached. Then your electrical wiring can be done so it is easy to plug in machines and drop cords can be correctly positioned over tables. Don't forget that people require space. If tables are set too close together, they cannot be used simultaneously.

Always allow more room, more storage space, and preferably more tables than you think you will need. If your business grows, you will have room to expand and you will not have to endure the trauma of moving so soon to a new location.

A very small workroom could be set up with one or two lock-stitch machines and a blind hemmer, but production would be slow as sheers would have to be french-seamed and pleats would have to be tacked by hand. A button sewer, or tacker, is the next most important machine to add. Not only does it tack pleats many times faster than can be done by hand, but the tack is more secure. If the shop will make a lot of unlined draperies, sheers, and casements, a serger with a lock-stitch should be the next investment. The purchase of a pleater would depend on the volume of work. If pleating becomes a bottleneck in production or if more than one person is required to pleat constantly, the expense of a pleater would be justified. A corner closer is an excellent device, particularly if a lot of commercial-type casements are made, but this is the least essential of the specialized machines.

If your shop is busy with a large volume of work, backup machines are almost a necessity. If your blind-stitch is out of order, production backs up in the whole shop. Four or five lock-stitch machines, and at least two each of sergers, blind-stitchers, and tackers keep production going if there should be a breakdown. An extra pleater is desirable too, but expense might prohibit having two.

Try at all times to be open-minded. Your employees may be more knowledgeable about work flow than you are. Listen to their suggestions and at least give them a try. Some of your best procedures may be developed this way.

DRAPERY ACCESSORIES

Drapery accessories are anything having to do with the making of a drapery other than the fabric and the lining.

Thread

Thread used to sew draperies should be heavy-duty, size 50 or larger if using ordinary sewing thread. Special threads are available to the trade. A mercerized thread in a color matching the fabric is still considered to be the best. A smaller size must be used on sheers and fine, lightweight fabrics, but usually a cotton thread is best even on these fabrics.

Some new threads have been put on the market in recent years. The polyester threads are fine for home sewing but are too expensive for workroom use. The Nylon or plastic threads were very popular when first introduced, largely for their see-through property—they matched everything so it was not necessary to keep a large stock or change them constantly. It is true that seams and hems looked great in most cases when the drapery was finished. However, within a short time, many of these seams began to pucker and no amount of pressing helped. The apparent cause for this seems to be that no matter how loosely tension is adjusted for sewing, these threads stretch slightly as they are sewn. After hanging or under certain conditions of moisture or heat, they shrink back to their original form, thus pulling the fabric and causing it to pucker. It is still possible to use these threads for stitching pleats and tacking since with crinoline in the heading, shrinking cannot take place to any noticeable degree.

Weights

Drapery weights are used to weight the seams, to avoid puckering, and to keep them from hiking up. At the leading edges they help the drapery to hang straight. Whether they are round or square makes little difference except that round ones are easier to insert in side hems.

The usual weight is made of lead in four round sizes, one square, and two triangular. All have perforations or openings to sew through to attach them to the drapery. The lead from an uncovered weight rubs off on the fabric, so most manufacturers now glue a covering to the weight that helps eliminate this problem. If you use uncovered weights, you may cover them with scraps of lining by using a zipper foot and sewing very closely around the weights. Then cut them apart, leaving a ¼-inch edge. You can sew through this to attach the weight.

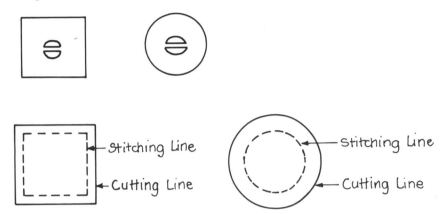

Some weights are now covered in cloth with a laminating process, leaving an edge or tab. These weights can be sewed into the seams as the widths are joined, thus eliminating the need for attaching later by hand.

Chain weights (often called "rat-tails") are sometimes used in sheers to stop billowing at the bottom. These weights are a series of BB shot covered in a woven rayon or cotton casing. They are made in a continuous chain and can be cut as needed. Some chain weights come in larger rectangular sizes for use in heavier fabrics or possibly for stage draperies, although ordinary chain is often used for this purpose.

Any chain weight will cause a bumpy appearance in the hem, but to achieve your purpose, appearance may have to be sacrificed to usefulness. Draperies or sheers hanging over air-conditioning convectors need these weights most often.

Pins (Hooks)

The terms "pin" and "hook" are generally used interchangeably. Their design varies slightly from one manufacturer to another. They can be bought in packages of 14 (not practical for workrooms), in bulk, or in cartridges for use in hand or machine pin-setters.

Pin-in hooks have a sharp pin at the opposite end from the hook that is pinned into the drapery at each side of the panel and behind each pleat. Sew-on hooks have eyelets that are sewn to the heading at the same points. Slip-in hooks slip into the heading at each pleat and must have pin-in hooks at each edge of the drapery. The two latter hooks have the disadvantage of not being adjustable on the job. Some variations of these that have adjustments are now made as a specialty item. The four-pronged hooks for pleater tape are also not adjustable. If this type of heading should be used by some stretch of the imagination for a custom drapery, the hooks must be inserted in the workroom and not left to the installer.

Hooks can be inserted with hand-held devices that measure as well as insert. You can use a machine but this must be done in the shop as the machine must be fastened down. If set correctly, these devices are more accurate and much faster to insert than pinning by hand. If hooks must be set by hand, a small wooden ruler will measure as well as help to pull the hooks into place.

The hook must be heavy enough to hold the drapery without bending. Small and lightweight hooks are useful only for lightweight sheers and delicate fabrics. If the fabric has been flame-proofed, the hook must also be rust-resistant.

Crinoline

Crinoline, or buckram, is the stiffening at the top of the drapery. It comes in several widths and grades. The size varies from 3 to 6 inches. The 3-inch size is used in very short draperies. The 4-inch size is standard. Other widths are used for special effects.

Nonpermanent is a heavily starched, woven crinoline that loses its stiffness if it is washed or cleaned. It is cheap but not practical for custom operations. A variation of this type is one that sticks to fabric when it is ironed. In general it is not satisfactory in the custom workroom except for stabilizing crinoline in slippery sheers.

Lightweight and heavyweight woven permanent-finish crinolines are staples for the workroom. Cheaper in price but quite satisfactory are the light- and heavyweight nonwoven permanent types. They are not as stiff and brittle to work with and hold up well.

Pellon is a stiffening that is nonwoven, permanent-finish, lightweight, and shrink-resistant. Because it is soft and resilient it is chosen by many decorators for sheers and other delicate fabrics. It is more expensive than other varieties.

Another type of drapery heading (that has little application to custom draperies) is pleater tape. This is a tape with woven pockets into which four-pronged hooks are inserted to form pleats. One type has only 23 pockets per yard that will pleat a 48-inch width of fabric to 24 inches. The other has 66 pockets per yard, giving greater flexibility in spacing pleats. Both have the advantage that the hooks can be removed and the draperies cleaned while flat. The disadvantage for custom draperies is that it is more difficult to control width than with regular pleating methods; moreover, two rows of stitching will show at the top on the face of the drapery. On a large volume, inserting these hooks would try the patience of a saint.

Tapes

Several different types of tapes are used on a regular basis in the workroom.

Roman shade tape is a twill-weave cotton tape about ⅝ inches wide with small plastic rings attached at 5-inch intervals. A series of these tapes is sewn vertically on a flat piece of fabric, with rings aligned, to make roman shades.

Single shirring tape is the same type of tape as roman shade with no rings and with one row of cord inserted in a woven pocket. When sewn flat on a piece of fabric along both edges, the cord can be pulled to gather or shirr the fabric. (Don't forget to fasten or knot one end of the cord before pulling.) Double shirring tape is similar except that there are two cords in woven pockets. This makes more controlled gathers that usually look more attractive. There is also a four-cord tape to form headings on sheers.

Austrian shade tape is a two-cord shirring tape with plastic rings sewed on at 13-inch intervals. When sewed vertically at intervals to a flat piece of fabric that is three times longer than the finished length desired, the fabric can be gathered to form an Austrian shade with rings spaced properly for rigging.

VELCRO® tape is used for fastening valances to boards, fastening tiebacks, and fastening panels to Paneltrac®. It consists of two parts, loop and pile, one of which is sewed to the valance, and the other glued, sewn, or stapled to the surface on which it is to fasten. The tape is nylon and virtually indestructible. It holds very well if no great strain is placed on it.

WORKROOM ACCESSORIES

Items used daily in the workroom are usually furnished by the management. In a large operation with many employees it may be necessary to ask them to furnish scissors for themselves as such implements have a way of disappearing. It is amazing how much more careful people are with their personal possessions than with yours.

Shears. Good quality shears are a necessity. Seven or eight inches is the most practical length as either is easily handled by most people. The quality must be good so the shears can be sharpened without deteriorating. Care must be taken not to drop them as this will ruin good shears very quickly. Each employee should have at least one pair.

Pins. Buy straight pins in bulk (1-pound boxes). Number 20 steel dressmaker pins are strong and long enough for the purpose. Distribute them in reasonable amounts into smaller boxes kept on the shelves near the tables. This encourages employees to be a little more careful with their supply and to reuse them when possible. It is also less disastrous when a box is dropped on the floor. It is not worth anyone's time to pick up pins that are dropped occasionally, but if a whole box goes, use a magnet to retrieve as many as possible.

Push Pins. If a clamp bar is not used when tabling, push pins must be used. These also should be distributed from the original box into smaller ones. Even if a clamp bar is used, a few of these pins should be at each table.

Rulers. Rulers of various sizes should be kept at each table. The standard 12-inch and a 6- or 7-inch one are musts. A ruler cut off to 8 inches is useful when pressing hems. If you have no pleating device, you will also need a ruler marked in tenths of inches.

Yardsticks. These are useful for many things other than measuring. They are particularly useful for smoothing out fabric and lining when tabling. They should be sturdy enough not to break easily.

Steel Tape. One or two 12-foot steel tapes must be available to check length measurements as tabling is done. These should be kept at the supervisor's desk as they also have a way of disappearing.

Irons. Keep a steam iron at each table. You do not need the fancy variety but a reliable make. Your best bet is to buy them on sale at discount houses as they wear out rapidly under constant use.

Razor Blades. Single-edge razor blades are the most effective ripping device. They should not be kept in boxes with pins because of the danger of accidentally cutting yourself, but they should be readily available.

Needles. Fairly long sharp needles are needed at tables where corner-closing is done. They are hard to keep up with but a pin cushion on the shelf would help.

Water Bottles. Plastic water bottles to fill the steam irons should be kept close to but not on the table. Dishwashing fluid bottles are good because their mouth easily fits the iron and can be closed to avoid spills.

Pencils. Use fluorescent crayons or pencils to mark pleats when pleating under a black light. Graphite pencils can be used but they leave unsightly marks on the heading.

MACHINE ACCESSORIES

Each machine should be equipped with all needed items for sewing.

Bobbins. Extra bobbins must be kept at each machine so time will not be wasted hunting for empty ones. Be sure not to mix sizes for different machines.

Needles. Each machine should have its own supply of needles. If more than one size is used, they all should be kept on hand. Bent or dull needles can cause bad stitches. A needle threader is helpful but many people do not need them.

Screwdriver. A screwdriver that fits the screw into the needle clamp should be provided for each machine. Be sure it is the right size so the slot in the screw will not be damaged.

Pins. A small supply of pins may be needed. A pin box is more necessary as pins are removed from draperies during stitching.

Magnet. A small magnet kept on the machine makes picking up pins much easier than using your fingers. Pins tend to collect in inaccessible places. To avoid this, store them in boxes.

Ruler. A 6-inch ruler is often useful. One marked in tenths of inches is a must if pleats are stitched on the lock-stitch machines.

Snips. Thread snips must be chained to each machine. Otherwise they will never be there when needed.

DRAPERY CONSTRUCTION TECHNIQUES

CUTTING DRAPERIES

Equipment Needed for Cutting

Steps in Cutting

Check all Information Pertaining
to the Job
Check for Flaws
Determine Right Side of Fabric
Check Condition of Fabric
Proceed with Cutting on Solid Fabrics
Pulling Threads
Splitting widths
Folding
Tagging
Cutting Lining
Cutting Printed Fabrics
*Determine hem line and alignment with
other draperies*
Check for pattern drift
Allowances when cutting printed fabrics
Fabrics lost between cuts
Dropped repeats
Other items to check

JOINING WIDTHS

Preparing to Sew

Sewing the Seam

Attaching Weights

Using Half-Widths

Matching Patterns

Completing the Seam

Joining Linings

Unlined Draperies

Serging
Enclosed Seams
Zigzag Seams

HEMS

Single Hems

Double Hems

Pressing Hems

Turning Hems with Pattern

Chain Weights in Hems

Stitching Hems

Special Hems

Heming Net Fabrics

Hems in Sheers

**PREPARING THE DRAPERY
FOR TABLING**

Lined Draperies

Unlined Draperies

TABLING

The Table

Unlined Draperies

Sheers and Casements
Heavier Fabrics

Lined Draperies

Lined Sheers and Casements

FINISHING THE DRAPERY

Closing Corners

Tacking the Lining

Pin Settings

Pressing

Folding

CUTTING DRAPERIES

The drapery cutter is a key person with tremendous responsibility who should try to be aware of it at all times. He or she must check fabrics, watch for flaws, allow the proper amount for cut lengths, calculate amounts for pattern repeats, and cut accurately.

Equipment Needed for Cutting

Every workroom should have a table used exclusively for cutting. It should be at least 5 feet wide and 12 or more feet long. The height should be comfortable for working but low enough to allow the cutter to reach across the table. The surface should be hard, slick, and free of snags. The side should be marked permanently in inches. A device to hold fabric rolls should be erected at one end. The table should be located where there is excellent light and be close to the fabric storage area.

The cutter should be provided with large, sharp shears (ten-inch length is best). An electric round knife can be used if the cutter can reach across the table and lift the knife easily with one hand. Long pencils in light and dark colors and a pencil sharpener are needed. If the table is not marked with lines at intervals, a T-square with a long extension is helpful. A straight, rigid 48- or 60-inch wooden ruler is a must. Use pressure tape in a color to contrast with the table to mark the cutting line. Use tags for marking leftover fabric.

Figure 43. Cutting table showing device used to hold rolls.

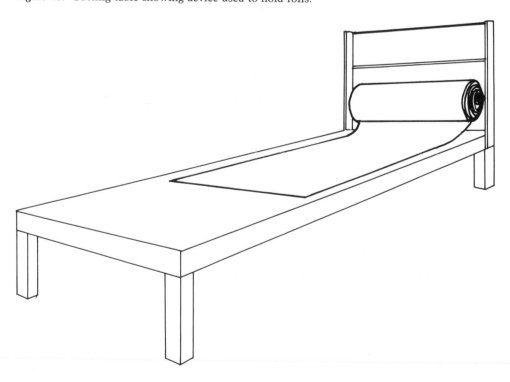

Steps in Cutting

Check all Information Pertaining to the Job. When starting to cut a job, the cutter should check the fabric source, pattern name or number, and color with the information on the cutting ticket. If it does not coincide, the reason should be found before any cutting is done.

Before cutting, check to find the finished length. Add the correct allowance for hems and headings and mark this spot at the side of the table with pressure tape. If there is a pattern repeat, the tape may have to be moved to compensate for this. At this point, unless someone else has already done so, check the cut length and the number of cuts needed with the yardage to make sure that you will have enough. When a large job with several cut lengths is being cut, it is best to cut the longest first. Then when you reach a flaw, it is often possible to work in a shorter length. Try to position flaws in hems and headings, thus saving a few inches of waste.

Check for Flaws. Checking for flaws must be done constantly. Most fabric lengths under 50 yards are designated as cut yardage and are inspected as they are cut and rerolled. Even then flaws do slip through. Most distributors will flag the flaws and allow extra yardage (¼ to ½ yard). Obviously if the flaw falls in the middle of a panel, this amount does little good and you must try to work the problem out.

Cut lengths should be specified when ordering, which puts the responsibility on the distributor, but do not expect the problem to be eliminated. On full rolls vigilance in looking for flaws must be even greater because the fabric is inspected only at the mill and not again at your source. A further discussion of flaws appears in the section on Problems with Fabrics in the chapter on Background Knowledge.

Determine Right Side of Fabric. There is seldom a question as to which side of the fabric is the right one. However, there are some reversible fabrics, and others, such as damasks, can be confusing. Certain casements and woven textures can also be hard to distinguish. This is the time to determine the right side and to make some notation or marking so the seamstress will join the widths correctly. Contrary to popular belief, you cannot tell the right side by the way the fabric is rolled or folded. The only safe thing to do when in doubt is to ask the designer or decorator who originated the job which side to use. If you have a sample book for the fabric, you should use it the way it was sampled.

Check Condition of Fabric. Most decorative fabrics now come rolled on tubes, though a few are still doubled and rolled; they are folded in half lengthwise and then rolled on a flat base. These fabrics will often have a crease down the center that cannot be pressed out. If this is true, be sure not to cut until the person who originates the job knows about it. Do not cut fabric rolled like this while it is folded. It must be opened and laid flat to be cut properly.

If a roll of fabric has been stored for any length of time standing on end, the fabric will frequently have creases in it caused by the material sagging toward the bottom of the roll. Before cutting, check to see whether these creases can be pressed out. If they can't be, reject the roll.

Proceed with Cutting on Solid Fabrics. *Pulling threads.* Having checked all of these things carefully, you are now ready to cut. First, straighten the edge of the fabric as it comes off the bolt. If the fabric is a solid color, you must cut with the grain of the fabric by pulling a thread across the fabric and cutting on the resulting line. To pull a thread, cut through the selvage edge, spread the fabric apart, and locate one of the individual threads. Grasp this thread and pull it gently across the fabric, breaking or cutting it at the opposite selvage. This leaves a clearly defined line that can be followed with the shears. Sometimes the thread you are pulling breaks in midwidth. In this case cut to that point and pull again. Some fabrics have such obvious threads that you can pick one with the eye and follow it across. After cutting the length, notch the bottom corner on each piece—always at the same corner. This enables the seamstress to know at which end to start the seam. This offers protection when fabrics have a nap or "shade" running from one direction to the other. There are times, when one or both selvages are very tight, that the cut will look very peculiar when following drawn threads. To check to see if this will be a problem, remove both selvages on one cut length and see whether the fabric straightens out. If it does, proceed with the cutting in this manner. If not, the fabric has some other problem and should be rejected.

It is very difficult, in some cases impossible, to pull threads in fabrics such as chintz, twill weaves, sateen weaves, foam-backed fabrics, laminated fabrics, and malimos. These should be squared off on the table and cut straight across. (This is where the T-square is used.)

Be sure to remember that some apparently solid color fabrics have repeats in weave that must be considered just like printed fabrics.

Splitting widths. If a pair calls for a split width, this is done when the drapery is cut. You should wait until all widths are cut before splitting any. Frequently minor flaws can be used in a split width and will not show since most of this portion is in the side hem or return, or will hang over wall where light doesn't show through. By waiting until all widths are cut, you can tell whether you have flaws to contend with. To split a width, fold in half lengthwise, selvage to selvage, carefully aligning edges. Hand press and cut along the crease while folded. It is easier to do this if tension is applied in front of and behind the shears. A clamp at the starting end will provide tension while you pull ahead of the shears. Be sure to notch both split widths.

Folding. To fold widths of fabric for ease of unfolding and sewing, stand at the end of the table where the fabric is lying. Grasp each side about 14 inches from the end and pull toward you while holding the fabric and grasp again at about 28 inches, holding all thicknesses. Continue until you have used the whole length. Fold in half and stack until a pair is completed and tagged. Folding in this manner makes it much easier to unfold when widths are joined.

Tagging. As the draperies are cut, each pair or panel should be tagged with a sewing ticket. Most workrooms have their own tickets, which should provide the following information:

Name of job

Room or room number (floor if the entire building)

JOB NAME		ROOM	
UNLINED	LINED		
PAIR	PANEL	WIDTHS	
WIDTH	LENGTH	ROLL	
SIDE HEMS	BOTTOM HEMS		
SET HOOKS	PLEATS	WEIGHTS	
CUSTOM	COMM.	FABRIC	
BAR			

JOB NAME	*Smith*	ROOM	*L.R.*
UNLINED	LINED	*Ivory*	
1 PAIR	PANEL	6 WIDTHS	
WIDTH 114	LENGTH 86	ROLL	
SIDE HEMS	BOTTOM HEMS D3		
SET HOOKS 2	PLEATS *reg*	WEIGHTS ✓	
CUSTOM ✓	COMM.	FABRIC *Delton*	
BAR 3.5			1800 *Banana*

Sewing tickets

Pair or panel (left or right if panel)

Widths per pair or panel

Lined or unlined (color of lining or type if lined)

Finished length

Finished width

Side hem (size and whether double or single)

Bottom hem (size and whether double or single)

Heading (rolled or otherwise, size if unusual)

Weights

Type of pleat

Type of finish (commercial, custom, or hand-made)

Fabric source, name, color, and so on.

When a job has been cut, tag leftover fabric before storing. The tag should indicate the job name, fabric source, and pattern. Fabric for cornices, valances, or tie-backs should also be tagged.

Cutting Lining. Lining is cut in the same way as solid fabric on which you do not draw a thread. Straighten the end and draw a line perpendicular to the edge at the cut length. Fold in the same manner as the face fabric and tag with the job name, length, and number of widths to the pair. Place with drapery cuts. Roc lon lining must be notched and marked for right side as there is a perceptible difference in the look of right and wrong sides. Linings must be tagged since they are often sewn at different times and by different people from those doing the face fabrics.

Cutting Printed Fabrics. *Determine hem line and alignment with other draperies.* Before cutting printed fabrics, several things other than pattern repeat should be checked. If the print has a definite design, it is desirable for this design to fall at the bottom of the drapery. To do this the amount needed for the hem should be allowed below the design and the cut made there. A little waste may occur before the first cut, so be sure to check yardage to find out whether you can afford the loss. If not, then you will have to cut as the pattern occurs at the beginning of the roll.

If long and short draperies are in the same room, you must check to see how they should line up. It is normal for the tops to be at the same point as in a room with a short window and a sliding glass door. In this case plan how the pattern should fall for the long ones, see where you will cut for the tops, then figure down from this point to determine where the cut must be for the bottom of the short ones. Any other alignment would be worked out from the point where the patterns should coincide.

Check for pattern drift. Very few prints are printed exactly square on the fabric. The distance that this differs from the parallel to the grain of the fabric is called "drift." A drift of 1½ inches is "allowable," and though it causes some workroom problems, it can usually be worked out unless draperies are very wide. If the drift is more than this, reject the fabric. With a 3-inch drift, if each width were cut by the same pattern from one side to the other and the pattern matched, this situation would occur:

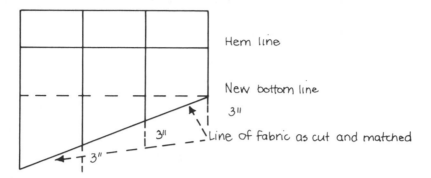

The drift would be multiplied to 9 inches when three widths were matched, and the new bottom would have to be drawn at that point. Nine inches would be lost from your cut length and the hem obviously could not follow the pattern. You cannot hem according to the pattern because the hem would be on the bias and the drapery could not be squared on the table. It would have to be made perpendicular to the edge regardless of pattern, and the pattern would then seem to drift upward or downward. The second half of the pair would have to be cut to coincide with the new bottom. If all widths were cut alike and sewed as were the first half, the leading edges would be mismatched or a total of 18 inches would have to be lost to position hems correctly. This is why you must reject a fabric that has a bad drift.

Allowances when cutting printed fabrics. When cutting draperies with a pattern, each width is cut the proper length plus the amount needed to take it to the point on the pattern where the first cut was made. Each cut in a pair must have the same pattern at the bottom. If the yardages are figured correctly, this is no problem. (See the section on Pattern Repeats in the chapter on Measuring and Estimating.) To straighten the bottom, find the point on one edge that matches the pattern on the other edge and draw a line from one to the other (for instance, the bottom of a leaf, the top of a flower, or a certain geometric point). If this pattern occurs several times across the fabric, the line you draw will not necessarily touch that point each time it occurs, but it must be correct at the edges where it will match. The eye is not accurate enough to follow the pattern when you want to make a straight cut. Unless there is a reason not to, it is a good idea to leave any excess at the top until the drapery is tabled, in case you run into the need to adjust hems and so forth.

Fabric lost between cuts. There are times when using this excess fabric in conjunction with the next pattern repeat can give you enough length for a cornice or valance cut, thus eliminating much waste. Saving fabric this way is quite sensible but must be planned carefully. Assume that the cut length of the drapery must be 109 inches. The pattern repeat is 20 inches, and therefore the cut allowing for repeat is 120 inches; you lose 11 inches. This 11 inches plus the next pattern repeat is 31 inches, sufficient for a 15- to 18-inch valance or for a cornice up to 26 inches deep. Thus drapery and valance cuts would be alternated, eliminating waste as well as the need to have two pattern repeats or 40 inches for each cornice or valance cut. If the decorator figured this way to save fabric, it must be specified; otherwise you would not know that your fabric has to be cut in this manner.

Another way to save printed fabric with considerable pattern repeat loss is to alternate cuts, using different bottoms. This can be done only if the draperies are for separate rooms, but on a large job such as a hotel or nursing home, this is no problem. To determine whether it would work, see if two cut lengths equal a number of pattern repeats that is less than would be needed to allow pattern loss on both widths. For a pattern with a 20-inch repeat and 110-inch cut length:

> To cut 110 inches, 120 inches are needed—two cuts take 240 inches or
> 12 repeats
> 110 inches + 110 inches = 220 inches, or 11 repeats.

Twenty inches would be saved each time two widths were cut. The bottoms on alternate lengths would be the same to match as pairs.

Dropped repeats. Cutting draperies to match with a step-up design is very difficult. The only sure way is to cut the first width and then match the next one to it before cutting again. Once you have established where the various cuts will be, it may not be necessary to match each cut to the next, but it may be necessary to pin them for the seamstresses.

Other items to check. If part of a pattern has been left out in printing (as occurs when a pattern designed for 48-inch fabric is printed on 45-inch goods), so the pattern does not match selvage to selvage, cut each width with the same bottom and just align the patterns when sewing. With seams behind the pleats, the lack of match should not be very noticeable.

If a job using a patterned fabric is large enough to have more than one bolt, check dye lot and pattern repeat on each bolt before cutting. You should already be familiar with dye lot problems, but it is also possible for pattern repeats to vary from one bolt to another. Even ¼ inch can create havoc when matching since this multiplies to 1½ inches if there are six repeats in a cut. It is essential that only widths from the same bolt be used together.

As a cutter gains experience, these things become almost second nature, but even then it is important to remember that a lot of material can be ruined if the cutter is careless.

JOINING WIDTHS

Preparing to Sew

Before joining widths, thread the machine with appropriate thread, matching color of fabric as closely as possible. (Nylon or monofilament thread is not recommended for any drapery process other than pleating. Although it eliminates the need to change threads often, seams and hems sewed with this thread often pucker or draw after the draperies are hung.) Next check to be sure there is no oil or grease on the machine. Then check the tension on a doubled scrap of the material to be used so the machine can be adjusted before you begin sewing.

Sewing the Seam

Read the sewing ticket to be sure how many widths you will need for each side of the pair. Unfold your first two cuts, laying them out with right sides together and end notches at the top where you will begin sewing. The notched side is sewed to the unnotched side. Align corners and sew a few inches to hold, making the seam wide enough to allow for cutting selvages. (If selvages are badly drawn, you may have to remove them before sewing.) Then smooth the two sides together for about 18 inches, placing your right hand at this point. With your left hand reach behind the presser foot and hold the material. Pull the fabric with slight tension with your left hand while holding firmly and guiding with your right. Sew as quickly as possible for accuracy to the point your right hand holds. Repeat this process as necessary, remembering that the longer the runs you can make the better it will be. There is usually a little change in tension when the machine starts and stops, so it is desirable to do this as seldom as possible. Also the longer the runs the faster the seam will be sewn. This holds true on seams using any machine—lock-stitch, serger, or blind-stitch. Do not be concerned if widths do not come out even at the top unless there is a great difference. A slight take-up or a slight variation in cutting is normal. If the difference is large, you might have widths intended for two different pairs or a large cutting error may have been made.

Attaching Weights

If weights are to be sewed into the seams, mark a point 8¼ inches from the bottom of the seam before starting to sew. Sew almost to this point. Lay the weight at the seam line so the tab is caught by the line of stitching and complete the seam as described, catching the weight into the seam. The amount to mark varies for hem sizes other than double 4-inch hems. If there are more widths to the panel, push both widths to the side, right sides up, and lay the next width out right side down with the notch at the same end as the others. Repeat the joining process as before.

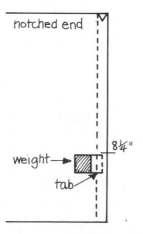

Using Half-Widths

If the panel has half-widths, start with the first half-width, adding enough full widths to complete one-half the pair. This will be the right side of the drapery. Then start with full widths and add the other half-width last for the other side of the pair. No matter what size the pair, this is the best way to avoid confusion. (Anything done in a routine manner speeds production.) Remember that for a right panel, you use the half-width first. For a left, use it last.

Matching Patterns

If patterns have to be matched, do this before starting to sew. Very few people can do this correctly without pinning the seam, so it should be standard to pin-match first. A correctly matched seam is almost impossible to detect. To pin-match, press the seam allowance under on one edge of the drapery. With right sides up, lay this seam down on the opposite edge of the next panel, matching each segment of the pattern. With straight pins, pin at the exact crease line through the pressed-under seam allowance and through the seam allowance on the other width. (It is easier to do this on a padded surface.) Pin at as many points as necessary to assure that the pattern will not shift as it is sewn. Leaving the pins in position, fold so that the right sides are together and sew on the crease line, sewing over the pins. Turn and check for a correct match. If correct, remove the pins and proceed to the next seam. If not, remove the pins, take out the seam, and try again. Experience is the best teacher for this process.

Completing the Seam

After all widths for a pair are joined, cut off the selvages and press the seams open, being sure that the iron is not too hot for the fabric. If it is, the fabric will shrink at the point that the iron touches and you will have ruined two widths since shrinkage cannot be reversed.

Joining Linings

Linings are joined in the same way as the fabric. It is seldom necessary to remove selvages, but if they are tight, remove them the same way that you do on the face fabric. Linings can be serged together, thus removing selvages and eliminating the necessity of pressing open the seams.

Unlined Draperies

Serging. Unlined draperies are ideally joined with a serger, preferably one having a lock-stitch. This machine sews the widths together, cuts off the selvage, and overcasts seams. With closely matching thread, this seam is very unobtrusive and much less bulky than other types of seams. On closely woven sheers the lock-stitch can often be left off to make the seam even smaller. Serged seams are joined the same way as described for the lock-stitch and weights are inserted the same way.

For some fabrics the selvage cannot be cut. These include many hand-woven fabrics, architectural nets, and some fiberglass weaves. Some casements ravel so badly that it is not practical to remove the selvages. In these cases, sew them together on the lock-stitch machine as close to the selvage as possible and do nothing else. Where the lock-stitch serger will hold the fabrics, it is best to use it. If you doubt that this seam will hold, it is best to serge it together with the wrong sides facing. Then turn with right sides together and make a sort of french seam by stitching inside the serging on the lock-stitch machine. A true french seam has to be used if you have no serger. Some designers prefer this on sheers even if a serger is available.

Enclosed Seams. The true french seam is made by joining the widths, wrong sides together. Trim the seam back to ⅛ inch and press open. Then fold the drapery at the seam line so the right sides are together and stitch again at ⅜ inch so that the raw edge is completely enclosed in the seam. Great care must be taken that no puckering take place because two rows of stitching would compound the problem. Always stitch from the same end.

A simpler way to make an enclosed seam is to remove the selvages, align the edges, and then make a double ¼ inch fold (like a hem) with both edges together, stitching as close to the edge as possible. This is best done on sheer fabrics and can be done with a narrow hemmer if the operator is skillful. If the fabric is bulky, align the edges so that the top width is set back ½ inch from the edge of the underneath width. Then turn the single edge over ¼ inch to meet the edge of the top width. Then turn over one more time so the raw edge is covered. Stitch as before.

Zigzag Seams. Some net fabrics have virtually nothing to sew to. If the fabric has nothing but vertical threads at the side, you can join it by placing the wrong side of one width over the right side of the other, selvages intact, and overlapping only the amount of the selvage. Then zigzag the seam, catching as many vertical threads as possible.

After joining, fold the panels and place them in pairs, making sure the sewing tickets are attached prominently. Proceed to the next job.

HEMS

Hems are used to finish the bottoms and sides of draperies.

Single Hems

In ready-made and budget draperies single hems are used to save fabric. A saving of 3 to 4 inches can be achieved on each cut, which amounts to considerable yardage on a large job. These hems are often done with a single-fold hemmer or folder. A skilled operator is required for this job and a device called a "puller" is frequently used to eliminate take-up on the machine. These hems may be done with a lock-stitch or a blind-stitch. With no folder, you would measure the width of the hem plus ½ inch for fold-under. Place the hem with edge folded under beneath the presser foot. Measure and form the hem about 12 inches from the machine and stitch, repeating for the length of the hem. Check

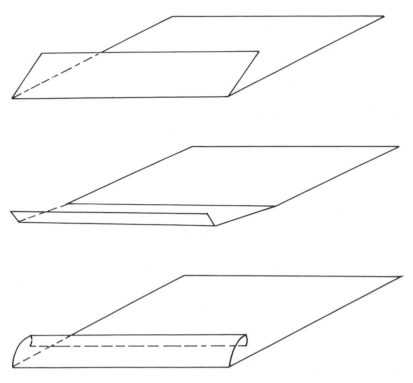

Figure 44. Turning single hem.

often to be sure the hem is not rolling or taking up underneath. On bottom hems be sure drapery seams and hem are aligned. If your operators are not skillful, press and pin the hems before sewing.

Double Hems

Double hems on solid fabrics can be done directly at the machine without pressing if the operator is skillful, but great care must be taken that the hems are completely double, that they do not roll, and that the seams are correctly aligned. This is more difficult with a double than a single hem, and if it cannot be done accurately and rapidly, the hems should be pressed as they are on printed fabrics. One advantage to hemming without pressing is that if a change needs to be made, there is no crease to press out.

Pressing Hems

Hems on printed fabrics should be pressed since there is often a need for adjustment when following the pattern. To press a double 4-inch hem, lay the fabric flat wrong side up, stretching out as many widths as possible on your table. Then turn up 8 inches, with edges and seams aligned. It is easier to do this with an 8-inch ruler. Then you will not have to check inches as you measure. Press the crease at this point, turn the fabric back down, bring the edge up to the crease, press, turn up to the original crease, and pin perpendicu-

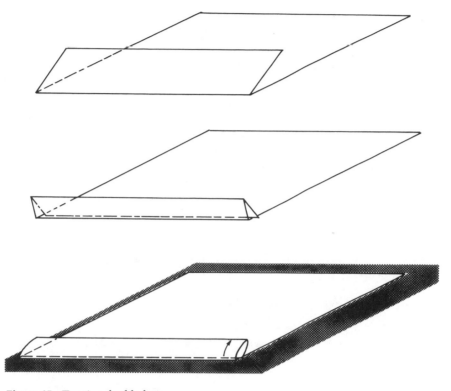

Figure 45. Turning double hem.

Figure 46. Pressing seam open.

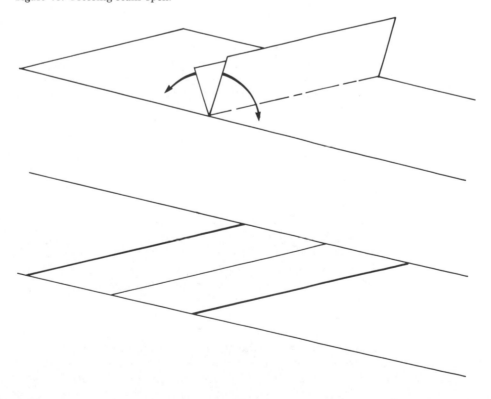

larly to the hem line with pin heads toward the top of the drapery for easy removal while hemming. Shift the fabric and continue until the hem is complete. Other size hems—3 inch, 1½ inch, 1 inch, and so on—are done the same way, with the true hem line always pressed first.

Turning Hems with Pattern

If you are following the pattern instead of measuring, choose a place on the pattern to turn the hem and turn at this point as you press. Occasionally the pattern will vary across the fabric. In that case, work from seam to seam using the pattern at that point only. There are times when a pattern has been printed so crooked on a fabric that a bias hem would result from following the pattern. (See the section on cutting in this chapter.) When this happens, a hem is pressed perpendicular to the sides of the fabric without regard for pattern. Be sure to make adjustments so the patterns match vertically at the leading edges. It is much better to reject the fabric before cutting and return it to the source.

Chain Weights in Hems

If chain weights are used in the drapery, lay them into the hem before it is stitched. In this case the hem must be pressed first, the weights laid in loosely (never stretched tightly), and then tacked at seams and edges to avoid shifting. It is possible to insert them in a stitched hem, but this is much more difficult to do, and tacking at seams would have to be done blindly from the outside.

Stitching Hems

Hems should be blind-stitched if possible because of the speed and excellent appearance. Every workroom, no matter how small, should have a blind-stitch machine. Properly done with matching thread and carefully adjusted bite and tension, the blind-stitched hem looks as good as or better than a hem done by hand. The operation is exceedingly fast and uses only one thread.

If you must hem with the lock-stitch machine, be sure the hem does not pucker as it is sewn. Many fabrics sew quite differently horizontally than vertically, and your machine may require an adjustment in tension after seams are joined and side hems stitched. The bobbin thread is the one that most often looks bad if the machine is out of adjustment. Above all, be accurate so you will not have to remove the hem. Removing it often leaves a mark that cannot be removed.

Hand hems properly done are almost imperceptible from either side, but many people do not hem properly, and the hem is neither as accurate (stitches evenly placed) nor as secure as a blind-stitched hem. Most people do not hem well or consistently when faced with yards of hems. Hand hems are very time-consuming, so if they are required, extra labor must be charged.

Special Hems

There are times when the appearance of a drapery on the outside of a building is particularly important. Some of the new casements have two "sides" that look completely different. When a conventional hem is turned, the face of the fabric shows on the back and distorts the uniform appearance of the drapery. A special hem can be turned to eliminate this problem. On the front side of the drapery, turn a single hem of the size desired and stitch using either kind of machine. Then fold this hem to the back side so the stitched edge is at the bottom of the drapery panel, press, and hem as usual. The same procedure can be used for the side hems.

Hemming Net Fabrics

Some net or open-weave patterns look better with a single hem. Turn nets with a wide hem, being careful to match holes. At the hem line zigzag across the hem on one of the heavy threads. Any raw edges can be clipped off. It is virtually impossible to hem these any other way since there is nothing to sew to. Geometric patterns in open weaves look better done this way with carefully matched designs, though it is often possible to use a conventional hem.

Hems in Sheers

Hems in sheers must be very carefully doubled since any deviations are quite noticeable. Selvages must be removed with a smooth cut and stitching must be accurate. A nice touch on sheers is to sew a 1-inch tuck just above the hem line. A series of spaced tucks can also be used. Remember to allow extra fabric for each tuck in your cutting allowance.

PREPARING THE DRAPERY FOR TABLING

Lined Draperies

Follow the appropriate steps in the section on Joining Widths and on Hems.

Solid fabric—sew seams on regular lock-stitch machine	p. 139
Printed fabrics—match patterns before sewing	p. 140
Trim selvages	p. 140
Press seams open	p. 140
Press in hems if necessary	p. 142
Attach weights if they were not inserted in seams, as on	p. 139

Weights are sewed in after the hem is pressed if they were not inserted in the seams as they were joined. They must be sewed to the seams on the drapery just above the hem line in order to weight the seam. If this is not done properly, the weight will be useless as it will be just lying in the hem, not weighting the seam.

Hem bottom	p. 144
Prepare lining	p. 140

The linings can be sewed together just like the drapery, selvages removed, and seams pressed open, or the widths can be serged together. When this is done the selvages are removed as they are sewed, the seams are overcast, and the resulting seam is small and unobtrusive. In either case the seams should be sewed so that each width of lining finishes the same width as the joined fabric. Since stocking several sizes of lining is expensive, this is not always possible.

Linings normally have a single 2-inch hem, usually done on the lock-stitch machine. They can be blind-stitched for appearance and speed, but the blind-stitch machines tend to be a bottleneck in the workroom; using them on linings causes delays. If linings show on the outside of the house, blind-stitched hems are a special touch. There are no weights in linings.

Unlined Draperies

Join widths   p. 140

Attach weights

If weights are used in a sheer or casement, they should be covered in self-fabric, doubled or tripled as necessary. These weights are sewed into the seams as widths are joined

Hem sides and bottoms   p. 142, p. 143

Side hems on sheers (usually double 1½ inches) are put in first. The bottom hem (usually double 4 inches but often double 6 inches) is completed next.

TABLING

Tabling is the process that determines the finished length of the drapery and squares it off to hang correctly. This process must be done accurately in all respects.

It was the practice for years in many shops to "pillowcase" lining and face fabric. This means that the overall lining is cut 5 inches narrower than the overall face fabric. The two are sewn together, right sides facing, either with lock-stitch or blind-stitch machines, starting at the bottom with the bottom of the lining set up 1½ inches from the bottom of the face fabric. Then the two are turned and put on the table for tabling. This leaves a limp front edge with a seam that shows through the finished drapery. Most factory or semicustom draperies are still made this way.

The accepted practice now is to let the lining come to the hem line at the sides, pin the side hem in while tabling, and blind-stitch later. Accessories necessary for the tabling process aside from the tables themselves are clamp bar or push pins, 12-foot steel tape, crinoline, steam iron, straight pins, shears, and yardstick.

The Table

The tables used for this purpose should be at least 8 feet by 12 feet and 30 inches high. They should never be fewer than 4 feet by 8 feet. They should be of sturdy construction and free of rough edges. It is desirable to have one table with a smooth surface to which fabrics will not cling for tabling loose-weave fabrics. Another table should be lightly padded and covered with canvas so that it can also be used for pressing. If the workroom has no clamp bars, the tops of the tables should be of pressed board, padded and covered so pins can be stuck into them. In this case too there must be a rigid piece of belting or something

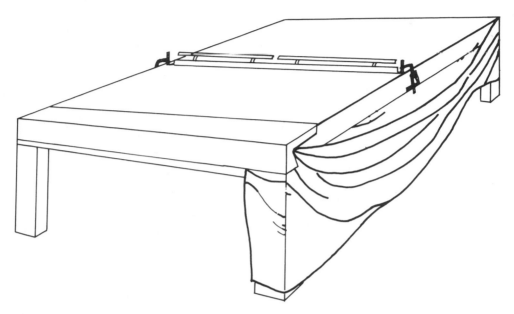

Figure 47. Tabling table showing side pocket.

similar, about 2 inches wide, that can be secured from side to side on the table to form a line at the correct length for tabling.

All tables including unpadded ones must have a canvas pressing surface at least 14 inches wide at the end where the heading is put in. This canvas must be stretched and secured very tightly. Approximately 2 inches from the edge of the table a line is drawn the width of the table. Draw two more lines parallel to this one, one 4 inches from it and one 8 inches from it. The last line is your tabling line, where the heading is completed. These must be drawn very straight and with indelible ink. If this is done on one short side and one long side of the table, the table can be used in either direction, depending on the length of the drapery. Three widths can usually be stretched flat in the 12-foot direction, only two in the 8-foot. The tables should have side pockets of canvas deep enough to allow the part of the drapery that will not fit on the table to drop into it.

Starting at the 8-inch or tabling line, mark the table in inches and half inches on each side by attaching steel tapes or marking directly on the table. These marks should be checked often to be sure they remain accurate.

Once the table is marked, the drapery can be tabled. If you use a clamp bar, set it at the correct finished length from the tabling line. If no bar is available, the rigid piece of belting must be attached tightly and securely across the table at the correct length.

Unlined Draperies

Sheers and Casements. Unlined draperies with a rolled top are tabled as follows. The joined and hemmed panel is laid on the table wrong side up. One side is close to and parallel to the right side of the table as you face it. The bottom hem is either secured under the clamp bar or is laid next to the belting strip and pinned to the table at about 1-inch intervals with push pins. (They must fasten securely into the table so the drapery can be pulled taut without pulling loose.) Pull the fabric taut and straighten it so that seams and side hems lie parallel to the edge of the table. Check for puckered seams and hems. Stretch the fabric gently to take out the "give"; then release. The unfinished edge of the drapery should come to the top of the table. Working from right to left, lay crinoline with 3 inches folded under across the table on the first line drawn starting no more than ¼ inch from the line of the side hem line. Holding the fabric firmly but not stretching it, lay it over the edge of the crinoline and press to hold. Then fold the entire heading over to the second line and press. Raw edges should now be turned under the crinoline. Then fold the entire heading over one more time so that the top of the drapery is at the 8-inch or tabling line. It should come exactly even with this line all the way across the table. Now any raw edges should be on the wrong side of the heading where they will not show through. At the left side of the drapery be sure to fold the crinoline under 3 inches and have it come to within ¼ inch of the side hem.

Press the heading carefully and pin at the edges of the drapery, several places across each width, and at the seams with pin heads toward the bottom of the panel. Seams should line up where the heading is turned. If the entire panel does not fit on the table, release the bottom and shift the panel so that all but about 4 inches of the tabled part is in the side pocket. Repeat the procedure described until all the drapery is tabled. You now know why a large table is best, since on a 4 foot by 8 foot table a panel would have to be shifted each time one width was tabled.

Heavier Fabrics. On unlined draperies made from fabric you cannot see through, your cutting allowance is 2 inches less and you do not turn down anything at the first line. Insert the crinoline even with the second line and turn the heading once more to be even with the tabling line. Do this also when lined draperies have a rolled heading as opposed to a continental heading. If this is done, the face fabric shows on the back of the drapery.

Lined Draperies

Lined drapery panels are laid on the table wrong side up. Then the lining is laid on top of the fabric, wrong side down (the wrong sides of both fabrics facing each other), with seams matching and the bottom of the lining hem 1½ inches from the bottom hem of the face fabric. Secure with a clamp bar or push pins. Lining seams cannot always be matched to face fabric seams. Stocking several widths of lining is expensive and the right size is not always available. If lining is narrower than face fabric, keep the seams near the front of the panel as close together as possible when tabling and let the seams work off to the back of the panel, where they will be concealed in the stack of the drapery much of the time or hang over the wall where no light comes through. For tie-back draperies the lining should be 3 inches from the bottom, and for sill-length draperies the lining should be only ½ inch from the bottom to improve the appearance from the outside. In this instance the lining hem should be blind-stitched.

At the side, turn a double 1½-inch hem with both lining and fabric included. Press, open out, and trim the lining at the hem line. Turn the fabric hem back

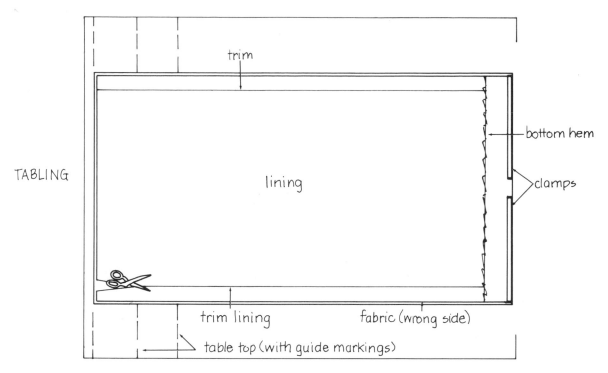

Figure 48. Trimming lining at hemline.

Figure 49. Turning double 1½ inch hem.

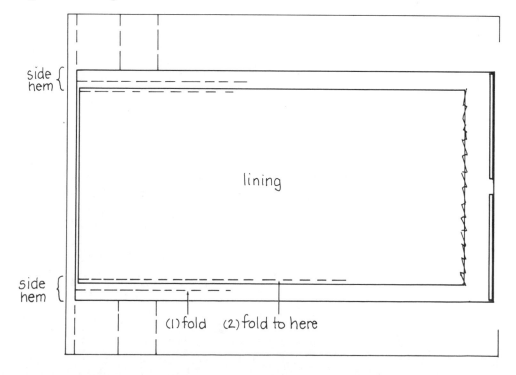

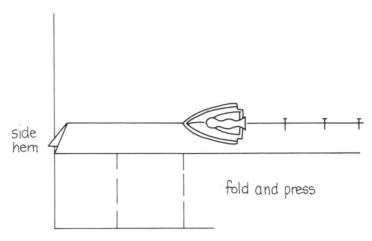

Figure 50. Tabling draperies—pressing side hem.

down over the lining and pin at 6-inch intervals with pins perpendicular to the side of the hem. Straighten the face fabric and the lining so that both are lying smoothly on the table with seams matching and parallel to the sides of the table. Stretch each until taut, as in unlined draperies, then release.

Slide crinoline with 3 inches turned under at the end between the fabric and the lining to the edge of the turned-under hem and even with the tabling line. (Fabric and lining should be about 4 inches longer.) Hold in place and turn the fabric over the crinoline so that it is even with the tabling line all the way across the panel. Press. Turn the lining under so that it comes to within ¼ inch

Figure 51. Insert buckram under face fabric.

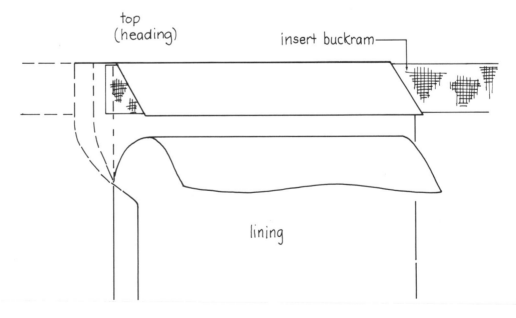

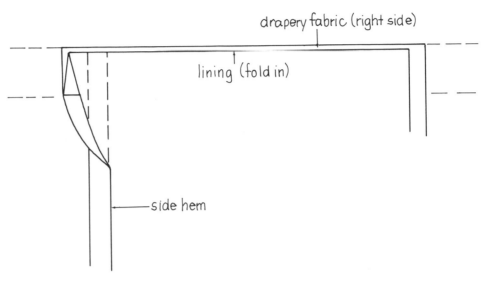

Figure 52. Turn lining in ¼ inch from top.

of the top of the drapery. Press all thicknesses and pin at intervals with pin heads toward the top. This is called a continental heading and is best for custom draperies since it lets the lining come to the top of the drapery and has as little bulk as possible.

If you desire a rolled heading, cut the fabric and lining 4 inches longer and finish the top like an unlined drapery of a heavy fabric that does not need to have raw edges concealed. Turn fabric and lining together over the crinoline on the 4-inch line and then turn them down again to finish on the tabling line. This is always done if a casement fabric must be lined.

Figure 53. Pin and set panel aside to pleat.

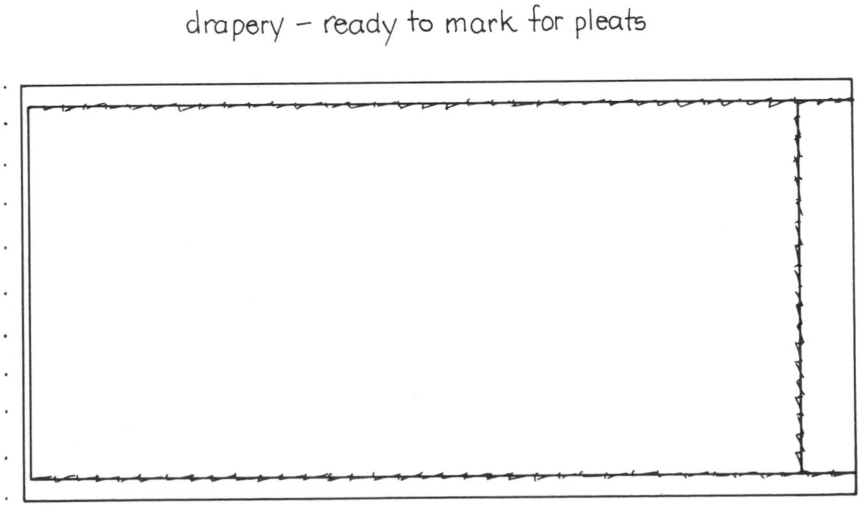

drapery – ready to mark for pleats

Continue tabling across the panel, finishing the second side like the first with the hem pressed and pinned in. Fold seam to seam and return to the blind-stitch machine to stitch the hems.

Very fine custom draperies and all interlined draperies have their linings put in by hand. This is started by laying the face fabric on the table wrong side up. The side hem allowance (single) is pressed down and loosely tacked at 4- to 6-inch intervals to the face. Then the lining, with seam allowance turned under and with wrong side down, is pinned to the hem approximately ⅜ inch from the edge and later slip-stitched by hand with an invisible stitch.

An interlined drapery has a piece of flannel lining between the lining and the face. This is brought to the crease at the front edge before the hem allowance is tacked and is tacked loosely at that point. The hem allowance is tacked to the face through the interlining. Lining is placed as previously. Interlining is pinked at the bottom rather than hemmed, thus eliminating bulk. Face fabric, interlining, and lining must be loosely tacked together the length of the drapery at half-widths and seams before the heading is inserted. This makes a fine drapery but the cost makes it unpopular with the average client.

Lined Sheers and Casements

If sheers or casements must be lined, there is an alternate method for attaching the sides that helps to eliminate the problem of lining and fabric that react differently to cause puckering and rolling. In this method lining and face fabric are hemmed separately so that the overall lining is 1½ inches narrower than the overall face fabric. When tabling, the process is similar to that used when tabling a drapery that is to have the lining put in by hand. The hemmed lining is brought to within ¾ inch of the hemmed edge of the face fabric, tacked to it with loose tailor's tacks at about 8-inch intervals, and left that way. This allows the lining to be tabled and pleated with the face fabric at the top, but it also allows the two fabrics to shrink or stretch a little at the sides without pulling against each other.

After the tabling process, fold the panel seam to seam and set it apart to mark pleats. If you have a pleating bar, pleats can be marked as the drapery is tabled, eliminating the need to fold and unfold the panel again.

FINISHING THE DRAPERY

Closing Corners

After the drapery had been tabled and blind-stitched, the pleats must be marked, stitched, and tacked. The corners must also be closed, by hand or with the corner closer. These two operations can be done in either order: corners can be closed before or after the drapery is pleated. Thus if the pleater is jammed up, someone can close corners, or if the tacker is behind, the corners can be closed between pleating and tacking. It is also possible to close corners while tabling but it slows the process down. When closing corners, be sure that they are square. If not the drapery will not hang well at the bottom corners.

Corners on sheers and casements are slip-stitched along the side of the bottom hem after the weight has been slipped into the side hem. It must be shifted to just above the hem line. The slip-stitching must also continue a short way across the hem line to complete the hem.

On lined draperies the weights are slipped into the bottom hem just past the side hem line. The side hem is turned and the corner mitered from corner to lining being certain that the corner is square. When hand finishing this corner, be sure to catch the covering of the weight with the needle to stabilize it in the corner.

Tacking the Lining

Tacking the lining to the drapery should be done during the tabling process but can be done later if the lining is pinned to the drapery at the seams and at the half-widths. This is done by making a loose tailor's tack about ¾ inch long that holds the fabric and lining together to prevent billowing but is not so tight that the two fabrics cannot give a little. This must be done at the seams and at the half-widths approximately 1 inch from the bottom of the lining.

Pin Settings

Pin settings on draperies are most important. If they are set too low or too high, the drapery will be too long or too short. If they are uneven, the drapery will be uneven.

Proper settings for pins are as follows:

½ inch from the top for most decorative rods. This allows the drapery to come just to the bottom of the ring. Pins must not be set lower since rods and rings are intended to be exposed. Drapery will tilt if they are set lower. Pins would also be set at ½ inch when a regular traverse drapery is intended to hang below the rod.

1½ inch from the top for ceiling mount. This allows the drapery to clear the ceiling. Pins would also be set at this height for rods in a valance board.

2 inches from the top for wall mount. This allows drapery to project ½ inch above the top of the rod for sure coverage.

These settings mean that the top of the hook comes that distance from the top of the drapery after being inserted. To figure where to start pinning the hook, add the measurement of the hook to the distance from the top of the drapery you wish to be and start pinning the hook at that point.

Hooks must be inserted behind each pleat and at each end of the heading. None of them should be allowed to show on the front of the drapery but they must be pinned securely through the crinoline. The hooks behind the pleats must not be pinned only into the stitching of the pleat as this will soon rip out. They should go into the fabric and crinoline immediately beside the line of stitching. If sew-on hooks are used, a heavy-duty thread must be used as the continual strain will soon break any ordinary thread.

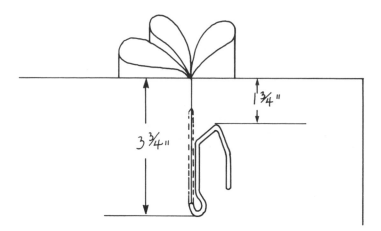

Figure 54. Inserting pins behind pleats.

Pressing

Pressing is very important for the final appearance of the drapery. Use a good steam iron set at an appropriate setting. (Do not forget that some fabrics cannot be steamed.) Be sure the iron is not too hot because the impression of a hot iron cannot be removed and will ruin a whole panel. Be sure the seam on unlined draperies is pressed to the same side for its entire length; otherwise an objectionable line will show through when the drapery is hung.

Folding

When folding using the fan-fold method, all folds must be straight from pleat to hem and the lining folded with the face fabric. If this is not done, the drapery will hang askew and the only thing that will straighten it is to be steamed again.

Tie-back draperies should be folded seam to seam because tied-back pleats do not follow a straight line down the length of the drapery.

If the drapery is to be put on a hanger, this is done before bands are attached to hold the folds in place. The sewing ticket should be securely pinned to the drapery in a prominent place, as on the band holding the folded drapery. Plastic tubing is convenient for packaging, as it can be slipped over the folded drapery and tied, top and bottom.

After packaging, check the order to be sure it is complete. If so, give the completion ticket to the workroom supervisor. It is helpful to have a listing made at the finishing table, showing date, name of client, and the size of each pair as it is completed. This allows easy checking on a large order and also allows the supervisor to count widths completed at any given time to check production.

FULLNESS AND PLEATING

FULLNESS

How to Figure Fullness

It is a popular misconception that if you use two 48-inch widths of fabric to cover a 48-inch window, you will have double fullness. This is not true since you must add 12 inches to the pleated width for returns and overlaps, and you will lose 6 inches of fabric on each width for side hems, making a total of 12 inches for hems for a pair. This is how it works:

48 inches	—rod width	48 inches		48 inches
× 2	—fullness	× 2½	×	3
96 inches		120 inches		144 inches
+ 12 inches	—returns and overlaps	+ 12 inches	+	12 inches
108 inches		132 inches		156 inches
+ 12 inches	—side hems	+ 12 inches	+	12 inches
120 inches	—amount of fabric needed	144 inches		168 inches
÷ 48 inches	—width of fabric	÷ 48 inches	÷	48 inches
2½	—widths per pair	3		3.5
or		or		or
1¼	—widths each side[a]	1½		1¾ [b]

[a]If ¼ widths cannot be used for some reason, it is best to go to 1½ widths. Otherwise spaces between pleats would be much too great with only one width.
[b]Two widths would have to be allowed for each side and this much could be used, but spaces would have to be calculated because this does not show on the chart.

How to Calculate the Spaces between Pleats

The importance of enough fullness is emphasized when you calculate the spaces between the pleats and the amount of fabric in the pleats with various numbers of widths. With a 48-inch rod width and 48-inch fabric it comes out like this:

		2 widths	2½ widths	3 widths
48 inches	—rod width			
+ 12 inches	—returns and overlaps			
60 inches	—overall width			
÷ 2				
30 inches	—finished width each side			
− 8 inches	—returns and overlaps[a]			
22 inches	—distance between end pleats	22 inches		22 inches
÷ 4	—number of spaces	÷ 5		÷ 6
5½ inches	—distance between pleats	4.4 inches		3.6 + inches

[a] See page 160 on pleating.

How to Calculate the Amount of Fabric in Each Pleat

The amount of fabric in the pleats would be as follows:

48 inches	—width of fabric	1¼	width	1½ width	
− 6 inches	—side hems	48 inches	—1 width	48 inches	
42 inches	—width of hemmed panel	+ 12 inches	—¼ width	+ 24 inches	
− 30 inches	—finished width of panel	60 inches	—1¼ width	72 inches	
12 inches	—amount left for pleats	− 1 inch	—for seams	− 1 inch	
÷ 5	—number of pleats	− 6 inches	—for hems	− 6 inches	
2.4 inches	in each pleat[a]	53 inches	—width of hemmed panel	65 inches	
		− 30 inches	—finished width of panel	− 30 inches	
		23 inches	—amount left for pleats	35 inches	
		÷ 6	—number of pleats	÷ 7	
		3.8 inches	in each pleat[b]	5 inches[c]	

[a]This amount could not be made into a pinch pleat.
[b]This amount would form a small skimpy pinch pleat.
[c]This amount is enough to make a good pleat.

Charts are included for fullness as well as spaces between pleats, but the amount left for pleats and the size of the pleats would still have to be calculated if you have no pleater bar.

Calculating for Different Widths of Fabric

There is little point to calculating the difference between 45-inch and 48-inch fabric when pleating. Unless the space is very wide, there is a minimal difference in the size of the pleats. However, with 54-inch fabrics it begins to change quite noticeably by the time you get to six widths. Use, for example, a window with a rod width of 175 inches with 2½ fullness. It would need 10 widths of 48-inch fabric.

175 inches	—rod width
× 2½	—fullness
437 inches	
+ 12 inches	—returns and overlaps
449 inches	—
+ 12 inches	—per pair for side hems
461 inches	—amount of fabric needed
÷ 48 inches	—width of fabric
9.6	or 10 widths needed

The pleat spacing is figured as before. Remember that with 45-inch, 48-inch, and 54-inch fabric there are always five pleats to the width.

```
 175 inches      —rod width
+  12 inches      —return and overlaps
 187 inches      —finished width for pair
÷   2
    93.5 inches   —finished width each side
−   8 inches      —returns and overlaps
    85.5 inches   —distance between end pleats
÷  24             —number of spaces between pleats
     3.5 + inches distance between pleats on 45 inch, 48 inch,
            and 54 inch fabrics.
```

The amount of fabric in the pleats would be as follows:

```
  45 inches  —width of fabric                    48 inches       54 inches
×   5        —number of widths per ½ pair  ×   5           ×   5
  225 inches —amount of fabric each side      240 inches      270 inches
−   3 inches —seams                          −   3 inches     −   3 inches
−   6 inches —side hems                       −   6 inches     −   6 inches
  216 inches —hemmed fabric                   231 inches      261 inches
−  93.5 inches—finished width per ½ pair     −  93.5 inches   −  93.5 inches
  122.5 inches—amount for pleats             137.5 inches    167.5 inches
÷  25                                         ÷  25            ÷  25
    4.9 inches —amount of fabric each pleat     5.5 inches       6.7 inches
```

The difference in the amount of fabric in the pleats in 54-inch fabric is considerable and would allow for cutting back one width on this pair if it were desirable to try to save yardage. This would be a matter of your judgment in the particular circumstance. Spaces would be further apart but pleats would still be very full.

```
  54 inches  —width of fabric             93.5 inches—pleated width
×   4½       —number of widths per ½ pair −   8 inches —returns and overlap
  243 inches —fabric each side             85.5 inches—distance between end pleats
−   3 inches —seams                       ÷  21        —number of spaces
−   6 inches —side hems                       4 inches —distance between pleats
  234 inches —hemmed fabric
−  93½       —pleated width
  140½       —amount left for pleats
÷  22        —number of pleats
    6.3 inches —amount of fabric each pleat
```

This would be a nice full drapery even though the pleat spacing is a little wide.

PLEATING FOR THE WORKROOM

The finished width of a pair or panel of draperies is achieved by stitching the excess fabric over the amount needed to cover the rod into pleats. The finished width is determined by adding the amount for returns and overlaps to the width of the rod from one bracket to the other. Twelve inches is standard for a pair and 6 inches for a panel. (Each panel of a pair measures one-half the finished width of the pair.) The 12 inches come from 4 inches for each return and 4 inches for overlaps. This gives a little more flexibility than the 3½ inches frequently used, since it can be adapted to many types of rods with a slight adjustment of the pins. It also allows you to switch sides on pairs with full widths.

Each panel traverses either to the right or to the left. The seams should be hidden on the side to which it opens. A pair has two panels, a left and a right, so seams would be hidden on opposite sides of the pleats.

Each width of drapery (45 to 54 inches) will have five pleats in full widths and two pleats in half-widths. The pleats themselves will vary in size, but the inflexible rule is that all spaces between pleats must be the same size. Do not worry about the variation in pleats. When stitched and broken into folds, it will be barely discernible.

After the drapery is seamed, hemmed, (lined), and tabled, it is ready to be pleated. There are several old methods of pleating that involve a sort of trial-and-error method of determining sizes of spaces and pleats. However, the arithmetical method is the most accurate and needs less adjustment. In these days of inexpensive calculators, it should present no problem at all even to those who were rotten in mathematics.

Number of Pleats to Use

This method is based on the fact that all draperies made of 45- to 54-inch fabric have a set number of pleats and spaces for each size panel (1 width, 1½ width, 2 widths, and so on). The same is true fo 36-inch fabrics. A chart is included to tell how many spaces and pleats there are in the various sizes. Note that all center widths of draperies having half-widths always have five pleats and five spaces, while those panels with full widths show a variation only in the next-to-last width.

Returns and Overlaps

Before starting to pleat you must understand about returns and overlaps in relation to the amount added to get finished width and the amount deducted when pleating.

If you are using a standard traverse rod that is 80 inches wide, you must allow for the drapery to return from the front of the rod to the wall. The standard is 3½ to 4 inches. To give a little leeway it is best to allow 4 inches. The master carriers overlap each other by 2 inches, so this must must be allowed on each half of the pair to compensate. Therefore the total amount added to the rod width to allow for returns and overlaps is 12 inches; 80 inches

+ 12 inches = 92 inches, or the finished width of the pair. If you are using a double bracket with two rods, it is not necessary to add returns on the under-drapery as it cannot return to the wall and does not need to. The amount added to this pair would be 4 inches, or the amount needed for two overlaps, making a total of 84 inches as the finished width of the pair. However, the overdrapery would need 6-inch returns to allow for the projection of the two rods, and you would add 6 inches for each return and 2 inches for each overlap, making a total of 16 inches or a finished width of 96 inches (80 inches + 16 inches) for the pair.

What we have calculated is called the "finished width" of the pair. Each panel or half of the pair is half that amount.

During the actual process of pleating, when calculating spaces and pleats, we deduct on one side of the panel 4 inches for overlaps and on the other, 4 inches for returns. All this refers to is the amount of heading left flat from the hemmed edge to the first pleat. So if you deduct 8 inches from the finished width, this gives you the distance between the two end pleats. Of course, if the drapery has a 6-inch return, one side will be 6 inches and the other 4 inches, and the amount deducted to find the distance between pleats would be 10 inches. The pleating chart is based on distances between end pleats.

To avoid confusing the seamstresses about addition and deduction, it is best if the sewing tickets give finished width and size of returns if different than usual. As seamstresses are familiar with this method, there should be no problems in pleating.

To start pleating you will need a wide work table, a steel tape for measuring sizes of widths and finished width, a small ruler marked in tenths of inches, and a supply of sturdy pins.

Single Panel

A single panel is the easiest to pleat as it has no seams. We have a 2-width pair that is to cover a 28-inch rod. Lay one hemmed and tabled panel flat on the table, wrong side up, and measure it from hemmed edge to hemmed edge. This might be 42 inches.

Calculate how wide the finished size of this panel must be. To the rod width of the pair add 12 inches for returns and overlaps and divide by 2; 28 inches + 12 inches = 40 inches ÷ 2 = 20 inches. From 20 inches subtract 8 inches for returns and overlaps (4-inch return and 4-inch overlap), leaving 12 inches. From the chart there are four spaces in one width. Divide 12 inches by 4 inches, determining that the spaces are 3 inches.

Since the hemmed panel measures 42 inches, we deduct the finished size of the panel (20 inches) from 42 inches, leaving 22 inches, the amount to be used in pleats. From the chart, there are five pleats in a single width, so the pleats are 22 inches ÷ 5, for a total of 4.4 inches in each one.

With the drapery lying flat, place a pin 4 inches from each finished edge (these are returns and overlaps). Next measure from the first pin 4.4 inches and place a second pin. This defines a pleat. Measure and pin 3 inches, the size of a space. Continue the process until your final measurement of 4.4 inches comes to the pin marking the overlap at the other side. If any adjustment is necessary, it must be done in the pleats. Spaces must always remain the same. To mark the second half of the pair, lay it face down, wrong sides together, on the marked width about 1 inch from the top of the heading and place pins to coincide with those in the first panel.

Two-and-one-half-width Panel

Now assume that you have a 2½-width panel that must pleat to a finished measure of 48 inches. Deduct 4 inches for the return and 4 inches for the overlap, leaving a total of 40 inches. (This is to determine the distance between end pleats.) This 2½-width panel will have 12 pleats and 11 spaces (from the chart). Thus 40 inches divided by 11 spaces means that each space will be just a fraction over 3.6 inches.

Lay the panel of the drapery on the table wrong side up with the top facing you. Starting from the center of the drapery, the full width on pairs having half-widths and opposite sides on pairs with full widths, measure the first full width from hemmed edge to seam. This could be 44.5 inches. Subtract the overlap from this, 44.5 inches − 4 inches = 40.5 inches. Multiply the number of spaces in this width by the predetermined size of the spaces, in this case 3.6 inches × 4 = 14.4 inches. Subtract 14.4 inches from 40.5 inches, leaving 26.1 inches to be divided into 5 pleats.

The amount 26.1 inches divided by 5 equals 5.2 inches, or the amount in each pleat in this width. Our first width will have a 4-inch overlap five pleats of 5.2 inches each and four spaces of 3.6 inches each. Mark with pins with the last pin being about ¼ inch to the left of the seam adjacent to the last pleat in this width if you started with a full width on the left. (The pin would be to the right of the seam on the other half of the pair.) The second width will be measured from seam to seam. It has no overlap or return—only five pleats and five spaces. If it measures 47 inches, deduct the amount of 5 spaces (5 × 3.6) or 18 inches from 47 inches (47 inches − 18 inches). You will have 29 inches to divide into five pleats: 29 inches ÷ 5 = 5.8 inches in each pleat. The second width will have five spaces of 3.6 inches each and five pleats, of 5.8 inches each. Mark with pins as before with the last pin ¼ inch to the left of the last seam.

The half-width is measured from seam to finished edge and should have about 20.5 inches. Deduct for one return (4 inches), leaving 16.5 inches. A half-width has 2 spaces, so we deduct 7.2 inches (3.6 inches × 2) from 16.5 inches, leaving 9.3 inches to put into pleats. There are two pleats in a half-width. These would have 4.6 inches each. The half-width will have two spaces of 3.6 inches, two pleats of 4.6 inches, and one return of 4 inches.

Place pins to correspond to these figures. Be sure pins at the seams are placed ¼ inch from the seam to allow for stitching without including the seam. The panel should then look like Figure A, below.

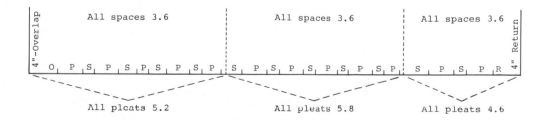

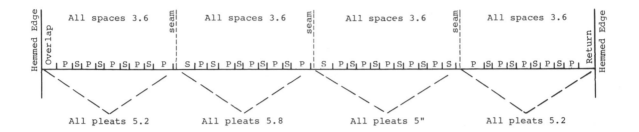

If this panel is half of a pair, simply lay the opposite panel on this panel, wrong sides together, and mark the second panel to correspond. The same method using charts to determine pleats and spaces is used on 36-inch fabrics.

Four-width Panel

A 4-width panel, or any panel having only full widths, is handled the same way with the exception of the next-to-last width (the third in this example). *See* figure B, above.

We are assuming an 8-width pair that has a finished measurement of 153 inches. One-half of this is 76.5 inches, for a 4-width panel. We know that there will be 20 pleats in four widths, which means 19 spaces. Deduct 8 inches from 76.5 inches for returns and overlaps, leaving 68.5 inches. Divide 68.5 inches by 19 (spaces), making the spaces a fraction over 3.6 inches. Disregard fractions of less than one-tenth.

Proceed with marking exactly as in the 2½-width panel, starting on the side that will be the center of the drapery. Follow the first two steps (first and second widths) and mark with pins. Measure the third width, and again it will be 47 inches. In this width, according to the chart, there must be six spaces and five pleats. Multiply 6 times 3.6 inches (the size of your spaces) to get 21.6 inches. Subtract this amount from 47 inches (47 inches − 21.6 inches) to see how much fabric will go into pleats. The remainder is 25.4 inches divided by 5 pleats, giving 5 inches and a negligible fraction in each pleat. Mark this width as you have the others but this time start and stop with a space.

On the last width, mark 4 inches from the edge to define the return. Here you will have four spaces and five pleats. To find the size of the pleats, measure from seam to edge of drapery, probably 44.5 inches, deduct 4 inches for the return and 4 × 3.6 inches, or 14.4 inches, for the spaces, leaving 26 inches (44.5 inches − 4 inches − 14.4 inches) to be used in 5 pleats. These pleats will be 5.2 inches each.

Pleating Unusual Widths

On other widths of fabrics, such as 60 inches, 72 inches, or 118 inches, you divide into increments approximately equal to 48-inch fabric and mark accordingly.

One width of 60-inch fabric is marked like 1¼ widths.
A 2-width panel like 2½ widths.
A 3-width panel like 3¾ widths.

A 3-width pair of 60-inch fabric has 90 inches on each side and is
   marked like two widths of 45-inch fabric.
One width of 72-inch fabric is like 1½ widths of 48-inch.
A 1½-width panel is like two widths.
A 2-width panel is like three widths, and so on.

Using a Pleater Bar

Many workrooms including ours now use a mechanical device to mark pleats.
There are several of these, all good, that come with charts, simplifying the
marking of pleats so that almost anyone can do it. With this system we mark
with special pencils instead of pins and pleat under a black light. No markings
show to the naked eye.

Stitching Pleats

To stitch pleats, fold the drapery so that pins marking pleats are together with
the top edge of the crinoline absolutely even. We recommend stitching from
this edge to the bottom of the pleat so that the drag of the feed will not cause
unevenness at the top of the drapery. However, it can be done in either direction so long as the top edges remain even. The stitching must be absolutely
parallel to the fold of the pleat and perpendicular to the top of the drapery. If
this is not done, the heading will be sloppy and the pleated width will be
inaccurate. If a regular lock-stitch machine must be used, graded markings on
the machine are helpful. Be sure to back-stitch both the top and bottom of the
pleat to insure holding.
   A better method is to use a machine designed to do nothing but stitch pleats.
Place the folded pleat under the bar at the desired depth. The machine is
tripped and stitches automatically twice from the center to the bottom, back to
the top, and returning to the center. Its stitching is absolutely straight and very
fast.
   Once the pleats are stitched, the drapery must be measured to check for
pleated width. A little slack (½ inch in 24 inches) is allowable, but if it is not
wide enough, it must be adjusted. This must never be done all in one or two
pleats because it will be obvious as a difference in spaces.

Forming Pleats

After checking the finished width, the pleats are formed and tacked. The for-
mation of pinch pleats and french pleats is the same, but they are tacked
differently. Lay the pleated drapery on the table with the pleated end at the left
(if you are right-handed). Place your left index finger inside the fold formed by
the stitching while holding the fold with your right hand. Firmly press the
seam of the pleat with your left hand to flatten it while lowering the fold
toward the seam with your right hand. Remove your left finger and help to
form a 3-folded pleat. Check to see that each section is equal by turning the
center fold to left and right over other folds. If all sections are equal, hold
together and press with your fingers to crease the crinoline. Follow the same
procedure with all pleats. The crinoline will remain creased until you are ready
to tack.

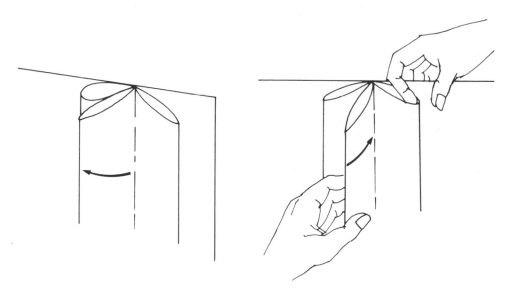

Figure 55. Forming and checking pleats.

Tacking Pleats

Tacking pleats means sewing back and forth through the folds of the pleat to hold them in position. A pinch pleat is tacked approximately ¾ inch from the bottom of the crinoline and in the center of the folded pleat. Tacking by hand is very difficult since at this point many thicknesses of material and crinoline must be sewed. If you must tack by hand, do so with heavy thread and a long, strong needle. You must sew back and forth several times through all thicknesses of the pleat and fasten the thread securely. It is not acceptable to sew over the front of the pleat or below the crinoline. It is almost impossible to tack a pleat on the lock-stitch machine.

Large workrooms use a bar-tacker (or button-sewer), which stitches back and forth automatically about ten times, making a very secure pleat. Nylon or plastic thread can be used for this operation since it does not show. This eliminates the need for constantly changing thread.

A french pleat is tacked so that all three folds remain separate. On a lock-stitch machine this can be done by using a zipper foot and sewing through all thicknesses on each side of the center fold. With a tacker you can tack top, center, and bottom on each side.

A cartridge pleat is opened and a small roll of crinoline is inserted to keep it in a rounded shape. This pleat must be tacked below the heading to keep the crinoline from falling out.

A box pleat is flattened and tacked under the top fold to hold it in place.

After pleats are tacked, trim all excess threads in the heading, and the drapery is ready to have pins inserted and to be pressed and folded.

DRAPERY CONSTRUCTION TECHNIQUES FOR SPECIAL TREATMENTS

SLANTED-TOP DRAPERIES

Measurements

Making the Pattern

Preparing the Drapery

Tabling

Pleating

CURVED-TOP DRAPERIES

Measurements

Making the Pattern

Tabling

Pleating

FABRICATION OF DECORATIVE SHADES

Roman Shades

Balloon Shades

Austrian Shades

RIGGING DECORATIVE SHADES

SLANTED-TOP DRAPERIES

There are occasions when you will be asked to make draperies for slanted windows, though in their original concept, these windows were probably intended to be undraped. Draperies for them are made the same way whether they traverse or remain stationary.

Measurements

Accurate measurements are essential and an absolutely accurate drapery must be made. Whereas in an ordinary traverse drapery, a small amount of extra fullness is unimportant, an inch or two of variation in pleated fullness on a slanted drapery can result in a very uneven hem line. These draperies are always made as panels.

Measurements must be as follows:

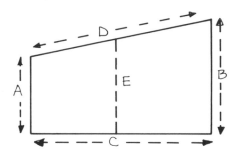

A—length at low point

B—length at high point

C—actual width

D—width on slant

E—length at half-way point

Making The Pattern

Patterns must be made for each different window, and it is of little use to save them since they can almost never be reused. To make a pattern, determine the fullness from the chart and decide how many widths of fabric should be used. Then cut that many widths of lining approximately 1 foot longer than the distance from A to B. If A is 80 inches and B is 112 inches, the cut lengths of lining should be 112 inches − 80 inches = 32 inches + 12 inches = 44 inches.

Lining scraps may be used. Stiff blackout lining makes a good pattern.

Suppose your width is 76 inches and you are using five widths. The actual fabric to be used should be measured and the amount for seams and side hems deducted. The pattern should measure that width with seams marked where they would be in the drapery.

No overlaps are needed on these draperies and returns are usually not necessary. If you do use a return, add it before looking up the pleat spacing. Pleats should start about 2 inches from the leading edge and be the same at the other side if there is no return. If there is a return, the pleat should be at the end of the rod.

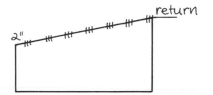

Look up pleat spacing on the chart and mark accordingly if you have a pleating device. If not, you can still look up the spaces on the chart but will have to mark the pleats according to the method explained in that chapter. Mark the other side of the long piece of fabric to correspond.

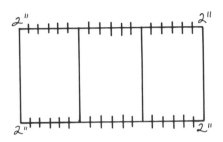

Pin in pleats top and bottom and arrange on a table so all pleats are lying toward what will be the high point of the panel. Press. From the high point measure down to the low point on the opposite side (the difference from A to B, in this case, 32). Draw a line from the low point to the high point across the pleated surface. Cut on this line. Mark where each pleat will be. (Pressing should have made marks you can follow.) Mark the middle of the drapery (point E) top and bottom.

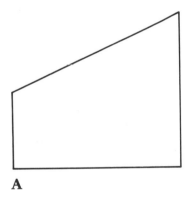

A

Unpin and unfold the pattern. It will look like this:

B

Cut straight across from one side of the pleat to the other so it will look this way:

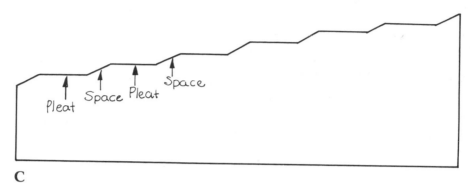

C

Preparing The Drapery

After the pattern is made, sew the fabric together, hem the sides and bottom, and put it on the table. It is best if the entire drapery can be laid out at once. If not, be sure that midpoint markings coincide with the middle of the drapery panel when shifted.

Tabling

If unlined, put the drapery on the table right side up and turn the fabric down along a line 1½ inches longer than the diagonal from point A to B. Lay 6 inches of crinoline, pellon, or other stiffening on top of this. Lay the pattern exactly on the finished line, straightening it from low to high point, and draw the pattern on the drapery. Cut the pellon 4 inches below the mark (for a 4-inch heading). Trim the excess at the top, leaving a seam allowance above the stitching mark, pin carefully, take it from the table, and stitch on the mark. Turn, fold the fabric under the crinoline, and press and pin it.

If lined, sew the lining and face the fabric together pillowcase style with the lining close to the edge, and put it on the table with right sides together and wrong side of lining up. The stiffening is laid on the diagonal, marked, and pinned. Trim the pellon 4 inches from the mark. Cut off the excess at the top, take the fabric from the table, and stitch and turn it.

Pleating

Fold the straight part of the pleat in half and stitch it on the mark. Be sure pleats are stitched parallel to the edge of the panel. After the pleats are stitched, put the fabric back on the table and be sure they fit the original pattern when pleated or the template if you have one.

Remember that total accuracy is essential to the hang of the completed drapery.

CURVED-TOP DRAPERIES

The procedure for making curved-top draperies is essentially the same as for slanted. You must have accurate measurements so you can make a template. These measurements are essential.

Measurements

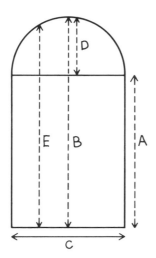

A— length from break in arch to floor

B— length from top of arch to floor

C— width

D— length from top of arch to break in arch

E— length from point at top of window half-way between A and B, necessary only if D is not equal to half of C.

Making the Pattern

Prepare the lining for the pattern as in slanted draperies, the cut length being the measurement D. The pattern has to be only for half the window as it can be reversed for the other half. Pleat the fabric exactly as in slanted draperies and press, with pleats turned toward the center of the window. There are usually no returns on curved-top draperies. Lay the template on the pattern and draw the curve across the pleats.

Template for half of window

A—half-width of window

B—length from top to break in curve

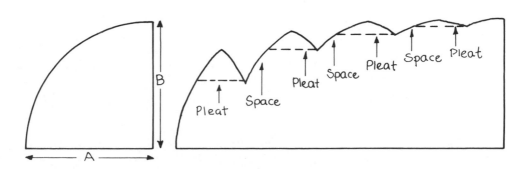

The pattern differs from the slanted-top variety only in the spaces, which are curved instead of diagonal.

Tabling

The tabling process is the same except that you lay the lower edge of the pattern straight across the table at point A distance from the break in the circle to the bottom of the drapery.

Pleating

It is more difficult in curved-top draperies to stitch pleats straight, but they must be perpendicular to the bottom of the drapery. This is why it is important to cut the pleats straight across from one mark to the other when the original pattern is unfolded. The top of the pleat will act as a guide where to stitch.

Before tacking the pleats, check the drapery against the template for accuracy. The last pleat should fall 2 inches above the break in the circle unless there is a return, in which case it is at the break.

These draperies can be hung on flex rod or screw eyes placed to correspond with the pleats. Slanted-top draperies can go on regular rodding with slides but must be fastened at the high point so they won't slide down the rod.

FABRICATION OF DECORATIVE SHADES

The fabrication of decorative shades is relatively simple but very time-consuming and requires meticulous workmanship. Do not be misled by the simplicity of the process. It is more costly to make them than most people realize.

Roman Shades

The flat roman shade is the easiest to make and requires the least amount of fabric. When cut, the fabric must be 3 inches wider and 10 inches longer than the finished size. The tapes can be spaced from 10 to 18 inches apart, the usual distance being 12 to 15 inches. If the tapes are too far apart, the folds tend to sag when you raise the shade. When the shade is wider than one width of fabric, the spacing is often determined by the width of the fabric, as the seam must fall behind a tape. You never add just a few inches to the side of any shade. The amount you add must be equal to a multiple of the shade spacing plus 1½ inches for the side hem.

Roman shades are usually lined to add body and provide privacy. Lining and fabric are cut the same size and laid on the table wrong sides together and the lining on top. On each side of the shade carefully turn both fabrics 1½ inches to the lining side, press down, and pin. Next draw a line from top to bottom of the shade on each side, 1⅛ inch from the pressed edge. This line should go to within 9 inches of the bottom of the unhemmed shade. Divide the distance between these lines by the number of divisions the shade will have. This is the distance to space the other lines. For example, the distance between the lines is 42 inches. You want three divisions in your shade. Thus 42 inches divided by 3 equals 14 inches. The next two lines will be drawn 14 inches from existing lines and 14 inches apart. Pin the lining and the fabric together at intervals along these lines to keep them from shifting while the tapes are sewed on.

Roman shade tape is a twill tape about ⅝ inch wide with white plastic rings attached at 5-inch intervals. Measure the lengths of tape 5 inches shorter than the length to which the fabric was cut and with the first ring (where it is attached to the tape) 1½ inches from the end.

The lines you have drawn are where the center of the tape will go. Lay the end of the cut tape on the line 9 inches from the bottom edge of the shade. The outer edge of the side tapes should be about ¾ inch from the edge of the shade. Sewing on the side tapes covers the raw edges of the fabric and the lining. Sew all tapes on each side as accurately as possible so the lines of stitching on the front of the shade are parallel. Start all tapes at the same point at the bottom and check from time to time to see that the rings are aligned horizontally at the point where they are joined to the tape. If they are not, the folds will not be level as they pull up. Sew all seams in the same direction. If the fabric and the lining had to be seamed to make the shade wide enough, be sure the seams, pressed open and flat, are under one of the tapes.

Fold 5 inches of fabric and lining together to the wrong side of the shade at the bottom and pin. Close the sides with a slip stitch as neatly as possible. This forms a self-lined flap at the bottom of the shade.

Turn up the flap another 5 inches, making sure that the raw edge stays flat in the hem. Sew a 1-inch tuck across the shade so that the ends of the tapes are in the tuck and back-stitch at each end of the seam. This is the pocket through which you will insert a ⅜-inch brass rod for weight.

Table the shade to the correct length, turning extra at the top down on the tabling line. Press across it at that point. Check to be sure the shade is square at all corners and that tapes are properly aligned. Stitch across the crease, finish the top edge, and attach to a 1 inch by 2 inch board that has previously been covered with lining. It may be stapled or VELCRO® Tape may be used.

A tie-folded or pre-pleated roman shade is made the same way except that it must be made twice as long as the finished length. When you have completed all steps, start at the bottom with a piece of fishline and tie the rings so they are held 2½ inches apart. This makes folds in the fabric that stay, even when the shade is down. Another way to achieve this effect is to blind-stitch a 2-inch hem on each side of the shade. Then instead of drawing lines, start 10½ inches from the bottom of the shade and make marks 5 inches apart where the lines would be. These must line up with each other in both directions. Now sew additional rings on the tapes so that all rings are spaced 2½ inches apart. This can be done by hand or on the bar-tacker.

Starting as before, position the first ring on the tape at the first mark and tack securely through fabric and lining. Proceed with the next ring up the length of the shade, forming tucks as you go. The tape is not sewn to the shade except at the very bottom below the first ring. This is a good method when the lines of stitching would be objectionable on the face of the fabric. All that shows are the tacks.

If the shade is to have bands of trim down the front where the tapes go, these are sewed to the face fabric at the tape lines before the shade is constructed.

Balloon Shades

Balloon shades are constructed in a similar manner to roman shades. The length allowance is the same, but you must allow approximately double fullness across the window or 12 inches for each pleat and 6 inches for each half-pleat. This may vary according to the fullness you want and the size of the spaces. On the same window that has 42 inches between the outside tapes, each section of fabric has to be 12 inches wider than on a roman shade, so this shade would require two widths of 48- or 54-inch fabric to construct.

```
    42 inches—width of finished shade
+    3 inches—for side hems
+  24 inches—for two full pleats
+  12 inches—for two half-pleats
+    1 inch—for seams
    82 inches—amount of fabric needed
```

Seam the fabric together and press the seams open. This type of seam must fall behind a tape, so spaces must be laid out accordingly. If the fabric is 54 inches wide, this works out well, as the amount of fabric needed for the first space is 1½ inches for the side hem, 14 inches for space, and 12 inches for pleats, or 27½ inches. It would then be 25½ inches to the seam. A 14-inch space and 12 inches for pleats comes to 26 inches and the tape could be placed over the seam, the small discrepancy being absorbed in the pleat. The other space has a full width so it is no problem.

If the fabric were only 48 inches wide, the pleats would have to be adjusted to have only 9 inches or there could be only two divisions in the shade. The first width would use 1½ inches for the side hem, 28 inches for two spaces, and 18 inches for pleats. The other space and pleats would come from the second width. It would be less trouble to cut the number of divisions to two and make large pleats, unless this would cause a problem with balancing other shades. It would still require two widths of fabric.

Press the side hems as on romans and pin. Mark pleats and spaces both at top and bottom of the shade with pins, being sure the marks are parallel to each other and that the pins are visible from the right and wrong sides of the shade. Draw lines for tapes and pin the lining (if any) and fabric together as in romans. Balloons are often made unlined so creases can be used for marking, as in Austrians.

Turn the shade over and lift the fabric at the first pleat marking, bring it to the first tape line, forming half of an inverted pleat at the side tape. Go to the next tape and form a full pleat with the tape line at the center. Continue with full pleats until you reach the other side, where there is another half-pleat. Be sure all pleats are straight from top to bottom. Then press carefully.

Turn the shade back to the wrong side and release the pleats so that tapes can be sewn as in romans but with the first ring 2½ inches from the bottom. Check for horizontal alignment and always sew in the same direction. Again working from the front side, lay the pleats back in, following the creases, and pin them in place to hold, pinning carefully at top and bottom. Form a double 1-inch bottom hem on the wrong side, keeping the pleats in place as you do so. Unfold, trim out as much of the pleats as possible to remove bulk, and stitch-hem, back-stitching to secure the ends. Slip a ⅜-inch brass rod into the hem for weight and close the ends of the pocket by hand. Table for correct length, stitching across the top at this point, keeping the pleats in place. Finish the top with a double hem and attach it to the board for rigging.

Austrian Shades

Austrian shades should be made of a soft fabric, preferably a sheer. They can be made from a heavier fabric and lined but they then lose some of their effectiveness. Once the size is determined, add 4 inches to the width for each section you will have and triple the length. Spacing for sections is usually 12 inches but can vary from 10 to 18 inches. Do not forget that tapes are spaced 4 inches further apart than you want the scallops to be.

For side hems turn under 1¼ inch on each side, press, and pin. Mark lines for tapes as in roman shades, but the lines should go all the way to the bottom. Instead of drawing lines that might show through the fabric, you can press a crease to use as a guide.

Austrian shade tape is 2-cord shirring tape with rings sewed at 13-inch intervals. Start the tape at the bottom of the shade with 1½ inches of tape below the first ring. Sew as on romans, as accurately as possible and always in the same direction. Knot the cords at the bottom of the tape and then stitch a shirt-tail or double ½ inch hem across the bottom. Fringe or trim may be sewed at this point.

To shirr the Austrian, pull up the two cords on each tape, holding both cords taut while you pull. When you feel the approximate length has been reached, lay the shade on the table wrong side up with the bottom under the tabling bar at the correct length. Pull some more if it is too long or let some fullness out if it is too short. Leave 2 inches ungathered above the tabling line. Knot the cords securely and cut off the excess fabric. Press the crease at the tabling line.

Adjust gathers up and down the tapes until they are evenly distributed and all rings align horizontally. Cut a rod the correct width of the shade minus ½ inch. Cover it with a sleeve made of fabric and divide it into as many equal sections as there are spaces. Sew the rod to the tapes just below the first ring at the bottom at the division points.

At the top pin in 1-inch tucks behind the tapes on each side (on only one side on the side tapes). Adjust until the correct width is reached. Pin tucks and stitch across on the crease line. Hem the top with double hem, being sure to keep the tucks at the proper places.

Attach the shade to the board and rig it.

RIGGING DECORATIVE SHADES

All decorative shades are rigged alike. The board to which they are attached is 1 inch by 2 inches and covered with lining. For ceiling mount, screw eyes are attached on the 2-inch side about ½ inch from each end and at points where other tapes will fall. For wall mount, the screw eyes go in the 1-inch side. Thin nylon cord is used and the cord should be long enough to tie to the bottom ring and go up the length of the shade through the rings and across the board at the top with about 6 inches to spare. Each cord will be a different length. When you go through the last ring at the top, go through the screw eye above it and through all remaining screw eyes to the other side of the board. All cords go to the same side of the board. If you have four tapes, there will be four cords through the last screw eye. When this has been completed, have someone hold the bottom of the shade while you pull all the cords to remove the slack in them. When this has been done, knot all the cords together securely. Tie a single cord to this knot and make it long enough to reach easily from the floor when the shade is down. Attach a traverse cord weight at the end and the shade is ready to install. A cleat must be used to anchor the cord when the shade is raised.

APPENDIX
CHARTS FOR PLEATING

SPACE AND PLEAT CHART—45 TO 54 INCH FABRIC

SPACE AND PLEAT CHART—36 INCH FABRIC

SPACE SETTER CHART—45 TO 54 INCH FABRICS FOR FULL AND HALF WIDTH DRAPERIES

SPACE SETTER CHART—45 TO 54 INCH FABRICS FOR DRAPERIES CONTAINING ⅓ AND ⅔ WIDTHS

SPACE SETTER CHART—45 TO 54 INCH FABRICS FOR DRAPERIES CONTAINING ¼ AND ¾ WIDTHS

SPACE SETTER CHART—36 INCH FABRICS FOR FULL AND HALF WIDTH DRAPERIES

SPACE SETTER CHARTS

To use the SPACE SETTER CHART, calculate the width of the panel and subtract 4 inches plus the size of the return (4 inches + 4 inches = 8 inches or 4 inches + 6 inches = 10 inches). This gives you the distance between end pleats.

Find the correct number of widths per panel and the correct distance between end pleats on the chart. Next to this number is the correct spacing

SPACE AND PLEAT CHART—45 TO 54 INCH FABRICS—DRAPERIES CONTAINING FULL AND HALF WIDTHS

Number widths	1st width	2nd width	3rd width	4th width	5th width	6th width	7th width	8th width	9th width	10th width
1	4S 5P									
1½	4S 5P	2S 2P								
2	4S 5P	5S 5P								
2½	4S 5P	5S 5P	2S 2P							
3	4S 5P	6S 5P	4S 5P							
3½	4S 5P	5S 5P	5S 5P	2S 2P						
4	4S 5P	5S 5P	6S 5P	4S 5P						
4½	4S 5P	5S 5P	5S 5P	5S 5P	2S 2P					
5	4S 5P	5S 5P	5S 5P	6S 5P	4S 5P					
5½	4S 5P	5S 5P	5S 5P	5S 5P	5S 5P	2S 2P				
6	4S 5P	5S 5P	5S 5P	5S 5P	6S 5P	4S 5P				
6½	4S 5P	5S 5P	5S 5P	5S 5P	5S 5P	5S 5P	2S 2P			
7	4S 5P	5S 5P	5S 5P	5S 5P	5S 5P	6S 5P	4S 5P			
7½	4S 5P	5S 5P	5S 5P	5S 5P	5S 5P	5S 5P	5S 5P	2S 2P		
8	4S 5P	5S 5P	5S 5P	5S 5P	5S 5P	5S 5P	6S 5P	4S 5P		
8½	4S 5P	5S 5P	5S 5P	5S 5P	5S 5P	5S 5P	5S 5P	5S 5P	2S 2P	
9	4S 5P	5S 5P	5S 5P	5S 5P	5S 5P	5S 5P	5S 5P	6S 5P	4S 5P	
9½	4S 5P	5S 5P	5S 5P	5S 5P	5S 5P	5S 5P	5S 5P	5S 5P	2S 2P	
10	4S 4P	5S 5P	5S 5P	5S 5P	5S 5P	5S 5P	5S 5P	6S 5P	4S 5P	

SPACE AND PLEAT CHART—45 TO 54 INCH FABRICS—DRAPERIES CONTAINING ¼ AND ¾ WIDTHS

Number widths	1st width	2nd width	3rd width	4th width	5th width	6th width
1–¼	5S 5P	1P				
1–¾	4S 5P	3S 3P				
2–¼	4S 5P	6S 5P	1P			
2–¾	4S 5P	5S 5P	3S 3P			
3–¼	4S 5P	5S 5P	6S 5P	1P		
3–¾	4S 5P	5S 5P	5S 5P	3S 3P		
4–¼	4S 5P	5S 5P	5S 5P	6S 5P	1P	
4–¾	4S 5P	5S 5P	5S 5P	5S 5P	3S 3P	
5–¼	4S 5P	5S 5P	5S 5P	5S 5P	6S 5P	1P
5–¾	4S 5P	5S 5P	5S 5P	5S 5P	5S 5P	3S 3P

between pleats in inches and tenths of inches. If there is a plus after the number such as 4+, you should make the space halfway between 4 and 4.1.

The SPACE AND PLEAT CHART shows the correct number of spaces in each width of the panel. S is for Space. P is for Pleat.

For right panel read chart from right to left.

For left panel read chart from left to right.

SPACE AND PLEAT CHART—45 TO 54 INCH FABRICS—DRAPERIES CONTAINING ⅓ AND ⅔ WIDTHS

Number widths	1st width	2nd width	3rd width	4th width	5th width	6th width
1–⅓	4S 5P	1S 1P				
1–⅔	4S 5P	3S 3P				
2–⅓	4S 5P	5S 5P	1S 1P			
2–⅔	4S 5P	5S 5P	3S 3P			
3–⅓	4S 5P	5S 5P	5S 5P	1S 1P		
3–⅔	4S 5P	5S 5P	5S 5P	3S 3P		
4–⅓	4S 5P	5S 5P	5S 5P	5S 5P	1S 1P	
4–⅔	4S 5P	5S 5P	5S 5P	5S 5P	3S 3P	
5–⅓	4S 5P	5S 5P	5S 5P	5S 5P	5S 5P	1S 1P
5–⅔	4S 5P	5S 5P	5S 5P	5S 5P	5S 5P	3S 3P

SPACE AND PLEAT CHART—36 INCH FABRIC—DRAPERIES CONTAINING FULL AND HALF WIDTHS

Number widths	1st width	2nd width	3rd width	4th width	5th width	6th width	7th width	8th width	9th width	10th width
1	3S 4P									
1½	4S 4P	1S 2P								
2	3S 4P	4S 4P								
2½	3S 4P	5S 4P	1S 2P							
3	3S 4P	5S 4P	3S 4P							
3½	3S 4P	4S 4P	5S 4P	1S 2P						
4	3S 4P	4S 4P	5S 4P	3S 4P						
4½	3S 4P	4S 4P	4S 4P	5S 4P	1S 2P					
5	3S 4P	4S 4P	4S 4P	5S 4P	3S 4P					
5½	3S 4P	4S 4P	4S 4P	4S 4P	5S 4P	1S 2P				
6	3S 4P	4S 4P	4S 4P	5S 4P	4S 4P	3S 4P				
6½	3S 4P	4S 4P	4S 4P	4S 4P	4S 4P	5S 4P	1S 2P			
7	3S 4P	4S 4P	4S 4P	5S 4P	4S 4P	4S 4P	3S 4P			
7½	3S 4P	4S 4P	4S 4P	4S 4P	4S 4P	4S 4P	5S 4P	1S 2P		
8	3S 4P	4S 4P	4S 4P	5S 4P	4S 4P	4S 4P	4S 4P	3S 4P		
8½	3S 4P	4S 4P	4S 4P	4S 4P	4S 4P	4S 4P	4S 4P	5S 4P	1S 2P	
9	3S 4P	4S 4P	4S 4P	5S 4P	4S 4P	4S 4P	4S 4P	4S 4P	3S 4P	
9½	3S 4P	4S 4P	4S 4P	4S 4P	4S 4P	4S 4P	4S 4P	4S 4P	5S 4P	1S 2P
10	3S 4P	4S 4P	4S 4P	5S 4P	4S 4P	4S 4P	4S 4P	4S 4P	4S 4P	3S 4P

SPACE SETTER CHART—45 TO 54 INCH FABRICS FOR FULL AND HALF WIDTH DRAPERIES

Number of Widths Per Panel							
Single width		1½ widths		2 widths		2½ widths	
Distance between end pleats	Set space	Distance between end pleats	Set space	Distance between end pleats	Set space	Distance between end pleats	Set space
9 inches	2.2½	16½ inches	2.7½	24 inches	2.7	31 inches	2.8½
9½ inches	2.4	17 inches	2.8½	24½ inches	2.7½	32 inches	2.9½
10 inches	2.5	17½ inches	2.9½	25 inches	2.8	33 inches	3.0
10½ inches	2.6½	18 inches	3.0	25½ inches	2.8½	34 inches	3.1
11 inches	2.8	18½ inches	3.1	26 inches	2.9	35 inches	3.2
11½ inches	2.9	19 inches	3.2	26½ inches	2.9½	36 inches	3.3
12 inches	3.0	19½ inches	3.2½	27 inches	3.0	37 inches	3.4
12½ inches	3.1½	20 inches	3.3½	27½ inches	3.1	38 inches	3.5
13 inches	3.2½	20½ inches	3.4½	28 inches	3.1½	39 inches	3.5½
13½ inches	3.4	21 inches	3.5	28½ inches	3.2	40 inches	3.6½
14 inches	3.5	21½ inches	3.6	29 inches	3.2½	41 inches	3.7½
14½ inches	3.6½	22 inches	3.7	29½ inches	3.3	42 inches	3.8½
15 inches	3.7½	22½ inches	3.7½	30 inches	3.3½	43 inches	3.9½
15½ inches	3.9	23 inches	3.8½	30½ inches	3.4	44 inches	4.0
16 inches	4.0	23½ inches	3.9½	31 inches	3.4½	45 inches	4.1
16½ inches	4.1½	24 inches	4.0	31½ inches	3.5	46 inches	4.2
17 inches	4.2½	24½ inches	4.1	32 inches	3.5½	47 inches	4.3
17½ inches	4.4	25 inches	4.2	32½ inches	3.6½	48 inches	4.4
18 inches	4.5	25½ inches	4.2½	33 inches	3.7	49 inches	4.5
18½ inches	4.6½	26 inches	4.3½	33½ inches	3.7½	50 inches	4.5½
19 inches	4.7½	26½ inches	4.4½	34 inches	3.8	51 inches	4.6½
19½ inches	4.9	27 inches	4.5	34½ inches	3.8½	52 inches	4.7½
20 inches	5.0	27½ inches	4.6	35 inches	3.9	53 inches	4.8½
20½ inches	5.1½	28 inches	4.7	35½ inches	3.9½	54 inches	4.9½
21 inches	5.2½	28½ inches	4.7½	36 inches	4.0	55 inches	5.0
		29 inches	4.8½	36½ inches	4.1	56 inches	5.1
		29½ inches	4.9½	37 inches	4.1½	57 inches	5.2
		30 inches	5.0	37½ inches	4.2	58 inches	5.3
		30½ inches	5.1	38 inches	4.2½	59 inches	5.4
		31 inches	5.2	38½ inches	4.3	60 inches	5.5
		31½ inches	5.2½	39 inches	4.3½	61 inches	5.5½
		32 inches	5.3½	39½ inches	4.4		
		32½ inches	5.4½	40 inches	4.4½		
		33 inches	5.5	40½ inches	4.5		
		33½ inches	5.6	41 inches	4.6		
		34 inches	5.7	41½ inches	4.6½		
		34½ inches	5.7½	42 inches	4.7		
				42½ inches	4.7½		
				43 inches	4.8		
				43½ inches	4.8½		
				44 inches	4.9		
				44½ inches	4.9½		
				45 inches	5.0		
				45½ inches	5.1		
				46 inches	5.1½		
				46½ inches	5.2		
				47 inches	5.2½		
				47½ inches	5.3		
				48 inches	5.3½		

SPACE SETTER CHART—45 TO 54 INCH FABRICS FOR FULL AND
HALF WIDTH DRAPERIES

Number of Widths Per Panel							
3 widths		3½ widths		4 widths			
Distance between end pleats	Set space	Distance between end pleats	Set space	Distance between end pleats	Set space	Distance between end pleats	Set space
39 inches	2.8	46 inches	2.9	54 inches	2.8½	97 inches	5.1½
40 inches	2.9	47 inches	2.9½	55 inches	2.9	98 inches	5.2
41 inches	2.9½	48 inches	3.0	56 inches	2.9½	99 inches	5.2½
42 inches	3.0	49 inches	3.1	57 inches	3.0	100 inches	5.3
43 inches	3.1	50 inches	3.1½	58 inches	3.1	101 inches	5.3½
44 inches	3.1½	51 inches	3.2	59 inches	3.1½	102 inches	5.4
45 inches	3.2½	52 inches	3.2½	60 inches	3.2		
46 inches	3.3	53 inches	3.3½	61 inches	3.2½		
47 inches	3.4	54 inches	3.4	62 inches	3.3		
48 inches	3.4½	55 inches	3.4½	63 inches	3.3½		
49 inches	3.5	56 inches	3.5	64 inches	3.4		
50 inches	3.6	57 inches	3.6	65 inches	3.4½		
51 inches	3.6½	58 inches	3.6½	66 inches	3.5		
52 inches	3.7½	59 inches	3.7	67 inches	3.5½		
53 inches	3.8	60 inches	3.7½	68 inches	3.6		
54 inches	3.9	61 inches	3.8½	69 inches	3.6½		
55 inches	3.9½	62 inches	3.9	70 inches	3.7		
56 inches	4.0	63 inches	3.9½	71 inches	3.7½		
57 inches	4.1	64 inches	4.0	72 inches	3.8		
58 inches	4.1½	65 inches	4.1	73 inches	3.8½		
59 inches	4.2½	66 inches	4.1½	74 inches	3.9		
60 inches	4.3	67 inches	4.2	75 inches	3.9½		
61 inches	4.4	68 inches	4.2½	76 inches	4.0		
62 inches	4.4½	69 inches	4.3½	77 inches	4.1		
63 inches	4.5	70 inches	4.4	78 inches	4.1½		
64 inches	4.6	71 inches	4.4½	79 inches	4.2		
65 inches	4.6½	72 inches	4.5	80 inches	4.2½		
66 inches	4.7½	73 inches	4.6	81 inches	4.3		
67 inches	4.8	74 inches	4.6½	82 inches	4.3½		
68 inches	4.9	75 inches	4.7	83 inches	4.4		
69 inches	4.9½	76 inches	4.7½	84 inches	4.4½		
70 inches	5.0	77 inches	4.8½	85 inches	4.5		
71 inches	5.1	78 inches	4.9	86 inches	4.5½		
72 inches	5.1½	79 inches	4.9½	87 inches	4.6		
73 inches	5.2½	80 inches	5.0	88 inches	4.6½		
74 inches	5.3	81 inches	5.1	89 inches	4.7		
75 inches	5.4	82 inches	5.1½	90 inches	4.7½		
		83 inches	5.2	91 inches	4.8		
		84 inches	5.2½	92 inches	4.8½		
		85 inches	5.3½	93 inches	4.9		
		86 inches	5.4	94 inches	4.9½		
		87 inches	5.4½	95 inches	5.0		
		88 inches	5.5	96 inches	5.1		

SPACE SETTER CHART—45 TO 54 INCH FABRICS FOR FULL AND HALF-WIDTH DRAPERIES

Number of Widths Per Panel							
4½ widths				5 widths			
Distance between end pleats	Set space	Distance between end pleats	Set space	Distance between end pleats	Set space	Distance between end pleats	Set space
61 inches	2.9½	105 inches	5.0	69 inches	2.9	113 inches	4.7½
62 inches	2.9½	106 inches	5.1	70 inches	2.9½	114 inches	4.8
63 inches	3.0	107 inches	5.1	71 inches	3.0	115 inches	4.8
64 inches	3.1	108 inches	5.1½	72 inches	3.0	116 inches	4.8½
65 inches	3.1	109 inches	5.2	73 inches	3.1	117 inches	4.9
66 inches	3.1½	110 inches	5.2½	74 inches	3.1	118 inches	4.9½
67 inches	3.2	111 inches	5.3	75 inches	3.1½	119 inches	5.0
68 inches	3.2½	112 inches	5.3½	76 inches	3.2	120 inches	5.0
69 inches	3.3	113 inches	5.4	77 inches	3.2½	121 inches	5.1
70 inches	3.3½	114 inches	5.4½	78 inches	3.3	122 inches	5.1
71 inches	3.4	115 inches	5.5	79 inches	3.3	123 inches	5.1½
72 inches	3.4½	116 inches	5.5½	80 inches	3.3½	124 inches	5.2
73 inches	3.5			81 inches	3.4	125 inches	5.2½
74 inches	3.5½			82 inches	3.4½	126 inches	5.2½
75 inches	3.6			83 inches	3.5	127 inches	5.3
76 inches	3.6½			84 inches	3.5	128 inches	5.3½
77 inches	3.7			85 inches	3.5½	129 inches	5.4
78 inches	3.7½			86 inches	3.6		
79 inches	3.8			87 inches	3.6½		
80 inches	3.8½			88 inches	3.7		
81 inches	3.9			89 inches	3.7½		
82 inches	3.9½			90 inches	3.8		
83 inches	3.9½			91 inches	3.8		
84 inches	4.0			92 inches	3.8½		
85 inches	4.1			93 inches	3.9		
86 inches	4.1			94 inches	3.9½		
87 inches	4.1½			95 inches	4.0		
88 inches	4.2			96 inches	4.0		
89 inches	4.2½			97 inches	4.1		
90 inches	4.3			98 inches	4.1		
91 inches	4.3½			99 inches	4.1½		
92 inches	4.4			100 inches	4.2		
93 inches	4.4½			101 inches	4.2½		
94 inches	4.5			102 inches	4.3		
95 inches	4.5½			103 inches	4.3		
96 inches	4.6			104 inches	4.3½		
97 inches	4.6½			105 inches	4.4		
98 inches	4.7			106 inches	4.4½		
99 inches	4.7½			107 inches	4.5		
100 inches	4.8			108 inches	4.5½		
101 inches	4.8			109 inches	4.5½		
102 inches	4.8½			110 inches	4.6		
103 inches	4.9			111 inches	4.6½		
104 inches	4.9½			112 inches	4.7		

SPACE SETTER CHART—45 TO 54 INCH FABRICS FOR FULL AND HALF WIDTH DRAPERIES

Number of Widths Per Panel							
5½ widths				*6 widths*			
Distance between end pleats	*Set space*	*Distance between end pleats*	*Set space*	*Distance between end pleats*	*Set space*	*Distance between end pleats*	*Set space*
76 inches	2.9½	120 inches	4.6½	84 inches	2.9	128 inches	4.4½
77 inches	3.0	121 inches	4.6½	85 inches	2.9½	129 inches	4.4½
78 inches	3.0	122 inches	4.7	86 inches	3.0	130 inches	4.5
79 inches	3.1	123 inches	4.7½	87 inches	3.0	131 inches	4.5½
80 inches	3.1	124 inches	4.8	88 inches	3.1	132 inches	4.5½
81 inches	3.1½	125 inches	4.8½	89 inches	3.1	133 inches	4.6
82 inches	3.2	126 inches	4.8½	90 inches	3.1½	134 inches	4.6½
83 inches	3.2	127 inches	4.9	91 inches	3.1½	135 inches	4.6½
84 inches	3.2½	128 inches	4.9½	92 inches	3.2	136 inches	4.7
85 inches	3.3	129 inches	5.0	93 inches	3.2½	137 inches	4.7½
86 inches	3.3½	130 inches	5.0	94 inches	3.2½	138 inches	4.8
87 inches	3.3½	131 inches	5.1	95 inches	3.3	139 inches	4.8
88 inches	3.4	132 inches	5.1	96 inches	3.3½	140 inches	4.8½
89 inches	3.4½	133 inches	5.1½	97 inches	3.3½	141 inches	4.9
90 inches	3.5	134 inches	5.1½	98 inches	3.4	142 inches	4.9
91 inches	3.5	135 inches	5.2	99 inches	3.4½	143 inches	4.9½
92 inches	3.5½	136 inches	5.2½	100 inches	3.4½	144 inches	5.0
93 inches	3.6	137 inches	5.3	101 inches	3.5	145 inches	5.0
94 inches	3.6½	138 inches	5.3½	102 inches	3.5½	146 inches	5.+
95 inches	3.6½	139 inches	5.3½	103 inches	3.5½	147 inches	5.1
96 inches	3.7	140 inches	5.4	104 inches	3.6	148 inches	5.1
97 inches	3.7½	141 inches	5.4½	105 inches	3.6½	149 inches	5.1½
98 inches	3.8	142 inches	5.5	106 inches	3.6½	150 inches	5.2
99 inches	3.8½	143 inches	5.5	107 inches	3.7	151 inches	5.2
100 inches	3.8½			108 inches	3.7½	152 inches	5.2½
101 inches	3.9			109 inches	3.8	153 inches	5.3
102 inches	3.9½			110 inches	3.8	154 inches	5.3½
103 inches	4.0			111 inches	3.8½	155 inches	5.3½
104 inches	4.0			112 inches	3.9	156 inches	5.4
105 inches	4.1			113 inches	3.9		
106 inches	4.1			114 inches	3.9½		
107 inches	4.1½			115 inches	4.0		
108 inches	4.2			116 inches	4.0		
109 inches	4.2			117 inches	4.+		
110 inches	4.2½			118 inches	4.1		
111 inches	4.3			119 inches	4.1		
112 inches	4.3½			120 inches	4.1½		
113 inches	4.3½			121 inches	4.2		
114 inches	4.4			122 inches	4.2½		
115 inches	4.4½			123 inches	4.2½		
116 inches	4.5			124 inches	4.3		
117 inches	4.5			125 inches	4.3½		
118 inches	4.5½			126 inches	4.3½		
119 inches	4.6			127 inches	4.4		

Note: 4+ means set space half way between 4 and 4.1
5+ means set space half way between 5 and 5.1

SPACE SETTER CHART—45 TO 54 INCH FABRICS FOR FULL AND HALF WIDTH DRAPERIES

			Number of Widths Per Panel				
6½ widths				*7 widths*			
Distance between end pleats	*Set space*	*Distance between end pleats*	*Set space*	*Distance between end pleats*	*Set space*	*Distance between end pleats*	*Set space*
91 inches	2.9½	135 inches	4.4	99 inches	2.9½	143 inches	4.2½
92 inches	3.0	136 inches	4.4	100 inches	2.9½	144 inches	4.2½
93 inches	3.0	137 inches	4.4½	101 inches	3.0	145 inches	4.3
94 inches	3.+	138 inches	4.5	102 inches	3.0	146 inches	4.3
95 inches	3.1	139 inches	4.5	103 inches	3.+	147 inches	4.3½
96 inches	3.1	140 inches	4.5½	104 inches	3.1	148 inches	4.4
97 inches	3.1½	141 inches	4.6	105 inches	3.1	149 inches	4.4
98 inches	3.2	142 inches	4.6	106 inches	3.1½	150 inches	4.4½
99 inches	3.2	143 inches	4.6½	107 inches	3.1½	151 inches	4.4½
100 inches	3.2½	144 inches	4.6½	108 inches	3.2	152 inches	4.5
101 inches	3.3	145 inches	4.7	109 inches	3.2½	153 inches	4.5½
102 inches	3.3	146 inches	4.7½	110 inches	3.2½	154 inches	4.5½
103 inches	3.3½	147 inches	4.7½	111 inches	3.3	155 inches	4.6
104 inches	3.4	148 inches	4.8	112 inches	3.3	156 inches	4.6
105 inches	3.4	149 inches	4.8½	113 inches	3.3½	157 inches	4.6½
106 inches	3.4½	150 inches	4.8½	114 inches	3.4	158 inches	4.7
107 inches	3.4½	151 inches	4.9	115 inches	3.4	159 inches	4.7
108 inches	3.5	152 inches	4.9½	116 inches	3.4½	160 inches	4.7½
109 inches	3.5½	153 inches	4.9½	117 inches	3.4½	161 inches	4.7½
110 inches	3.5½	154 inches	5.0	118 inches	3.5	162 inches	4.8
111 inches	3.6	155 inches	5.0	119 inches	3.5½	163 inches	4.8
112 inches	3.6½	156 inches	5.+	120 inches	3.5½	164 inches	4.8½
113 inches	3.6½	157 inches	5.1	121 inches	3.6	165 inches	4.9
114 inches	3.7	158 inches	5.1	122 inches	3.6	166 inches	4.9
115 inches	3.7½	159 inches	5.1½	123 inches	3.6½	167 inches	4.9½
116 inches	3.7½	160 inches	5.2	124 inches	3.7	168 inches	4.9½
117 inches	3.8	161 inches	5.2	125 inches	3.7	169 inches	5.0
118 inches	3.8½	162 inches	5.2½	126 inches	3.7½	170 inches	5.0
119 inches	3.8½	163 inches	5.3	127 inches	3.7½	171 inches	5.1
120 inches	3.9	164 inches	5.3	128 inches	3.8	172 inches	5.1
121 inches	3.9½	165 inches	5.3½	129 inches	3.8	173 inches	5.1
122 inches	3.9½	166 inches	5.4	130 inches	3.8½	174 inches	5.1½
123 inches	4.0	167 inches	5.4	131 inches	3.9	175 inches	5.1½
124 inches	4.0	168 inches	5.4½	132 inches	3.9	176 inches	5.2
125 inches	4.+	169 inches	5.5	133 inches	3.9½	177 inches	5.2
126 inches	4.1	170 inches	5.5½	134 inches	3.9½	178 inches	5.2½
127 inches	4.1			135 inches	4.0	179 inches	5.3
128 inches	4.1½			136 inches	4.0	180 inches	5.3
129 inches	4.2			137 inches	4.+	181 inches	5.3½
130 inches	4.2			138 inches	4.1	182 inches	5.3½
131 inches	4.2½			139 inches	4.1	183 inches	5.4
132 inches	4.3			140 inches	4.1½		
133 inches	4.3			141 inches	4.2		
134 inches	4.3½			142 inches	4.2		

Note: 3+ means set space half way between 3 and 3.1
4+ means set space half way between 4 and 4.1
5+ means set space half way between 5 and 5.1

SPACE SETTER CHART—45 TO 54 INCH FABRICS FOR FULL AND HALF WIDTH DRAPERIES

Number of Widths Per Panel							
7½ widths				8 widths			
Distance between end pleats	Set space	Distance between end pleats	Set space	Distance between end pleats	Set space	Distance between end pleats	Set space
106 inches	2.9½	155 inches	4.3½	114 inches	2.9½	163 inches	4.2
107 inches	3.0	156 inches	4.3½	115 inches	2.9½	164 inches	4.2½
108 inches	3.0	157 inches	4.4	116 inches	3.0	165 inches	4.2½
109 inches	3.+	158 inches	4.4	117 inches	3.0	166 inches	4.3
110 inches	3.1	159 inches	4.4½	118 inches	3.+	167 inches	4.3
111 inches	3.1	160 inches	4.4½	119 inches	3.1	168 inches	4.3½
112 inches	3.1½	161 inches	4.5	120 inches	3.1	169 inches	4.3½
113 inches	3.1½	162 inches	4.5	121 inches	3.1½	170 inches	4.4
114 inches	3.2	163 inches	4.5½	122 inches	3.1½	171 inches	4.4
115 inches	3.2	164 inches	4.6	123 inches	3.2	172 inches	4.4½
116 inches	3.2½	165 inches	4.6	124 inches	3.2	173 inches	4.4½
117 inches	3.2½	166 inches	4.6½	125 inches	3.2½	174 inches	4.5
118 inches	3.3	167 inches	4.6½	126 inches	3.2½	175 inches	4.5
119 inches	3.3½	168 inches	4.7	127 inches	3.3	176 inches	4.5½
120 inches	3.3½	169 inches	4.7	128 inches	3.3	177 inches	4.5½
121 inches	3.4	170 inches	4.7½	129 inches	3.3½	178 inches	4.6
122 inches	3.4	171 inches	4.7½	130 inches	3.3½	179 inches	4.6
123 inches	3.4½	172 inches	4.8	131 inches	3.4	180 inches	4.6½
124 inches	3.4½	173 inches	4.8½	132 inches	3.4	181 inches	4.6½
125 inches	3.5	174 inches	4.8½	133 inches	3.4½	182 inches	4.7
126 inches	3.5	175 inches	4.9	134 inches	3.4½	183 inches	4.7
127 inches	3.5½	176 inches	4.9	135 inches	3.5	184 inches	4.7½
128 inches	3.6	177 inches	4.9½	136 inches	3.5	185 inches	4.7½
129 inches	3.6	178 inches	4.9½	137 inches	3.5½	186 inches	4.8
130 inches	3.6½	179 inches	5.0	138 inches	3.5½	187 inches	4.8
131 inches	3.6½	180 inches	5.0	139 inches	3.6	188 inches	4.8½
132 inches	3.7	181 inches	5.1	140 inches	3.6	189 inches	4.8½
133 inches	3.7	182 inches	5.1	141 inches	3.6½	190 inches	4.9
134 inches	3.7½	183 inches	5.1	142 inches	3.6½	191 inches	4.9
135 inches	3.7½	184 inches	5.1½	143 inches	3.7	192 inches	4.9½
136 inches	3.8	185 inches	5.1½	144 inches	3.7½	193 inches	4.9½
137 inches	3.8½	186 inches	5.2	145 inches	3.7½	194 inches	5.0
138 inches	3.8½	187 inches	5.2	146 inches	3.7½	195 inches	5.0
139 inches	3.9	188 inches	5.2½	147 inches	3.8	196 inches	5.+
140 inches	3.9	189 inches	5.3	148 inches	3.8	197 inches	5.1
141 inches	3.9½	190 inches	5.3	149 inches	3.8½	198 inches	5.1
142 inches	3.9½	191 inches	5.3½	150 inches	3.8½	199 inches	5.1
143 inches	4.0	192 inches	5.3½	151 inches	3.9	200 inches	5.1½
144 inches	4.0	193 inches	5.4	152 inches	3.9	201 inches	5.1½
145 inches	4.+	194 inches	5.4	153 inches	3.9½	202 inches	5.2
146 inches	4.1	195 inches	5.4½	154 inches	3.9½	203 inches	5.2
147 inches	4.1	196 inches	5.4½	155 inches	4	204 inches	5.2½
148 inches	4.1½	197 inches	5.5	156 inches	4	205 inches	5.2½
149 inches	4.1½			157 inches	4.+	206 inches	5.3
150 inches	4.2			158 inches	4.1	207 inches	5.3
151 inches	4.2			159 inches	4.1	208 inches	5.3½
152 inches	4.2½			160 inches	4.1½	209 inches	5.3½
153 inches	4.3			161 inches	4.1½	210 inches	5.4
154 inches	4.3			162 inches	4.2		

Note: 3+ means set space half way between 3 and 3.1   4+ means set space half way between 4 and 4.1
5+ means set space half way between 5 and 5.1

SPACE SETTER CHART—45 TO 54 INCH FABRICS FOR FULL AND HALF WIDTH DRAPERIES

Number of Widths Per Panel					
8½ widths					
Distance between end pleats	Set space	Distance between end pleats	Set space	Distance between end pleats	Set space
128 inches	3.1½	172 inches	4.2	216 inches	5.3
129 inches	3.1½	173 inches	4.2½	217 inches	5.3
130 inches	3.2	174 inches	4.2½	218 inches	5.3½
131 inches	3.2	175 inches	4.3	219 inches	5.3½
132 inches	3.2½	176 inches	4.3	220 inches	5.4
133 inches	3.2½	177 inches	4.3½	221 inches	5.4
134 inches	3.3	178 inches	4.3½	222 inches	5.4½
135 inches	3.3	179 inches	4.4	223 inches	5.4½
136 inches	3.3½	180 inches	4.4	224 inches	5.5
137 inches	3.3½	181 inches	4.4½	225 inches	5.5
138 inches	3.4	182 inches	4.4½	226 inches	5.5½
139 inches	3.4	183 inches	4.5	227 inches	5.5½
140 inches	3.4½	184 inches	4.5	228 inches	5.6
141 inches	3.4½	185 inches	4.5½		
142 inches	3.5	186 inches	4.5½		
143 inches	3.5	187 inches	4.6		
144 inches	3.5½	188 inches	4.6		
145 inches	3.5½	189 inches	4.6½		
146 inches	3.6	190 inches	4.6½		
147 inches	3.6	191 inches	4.7		
148 inches	3.6½	192 inches	4.7		
149 inches	3.6½	193 inches	4.7½		
150 inches	3.7	194 inches	4.7½		
151 inches	3.7	195 inches	4.8		
152 inches	3.7½	196 inches	4.8		
153 inches	3.7½	197 inches	4.8½		
154 inches	3.8	198 inches	4.8½		
155 inches	3.8	199 inches	4.9		
156 inches	3.8½	200 inches	4.9		
157 inches	3.8½	201 inches	4.9		
158 inches	3.9	202 inches	4.9½		
159 inches	3.9	203 inches	4.9½		
160 inches	3.9½	204 inches	5.0		
161 inches	3.9½	205 inches	5.0		
162 inches	4.0	206 inches	5.+		
163 inches	4.0	207 inches	5.+		
164 inches	4.0	208 inches	5.1		
165 inches	4.+	209 inches	5.1		
166 inches	4.+	210 inches	5.1½		
167 inches	4.1	211 inches	5.1½		
168 inches	4.1	212 inches	5.2		
169 inches	4.1½	213 inches	5.2		
170 inches	4.1½	214 inches	5.2½		
171 inches	4.2	215 inches	5.2½		

Note: 4+ means set space half way between 4 and 4.1
5+ means set space half way between 5 and 5.1

SPACE SETTER CHART—45 TO 54 INCH FABRICS FOR FULL AND HALF WIDTH DRAPERIES

	Number of Widths Per Panel				
	9 widths				
Distance between end pleats	Set space	Distance between end pleats	Set space	Distance between end pleats	Set space
135 inches	3.1	178 inches	4.+	221 inches	5.+
136 inches	3.1	179 inches	4.1	222 inches	5.+
137 inches	3.1½	180 inches	4.1	223 inches	5.1
138 inches	3.1½	181 inches	4.1½	224 inches	5.1
139 inches	3.2	182 inches	4.1½	225 inches	5.1½
140 inches	3.2	183 inches	4.2	226 inches	5.1½
141 inches	3.2½	184 inches	4.2	227 inches	5.2
142 inches	3.2½	185 inches	4.2½	228 inches	5.2
143 inches	3.3	186 inches	4.2½	229 inches	5.2
144 inches	3.3	187 inches	4.3	230 inches	5.2½
145 inches	3.3	188 inches	4.3	231 inches	5.2½
146 inches	3.3½	189 inches	4.3	232 inches	5.3
147 inches	3.3½	190 inches	4.3½	233 inches	5.3
148 inches	3.4	191 inches	4.3½	234 inches	5.3½
149 inches	3.4	192 inches	4.4	235 inches	5.3½
150 inches	3.4½	193 inches	4.4	236 inches	5.4
151 inches	3.4½	194 inches	4.4½	237 inches	5.4
152 inches	3.5	195 inches	4.4½	238 inches	5.4½
153 inches	3.5	196 inches	4.5	239 inches	5.4½
154 inches	3.5½	197 inches	4.5	240 inches	5.5
155 inches	3.5½	198 inches	4.5½	241 inches	5.5
156 inches	3.5½	199 inches	4.5½	242 inches	5.5
157 inches	3.6	200 inches	4.5½	243 inches	5.5½
158 inches	3.6	201 inches	4.6		
159 inches	3.6½	202 inches	4.6		
160 inches	3.6½	203 inches	4.6½		
161 inches	3.7	204 inches	4.6½		
162 inches	3.7	205 inches	4.7		
163 inches	3.7½	206 inches	4.7		
164 inches	3.7½	207 inches	4.7½		
165 inches	3.8	208 inches	4.7½		
166 inches	3.8	209 inches	4.8		
167 inches	3.8	210 inches	4.8		
168 inches	3.8½	211 inches	4.8		
169 inches	3.8½	212 inches	4.8½		
170 inches	3.9	213 inches	4.8½		
171 inches	3.9	214 inches	4.9		
172 inches	3.9½	215 inches	4.9		
173 inches	3.9½	216 inches	4.9½		
174 inches	4.0	217 inches	4.9½		
175 inches	4.0	218 inches	5.0		
176 inches	4.+	219 inches	5.0		
177 inches	4.+	220 inches	5.0		

Note: 4+ means set space half way between 4 and 4.1
5+ means set space half way between 5 and 5.1

SPACE SETTER CHART—45 TO 54 INCH FABRICS FOR FULL AND HALF WIDTH DRAPERIES

		Number of Widths Per Panel			
		9½ widths			
Distance between end pleats	Set space	Distance between end pleats	Set space	Distance between end pleats	Set space
143 inches	3.1½	186 inches	4.+	229 inches	5.0
144 inches	3.1½	187 inches	4.1	230 inches	5.0
145 inches	3.2	188 inches	4.1	231 inches	5.+
146 inches	3.2	189 inches	4.1½	232 inches	5.+
147 inches	3.2	190 inches	4.1½	233 inches	5.1
148 inches	3.2½	191 inches	4.2	234 inches	5.1
149 inches	3.2½	192 inches	4.2	235 inches	5.1½
150 inches	3.3	193 inches	4.2	236 inches	5.1½
151 inches	3.3	194 inches	4.2½	237 inches	5.1½
152 inches	3.3½	195 inches	4.2½	238 inches	5.2
153 inches	3.3½	196 inches	4.3	239 inches	5.2
154 inches	3.3½	197 inches	4.3	240 inches	5.2½
155 inches	3.4	198 inches	4.3½	241 inches	5.2½
156 inches	3.4	199 inches	4.3½	242 inches	5.3
157 inches	3.4½	200 inches	4.3½	243 inches	5.3
158 inches	3.4½	201 inches	4.4	244 inches	5.3½
159 inches	3.5	202 inches	4.4	245 inches	5.3½
160 inches	3.5	203 inches	4.4½	246 inches	5.3½
161 inches	3.5½	204 inches	4.4½	247 inches	5.4
162 inches	3.5½	205 inches	4.5	248 inches	5.4
163 inches	3.5½	206 inches	4.5	249 inches	5.4½
164 inches	3.6	207 inches	4.5	250 inches	5.4½
165 inches	3.6	208 inches	4.5½	251 inches	5.5
166 inches	3.6½	209 inches	4.5½	252 inches	5.5
167 inches	3.6½	210 inches	4.6	253 inches	5.5
168 inches	3.7	211 inches	4.6	254 inches	5.5½
169 inches	3.7	212 inches	4.6½	255 inches	5.5½
170 inches	3.7	213 inches	4.6½	256 inches	5.6
171 inches	3.7½	214 inches	4.6½	257 inches	5.6
172 inches	3.7½	215 inches	4.7		
173 inches	3.8	216 inches	4.7		
174 inches	3.8	217 inches	4.7½		
175 inches	3.8½	218 inches	4.7½		
176 inches	3.8½	219 inches	4.8		
177 inches	3.8½	220 inches	4.8		
178 inches	3.9	221 inches	4.8½		
179 inches	3.9	222 inches	4.8½		
180 inches	3.9½	223 inches	4.8½		
181 inches	3.9½	224 inches	4.9		
182 inches	4.0	225 inches	4.9		
183 inches	4.0	226 inches	4.9½		
184 inches	4.0	227 inches	4.9½		
185 inches	4.+	228 inches	5.0		

Note: 4+ means set space half way between 4 and 4.1
      5+ means set space half way between 5 and 5.1

SPACE SETTER CHART—45 TO 54 INCH FABRICS FOR FULL AND HALF WIDTH DRAPERIES

		Number of Widths Per Panel			
		10 widths			
Distance between end pleats	*Set space*	*Distance between end pleats*	*Set space*	*Distance between end pleats*	*Set space*
150 inches	3.1	193 inches	3.9½	236 inches	4.8½
151 inches	3.1	194 inches	4.0	237 inches	4.8½
152 inches	3.1	195 inches	4.0	238 inches	4.9
153 inches	3.1½	196 inches	4.0	239 inches	4.9
154 inches	3.1½	197 inches	4.+	240 inches	4.9
155 inches	3.2	198 inches	4.+	241 inches	4.9½
156 inches	3.2	199 inches	4.1	242 inches	4.9½
157 inches	3.2	200 inches	4.1	243 inches	5.0
158 inches	3.2½	201 inches	4.1	244 inches	5.0
159 inches	3.2½	202 inches	4.1½	245 inches	5.0
160 inches	3.3	203 inches	4.1½	246 inches	5.+
161 inches	3.3	204 inches	4.2	247 inches	5.+
162 inches	3.3½	205 inches	4.2	248 inches	5.1
163 inches	3.3½	206 inches	4.2	249 inches	5.1
164 inches	3.3½	207 inches	4.2½	250 inches	5.1
165 inches	3.4	208 inches	4.2½	251 inches	5.1½
166 inches	3.4	209 inches	4.3	252 inches	5.1½
167 inches	3.4½	210 inches	4.3	253 inches	5.2
168 inches	3.4½	211 inches	4.3	254 inches	5.2
169 inches	3.4½	212 inches	4.3½	255 inches	5.2
170 inches	3.5	213 inches	4.3½	256 inches	5.2½
171 inches	3.5	214 inches	4.4	257 inches	5.2½
172 inches	3.5½	215 inches	4.4	258 inches	5.3
173 inches	3.5½	216 inches	4.4½	259 inches	5.3
174 inches	3.5½	217 inches	4.4½	260 inches	5.3
175 inches	3.6	218 inches	4.4½	261 inches	5.3½
176 inches	3.6	219 inches	4.5	262 inches	5.3½
177 inches	3.6½	220 inches	4.5	263 inches	5.4
178 inches	3.6½	221 inches	4.5½	264 inches	5.4
179 inches	3.6½	222 inches	4.5½	265 inches	5.4½
180 inches	3.7	223 inches	4.5½	266 inches	5.4½
181 inches	3.7	224 inches	4.6	267 inches	5.4½
182 inches	3.7½	225 inches	4.6	268 inches	5.5
183 inches	3.7½	226 inches	4.6½	269 inches	5.5
184 inches	3.7½	227 inches	4.6½	270 inches	5.5½
185 inches	3.8	228 inches	4.6½		
186 inches	3.8	229 inches	4.7		
187 inches	3.8½	230 inches	4.7		
188 inches	3.8½	231 inches	4.7½		
189 inches	3.9	232 inches	4.7½		
190 inches	3.9	233 inches	4.8		
191 inches	3.9	234 inches	4.8		
192 inches	3.9½	235 inches	4.8		

Note: 4+ means set space half way between 4 and 4.1
5+ means set space half way between 5 and 5.1

SPACE SETTER CHART—45 TO 54 INCH FABRICS FOR DRAPERIES
CONTAINING ⅓ AND ⅔ WIDTHS

			Number of Widths Per Panel				
1–⅓ widths		1–⅔ widths				2–⅓ widths	
Distance between end pleats	Set space	Distance between end pleats	Set space	Distance between end pleats	Set space	Distance between end pleats	Set space
14 inches	2.8	19 inches	2.7½	29 inches	2.9	50 inches	5.0
14½ inches	2.9	19½ inches	2.8	29½ inches	2.9½	50½ inches	5.+
15 inches	3.0	20 inches	2.9	30 inches	3.0	51 inches	5.1
15½ inches	3.1	20½ inches	2.9½	30½ inches	3.+	51½ inches	5.1½
16 inches	3.2	21 inches	3.0	31 inches	3.1	52 inches	5.2
16½ inches	3.3	21½ inches	3.1	31½ inches	3.1½	52¼ inches	5.2½
17 inches	3.4	22 inches	3.2	32 inches	3.2	53 inches	5.3
17½ inches	3.5	22½ inches	3.2½	32½ inches	3.2½	53½ inches	5.3½
18 inches	3.6	23 inches	3.3	33 inches	3.3	54 inches	5.4
18½ inches	3.7	23½ inches	3.4	33½ inches	3.3½	54½ inches	5.4½
19 inches	3.8	24 inches	3.4½	34 inches	3.4	55 inches	5.5
19½ inches	3.9	24½ inches	3.5	34½ inches	3.4½	55½ inches	5.5½
20 inches	4.0	25 inches	3.6	35 inches	3.5	56 inches	5.6
20½ inches	4.1	25½ inches	3.6½	35½ inches	3.5½	56½ inches	5.6½
21 inches	4.2	26 inches	3.7½	36 inches	3.6	57 inches	5.7
21½ inches	4.3	26½ inches	3.8	36½ inches	3.6½		
22 inches	4.4	27 inches	3.9	37 inches	3.7		
22½ inches	4.5	27½ inches	3.9½	37½ inches	3.7½		
23 inches	4.6	28 inches	4.0	38 inches	3.8		
23½ inches	4.7	28½ inches	4.1	38½ inches	3.8½		
24 inches	4.8	29 inches	4.1½	39 inches	3.9		
24½ inches	4.9	29½ inches	4.2½	39½ inches	3.9½		
25 inches	5.0	30 inches	4.3	40 inches	4.0		
25½ inches	5.1	30½ inches	4.4	40½ inches	4.+		
26 inches	5.2	31 inches	4.4½	41 inches	4.1		
26½ inches	5.3	31½ inches	4.5	41½ inches	4.1½		
27 inches	5.4	32 inches	4.6	42 inches	4.2		
27½ inches	5.5	32½ inches	4.6½	42½ inches	4.2½		
28 inches	5.6	33 inches	4.7½	43 inches	4.3		
28½ inches	5.7	33½ inches	4.8	43½ inches	4.3½		
29 inches	5.8	34 inches	4.9	44 inches	4.4		
29½ inches	5.9	34½ inches	4.9½	44½ inches	4.4½		
30 inches	6.0	35 inches	5.0	45 inches	4.5		
		35½ inches	5.1	45½ inches	4.5½		
		36 inches	5.1½	46 inches	4.6		
		36½ inches	5.2½	46½ inches	4.6½		
		37 inches	5.3	47 inches	4.7		
		37½ inches	5.4	47½ inches	4.7½		
		38 inches	5.4½	48 inches	4.8		
		38½ inches	5.5½	48½ inches	4.8½		
		39 inches	5.6	49 inches	4.9		
				49½ inches	4.9½		

Note: 3+ means set space half way between 3 and 3.1
      4+ means set space half way between 4 and 4.1
      5+ means set space half way between 5 and 5.1

SPACE SETTER CHART—45 TO 54 INCH FABRICS FOR DRAPERIES CONTAINING ⅓ AND ⅔ WIDTHS

Number of Widths Per Panel

2–⅔ widths		3–⅓ widths		3–⅔ widths	
Distance between end pleats	Set space	Distance between end pleats	Set space	Distance between end pleats	Set space
34 inches	2.8½	57 inches	4.7½	44 inches	2.9½	49 inches	2.9
34½ inches	2.9	57½ inches	4.8	45 inches	3.0	50 inches	2.9½
35 inches	2.9½	58 inches	4.8½	46 inches	3.1	51 inches	3.0
35½ inches	3.0	58½ inches	4.9	47 inches	3.1½	52 inches	3.1
36 inches	3.0	59 inches	4.9½	48 inches	3.2	53 inches	3.1½
36½ inches	3.+	59½ inches	5.0	49 inches	3.3	54 inches	3.2
37 inches	3.1	60 inches	5.0	50 inches	3.3½	55 inches	3.2½
37½ inches	3.1½	60½ inches	5.+	51 inches	3.4	56 inches	3.3
38 inches	3.2	61 inches	5.1	52 inches	3.5	57 inches	3.3½
38½ inches	3.2½	61½ inches	5.1½	53 inches	3.5½	58 inches	3.4½
39 inches	3.2½	62 inches	5.2	54 inches	3.6	59 inches	3.5
39½ inches	3.3	62½ inches	5.2½	55 inches	3.7	60 inches	3.5½
40 inches	3.3½	63 inches	5.2½	56 inches	3.7½	61 inches	3.6
40½ inches	3.4	63½ inches	5.3	57 inches	3.8	62 inches	3.6½
41 inches	3.4½	64 inches	5.3½	58 inches	3.9	63 inches	3.7
41½ inches	3.5	64½ inches	5.4	59 inches	3.9½	64 inches	3.8
42 inches	3.5	65 inches	5.4½	60 inches	4.0	65 inches	3.8½
42½ inches	3.5½	65½ inches	5.5	61 inches	4.1	66 inches	3.9
43 inches	3.6	66 inches	5.5	62 inches	4.1½	67 inches	3.9½
43½ inches	3.6½			63 inches	4.2	68 inches	4.0
44 inches	3.7			64 inches	4.3	69 inches	4.1
44½ inches	3.7½			65 inches	4.3½	70 inches	4.1½
45 inches	3.7½			66 inches	4.4	71 inches	4.2
45½ inches	3.8			67 inches	4.5	72 inches	4.2½
46 inches	3.8½			68 inches	4.5½	73 inches	4.3
46½ inches	3.9			69 inches	4.6	74 inches	4.3½
47 inches	3.9½			70 inches	4.7	75 inches	4.4½
47½ inches	4.0			71 inches	4.7½	76 inches	4.5
48 inches	4.0			72 inches	4.8	77 inches	4.5½
48½ inches	4.+			73 inches	4.9	78 inches	4.6
49 inches	4.1			74 inches	4.9½	79 inches	4.6½
49½ inches	4.1½			75 inches	5.0	80 inches	4.7
50 inches	4.2			76 inches	5.1	81 inches	4.8
50½ inches	4.2½			77 inches	5.1½	82 inches	4.8½
51 inches	4.2½			78 inches	5.2	83 inches	4.9
51½ inches	4.3			79 inches	5.3	84 inches	4.9½
52 inches	4.3½			80 inches	5.3½	85 inches	5.0
52½ inches	4.4			81 inches	5.4	86 inches	5.1
53 inches	4.4½			82 inches	5.5	87 inches	5.1½
53½ inches	4.5			83 inches	5.5½	88 inches	5.2
54 inches	4.5			84 inches	5.6	89 inches	5.2½
54½ inches	4.5½					90 inches	5.3
55 inches	4.6					91 inches	5.3½
55½ inches	4.6½					92 inches	5.4½
56 inches	4.7					93 inches	5.5
56½ inches	4.7½					94 inches	5.5½

Note: 3+ means set space half way between 3 and 3.1
   4+ means set space half way between 4 and 4.1
   5+ means set space half way between 5 and 5.1

SPACE SETTER CHART—45 TO 54 INCH FABRICS FOR DRAPERIES CONTAINING ⅓ AND ⅔ WIDTHS

Number of Widths Per Panel							
4–⅓ widths				4–⅔ widths			
Distance between end pleats	Set space	Distance between end pleats	Set space	Distance between end pleats	Set space	Distance between end pleats	Set space
59 inches	2.9 ½	100 inches	5.0	64 inches	2.9 ½	105 inches	4.8
60 inches	3.0	101 inches	5.+	65 inches	3.0	106 inches	4.8 ½
61 inches	3.+	102 inches	5.1	66 inches	3.0	107 inches	4.9
62 inches	3.1	103 inches	5.1 ½	67 inches	3.+	108 inches	4.9 ½
63 inches	3.1 ½	104 inches	5.2	68 inches	3.1	109 inches	5.0
64 inches	3.2	105 inches	5.2 ½	69 inches	3.1 ½	110 inches	5.0
65 inches	3.2 ½	106 inches	5.3	70 inches	3.2	111 inches	5.+
66 inches	3.3	107 inches	5.3 ½	71 inches	3.2 ½	112 inches	5.1
67 inches	3.3 ½	108 inches	5.4	72 inches	3.3	113 inches	5.1 ½
68 inches	3.4	109 inches	5.4 ½	73 inches	3.3 ½	114 inches	5.2
69 inches	3.4 ½	110 inches	5.5	74 inches	3.4	115 inches	5.2 ½
70 inches	3.5	111 inches	5.5 ½	75 inches	3.4 ½	116 inches	5.3
71 inches	3.5 ½			76 inches	3.5	117 inches	5.3 ½
72 inches	3.6			77 inches	3.5	118 inches	5.4
73 inches	3.6 ½			78 inches	3.5 ½	119 inches	5.4 ½
74 inches	3.7			79 inches	3.6	120 inches	5.5
75 inches	3.7 ½			80 inches	3.6 ½		
76 inches	3.8			81 inches	3.7		
77 inches	3.8 ½			82 inches	3.7 ½		
78 inches	3.9			83 inches	3.8		
79 inches	3.9 ½			84 inches	3.8 ½		
80 inches	4.0			85 inches	3.9		
81 inches	4.+			86 inches	3.9 ½		
82 inches	4.1			87 inches	4.0		
83 inches	4.1 ½			88 inches	4.0		
84 inches	4.2			89 inches	4.+		
85 inches	4.2 ½			90 inches	4.1		
86 inches	4.3			91 inches	4.1 ½		
87 inches	4.3 ½			92 inches	4.2		
88 inches	4.4			93 inches	4.2 ½		
89 inches	4.4 ½			94 inches	4.3		
90 inches	4.5			95 inches	4.3 ½		
91 inches	4.5 ½			96 inches	4.4		
92 inches	4.6			97 inches	4.4 ½		
93 inches	4.6 ½			98 inches	4.5		
94 inches	4.7			99 inches	4.5 ½		
95 inches	4.7 ½			100 inches	4.5 ½		
96 inches	4.8			101 inches	4.6		
97 inches	4.8 ½			102 inches	4.6 ½		
98 inches	4.9			103 inches	4.7		
99 inches	4.9 ½			104 inches	4.7 ½		

Note: 3+ means set space half way between 3 and 3.1
4+ means set space half way between 4 and 4.1
5+ means set space half way between 5 and 5.1

SPACE SETTER CHART—45 TO 54 INCH FABRICS FOR DRAPERIES CONTAINING ⅓ AND ⅔ WIDTHS

Number of Widths Per Panel

5–⅓ widths				5–⅔ widths			
Distance between end pleats	Set space	Distance between end pleats	Set space	Distance between end pleats	Set space	Distance between end pleats	Set space
74 inches	3.0	116 inches	4.6 ½	79 inches	2.9 ½	121 inches	4.5
75 inches	3.0	117 inches	4.7	80 inches	3.0	122 inches	4.5 ½
76 inches	3.+	118 inches	4.7 ½	81 inches	3.0	123 inches	4.5 ½
77 inches	3.1	119 inches	4.8	82 inches	3.+	124 inches	4.6
78 inches	3.1 ½	120 inches	4.8	83 inches	3.1	125 inches	4.6 ½
79 inches	3.2	121 inches	4.8 ½	84 inches	3.1 ½	126 inches	4.7
80 inches	3.2	122 inches	4.9	85 inches	3.1 ½	127 inches	4.7
81 inches	3.2 ½	123 inches	4.9 ½	86 inches	3.2	128 inches	4.7 ½
82 inches	3.3	124 inches	5.0	87 inches	3.2 ½	129 inches	4.8
83 inches	3.3 ½	125 inches	5.0	88 inches	3.3	130 inches	4.8 ½
84 inches	3.4	126 inches	5.+	89 inches	3.3	131 inches	4.8 ½
85 inches	3.4	127 inches	5.1	90 inches	3.3 ½	132 inches	4.9
86 inches	3.4 ½	128 inches	5.1 ½	91 inches	3.4	133 inches	4.9 ½
87 inches	3.5	129 inches	5.2	92 inches	3.4 ½	134 inches	5.0
88 inches	3.5 ½	130 inches	5.2	93 inches	3.4 ½	135 inches	5.0
89 inches	3.6	131 inches	5.2 ½	94 inches	3.5	136 inches	5.+
90 inches	3.6	132 inches	5.3	95 inches	3.5 ½	137 inches	5.1
91 inches	3.6 ½	133 inches	5.3 ½	96 inches	3.6	138 inches	5.1 ½
92 inches	3.7	134 inches	5.4	97 inches	3.6	139 inches	5.1 ½
93 inches	3.7 ½	135 inches	5.4	98 inches	3.6 ½	140 inches	5.2
94 inches	3.8	136 inches	5.4 ½	99 inches	3.7	141 inches	5.2 ½
95 inches	3.8	137 inches	5.5	100 inches	3.7	142 inches	5.3
96 inches	3.8 ½	138 inches	5.5 ½	101 inches	3.7 ½	143 inches	5.3
97 inches	3.9			102 inches	3.8	144 inches	5.3 ½
98 inches	3.9 ½			103 inches	3.8 ½	145 inches	5.4
99 inches	4.0			104 inches	3.8 ½	146 inches	5.4
100 inches	4.0			105 inches	3.9	147 inches	5.4 ½
101 inches	4.+			106 inches	3.9 ½		
102 inches	4.1			107 inches	4.0		
103 inches	4.1 ½			108 inches	4.0		
104 inches	4.2			109 inches	4.+		
105 inches	4.2			110 inches	4.1		
106 inches	4.2 ½			111 inches	4.1 ½		
107 inches	4.3			112 inches	4.1 ½		
108 inches	4.3 ½			113 inches	4.2		
109 inches	4.4			114 inches	4.2 ½		
110 inches	4.4			115 inches	4.3		
111 inches	4.4 ½			116 inches	4.3		
112 inches	4.5			117 inches	4.3 ½		
113 inches	4.5 ½			118 inches	4.4		
114 inches	4.6			119 inches	4.4		
115 inches	4.6			120 inches	4.4 ½		

Note: 3+ means set space half way between 3 and 3.1
4+ means set space half way between 4 and 4.1
5+ means set space half way between 5 and 5.1

SPACE SETTER CHART—45–54 INCH FABRICS FOR DRAPERIES CONTAINING ¼ AND ¾ WIDTHS

Number of Widths Per Panel							
1–¼ widths		*1–¾ widths*		*2–¼ widths*			
Distance between end pleats	*Set space*	*Distance between end pleats*	*Set space*	*Distance between end pleats*	*Set space*	*Distance between end pleats*	*Set space*
13 inches	2.6	21 inches	3.0	28 inches	2.8	49½ inches	4.9 ½
13½ inches	2.7	21½ inches	3.1	28½ inches	2.8 ½	50 inches	5.0
14 inches	2.8	22 inches	3.1½	29 inches	2.9	50½ inches	5.+
14½ inches	2.9	22½ inches	3.2½	29½ inches	2.9½	51 inches	5.1
15 inches	3.0	23 inches	3.3	30 inches	3.0	51½ inches	5.1½
15½ inches	3.1	23½ inches	3.4	30½ inches	3.+	52 inches	5.2
16 inches	3.2	24 inches	3.4½	31 inches	3.1	52½ inches	5.2½
16½ inches	3.3	24½ inches	3.5	31½ inches	3.1½	53 inches	5.3
17 inches	3.4	25 inches	3.6	32 inches	3.2	53½ inches	5.3½
17½ inches	3.5	25½ inches	3.6½	32½ inches	3.2½	54 inches	5.4
18 inches	3.6	26 inches	3.7½	33 inches	3.3	54½ inches	5.4½
18½ inches	3.7	26½ inches	3.8	33½ inches	3.3½	55 inches	5.5
19 inches	3.8	27 inches	3.9	34 inches	3.4		
19½ inches	3.9	27½ inches	3.9½	34½ inches	3.4½		
20 inches	4.0	28 inches	4.0	35 inches	3.5		
20½ inches	4.1	28½ inches	4.1	35½ inches	3.5½		
21 inches	4.2	29 inches	4.1½	36 inches	3.6		
21½ inches	4.3	29½ inches	4.2½	36½ inches	3.6½		
22 inches	4.4	30 inches	4.3	37 inches	3.7		
22½ inches	4.5	30½ inches	4.4	37½ inches	3.7½		
23 inches	4.6	31 inches	4.4½	38 inches	3.8		
23½ inches	4.7	31½ inches	4.5	38½ inches	3.8½		
24 inches	4.8	32 inches	4.6	39 inches	3.9		
24½ inches	4.9	32½ inches	4.6½	39½ inches	3.9½		
25 inches	5.0	33 inches	4.7½	40 inches	4.0		
25½ inches	5.1	33½ inches	4.8	40½ inches	4.+		
26 inches	5.2	34 inches	4.9	41 inches	4.1		
26½ inches	5.3	34½ inches	4.9½	41½ inches	4.1½		
27 inches	5.4	35 inches	5.0	42 inches	4.2		
27½ inches	5.5	35½ inches	5.1	42½ inches	4.2½		
28 inches	5.6	36 inches	5.1½	43 inches	4.3		
		36½ inches	5.2½	43½ inches	4.3½		
		37 inches	5.3	44 inches	4.4		
		37½ inches	5.4	44½ inches	4.4½		
		38 inches	5.4½	45 inches	4.5		
		38½ inches	5.5	45½ inches	4.5½		
		39 inches	5.6	46 inches	4.6		
		39½ inches	5.6½	46½ inches	4.6½		
		40 inches	5.7	47 inches	4.7		
		40½ inches	5.8	47½ inches	4.7½		
		41 inches	5.9	48 inches	4.8		
		41½ inches	5.9½	48½ inches	4.8½		
		42 inches	6.0	49 inches	4.9		

Note: 3+ means set space half way between 3 and 3.1
4+ means set space half way between 4 and 4.1
5+ means set space half way between 5 and 5.1

SPACE SETTER CHART—45 TO 54 INCH FABRICS FOR DRAPERIES
CONTAINING ¼ AND ¾ WIDTHS

Number of Widths Per Panel							
2–¾ widths				3–¼ widths		3–¾ widths	
Distance between end pleats	*Set space*	*Distance between end pleats*	*Set space*	*Distance between end pleats*	*Set space*	*Distance between end pleats*	*Set space*
36 inches	3.0	59 inches	4.9½	43 inches	2.9	51 inches	3.0
36½ inches	3.+	59½ inches	5.0	44 inches	2.9½	52 inches	3.1
37 inches	3.1	60 inches	5.0	45 inches	3.0	53 inches	3.1½
37½ inches	3.1½	60½ inches	5.+	46 inches	3.1	54 inches	3.2
38 inches	3.2	61 inches	5.1	47 inches	3.1½	55 inches	3.2½
38½ inches	3.2½	61½ inches	5.1½	48 inches	3.2	56 inches	3.3
39 inches	3.2½	62 inches	5.2	49 inches	3.3	57 inches	3.4
39½ inches	3.3	62½ inches	5.2½	50 inches	3.3½	58 inches	3.4½
40 inches	3.3½	63 inches	5.2½	51 inches	3.4	59 inches	3.5
40½ inches	3.4	63½ inches	5.3	52 inches	3.5	60 inches	3.5½
41 inches	3.4½	64 inches	5.3½	53 inches	3.5½	61 inches	3.6
41½ inches	3.5	64½ inches	5.4	54 inches	3.6	62 inches	3.6½
42 inches	3.5	65 inches	5.4½	55 inches	3.7	63 inches	3.7
42½ inches	3.5½	65½ inches	5.5	56 inches	3.7½	64 inches	3.8
43 inches	3.6	66 inches	5.5	57 inches	3.8	65 inches	3.8½
43½ inches	3.6½	66½ inches	5.5½	58 inches	3.9	66 inches	3.9
44 inches	3.7	67 inches	5.6	59 inches	3.9½	67 inches	3.9½
44½ inches	3.7½	67½ inches	5.6½	60 inches	4.0	68 inches	4.0
45 inches	3.7½	68 inches	5.7	61 inches	4.1	69 inches	4.1
45½ inches	3.8	68½ inches	5.7½	62 inches	4.1½	70 inches	4.1½
46 inches	3.8½	69 inches	5.7½	63 inches	4.2	71 inches	4.2
46½ inches	3.9			64 inches	4.3	72 inches	4.2½
47 inches	3.9½			65 inches	4.3½	73 inches	4.3
47½ inches	4.0			66 inches	4.4	74 inches	4.4
48 inches	4.0			67 inches	4.5	75 inches	4.4½
48½ inches	4.+			68 inches	4.5½	76 inches	4.5
49 inches	4.1			69 inches	4.6	77 inches	4.5½
49½ inches	4.1½			70 inches	4.7	78 inches	4.6
50 inches	4.2			71 inches	4.7½	79 inches	4.6½
50½ inches	4.2½			72 inches	4.8	80 inches	4.7½
51 inches	4.2½			73 inches	4.9	81 inches	4.8
51½ inches	4.3			74 inches	4.9½	82 inches	4.8½
52 inches	4.3½			75 inches	5.0	83 inches	4.9
52½ inches	4.4			76 inches	5.1	84 inches	4.9½
53 inches	4.4½			77 inches	5.1½	85 inches	5.0
53½ inches	4.5			78 inches	5.2	86 inches	5.1
54 inches	4.5			79 inches	5.3	87 inches	5.1½
54½ inches	4.5½			80 inches	5.3½	88 inches	5.2
55 inches	4.6			81 inches	5.4	89 inches	5.2½
55½ inches	4.6½			82 inches	5.5	90 inches	5.3
56 inches	4.7					91 inches	5.4
56½ inches	4.7½					92 inches	5.4½
57 inches	4.7½					93 inches	5.5
57½ inches	4.8					94 inches	5.5½
58 inches	4.8½					95 inches	5.6
58½ inches	4.9					96 inches	5.6½

Note: 3+ means set space half way between 3 and 3.1
4+ means set space half way between 4 and 4.1
5+ means set space half way between 5 and 5.1

SPACE SETTER CHART—45 TO 54 INCH FABRICS FOR DRAPERIES CONTAINING ¼ AND ¾ WIDTHS

Number of Widths Per Panel

4–¼ widths				4–¾ widths			
Distance between end pleats	Set space	Distance between end pleats	Set space	Distance between end pleats	Set space	Distance between end pleats	Set space
58 inches	2.9	101 inches	5.+	66 inches	3.0	109 inches	4.9½
59 inches	2.9½	102 inches	5.1	67 inches	3.+	110 inches	5.0
60 inches	3.0	103 inches	5.1½	68 inches	3.1	111 inches	5.+
61 inches	3.+	104 inches	5.2	69 inches	3.1½	112 inches	5.1
62 inches	3.1	105 inches	5.2½	70 inches	3.2	113 inches	5.1½
63 inches	3.1½	106 inches	5.3	71 inches	3.2½	114 inches	5.2
64 inches	3.2	107 inches	5.3½	72 inches	3.3	115 inches	5.2½
65 inches	3.2½	108 inches	5.4	73 inches	3.3½	116 inches	5.3
66 inches	3.3	109 inches	5.4½	74 inches	3.4	117 inches	5.3½
67 inches	3.3½			75 inches	3.4½	118 inches	5.4
68 inches	3.4			76 inches	3.4½	119 inches	5.4½
69 inches	3.4½			77 inches	3.5	120 inches	5.5
70 inches	3.5			78 inches	3.5½	121 inches	5.5
71 inches	3.5½			79 inches	3.6	122 inches	5.5½
72 inches	3.6			80 inches	3.6½	123 inches	5.6
73 inches	3.6½			81 inches	3.7		
74 inches	3.7			82 inches	3.7½		
75 inches	3.7½			83 inches	3.8		
76 inches	3.8			84 inches	3.8½		
77 inches	3.8½			85 inches	3.9		
78 inches	3.9			86 inches	3.9½		
79 inches	3.9½			87 inches	3.9½		
80 inches	4.0			88 inches	4.0		
81 inches	4.+			89 inches	4.+		
82 inches	4.1			90 inches	4.1		
83 inches	4.1½			91 inches	4.1½		
84 inches	4.2			92 inches	4.2		
85 inches	4.2½			93 inches	4.2½		
86 inches	4.3			94 inches	4.3		
87 inches	4.3½			95 inches	4.3½		
88 inches	4.4			96 inches	4.4		
89 inches	4.4½			97 inches	4.4½		
90 inches	4.5			98 inches	4.4½		
91 inches	4.5½			99 inches	4.5		
92 inches	4.6			100 inches	4.5½		
93 inches	4.6½			101 inches	4.6		
94 inches	4.7			102 inches	4.6½		
95 inches	4.7½			103 inches	4.7		
96 inches	4.8			104 inches	4.7½		
97 inches	4.8½			105 inches	4.8		
98 inches	4.9			106 inches	4.8½		
99 inches	4.9½			107 inches	4.9		
100 inches	5.0			108 inches	4.9		

Note: 3+ means set space half way between 3 and 3.1
       4+ means set space half way between 4 and 4.1
       5+ means set space half way between 5 and 5.1

SPACE SETTER CHART—45 TO 54 INCH FABRICS FOR DRAPERIES CONTAINING ¼ AND ¾ WIDTHS

				Number Widths Per Panel			
5–¼ widths				*5–¾ widths*			
Distance between end pleats	*Set space*	*Distance between end pleats*	*Set space*	*Distance between end pleats*	*Set space*	*Distance between end pleats*	*Set space*
73 inches	2.9½	114 inches	4.6	81 inches	3.0	122 inches	4.5½
74 inches	3.0	115 inches	4.6	82 inches	3.+	123 inches	4.6
75 inches	3.0	116 inches	4.6½	83 inches	3.1	124 inches	4.6
76 inches	3.+	117 inches	4.7	84 inches	3.1½	125 inches	4.6½
77 inches	3.1	118 inches	4.7½	85 inches	3.1½	126 inches	4.7
78 inches	3.1½	119 inches	4.8	86 inches	3.2	127 inches	4.7½
79 inches	3.2	120 inches	4.8	87 inches	3.2½	128 inches	4.7½
80 inches	3.2	121 inches	4.8½	88 inches	3.3	129 inches	4.8
81 inches	3.2½	122 inches	4.9	89 inches	3.3	130 inches	4.8½
82 inches	3.3	123 inches	4.9½	90 inches	3.3½	131 inches	4.9
83 inches	3.3½	124 inches	5.0	91 inches	3.4	132 inches	4.9
84 inches	3.4	125 inches	5.0	92 inches	3.4½	133 inches	4.9½
85 inches	3.4	126 inches	5.+	93 inches	3.4½	134 inches	5.0
86 inches	3.4½	127 inches	5.1	94 inches	3.5	135 inches	5.0
87 inches	3.5	128 inches	5.1½	95 inches	3.5½	136 inches	5.+
88 inches	3.5½	129 inches	5.2	96 inches	3.6	137 inches	5.1
89 inches	3.6	130 inches	5.2	97 inches	3.6	138 inches	5.1½
90 inches	3.6	131 inches	5.2½	98 inches	3.6½	139 inches	5.1½
91 inches	3.6½	132 inches	5.3	99 inches	3.7	140 inches	5.2
92 inches	3.7	133 inches	5.3½	100 inches	3.7½	141 inches	5.2½
93 inches	3.7½	134 inches	5.4	101 inches	3.7½	142 inches	5.3
94 inches	3.8	135 inches	5.4	102 inches	3.8	143 inches	5.3
95 inches	3.8	136 inches	5.4½	103 inches	3.8½	144 inches	5.3½
96 inches	3.8½			104 inches	3.9	145 inches	5.4
97 inches	3.9			105 inches	3.9	146 inches	5.4½
98 inches	3.9½			106 inches	3.9½	147 inches	5.4½
99 inches	4.0			107 inches	4.0	148 inches	5.5
100 inches	4.0			108 inches	4.0	149 inches	5.5½
101 inches	4.+			109 inches	4.+	150 inches	5.6
102 inches	4.1			110 inches	4.1		
103 inches	4.1½			111 inches	4.1½		
104 inches	4.2			112 inches	4.1½		
105 inches	4.2			113 inches	4.2		
106 inches	4.2½			114 inches	4.2½		
107 inches	4.3			115 inches	4.3		
108 inches	4.3½			116 inches	4.3		
109 inches	4.4			117 inches	4.3½		
110 inches	4.4			118 inches	4.4		
111 inches	4.4½			119 inches	4.4½		
112 inches	4.5			120 inches	4.4½		
113 inches	4.5½			121 inches	4.5		

Note: 3+ means set space half way between 3 and 3.1
    4+ means set space half way between 4 and 4.1
    5+ means set space half way between 5 and 5.1

SPACE SETTER CHART—36 INCH FABRICS FOR FULL AND HALF WIDTH DRAPERIES

Number of Widths Per Panel							
Full width		1–½ widths		2 widths		2–½ widths	
Distance between end pleats	Set space	Distance between end pleats	Set space	Distance between end pleats	Set space	Distance between end pleats	Set space
6 inches	2.0	12 inches	2.4	18 inches	2.6	24 inches	2.7
6½ inches	2.2	12½ inches	2.5	18½ inches	2.6½	24½ inches	2.7½
7 inches	2.3½	13 inches	2.6	19 inches	2.7½	25 inches	2.8
7½ inches	2.5	13½ inches	2.7	19½ inches	2.8	25½ inches	2.8½
8 inches	2.7	14 inches	2.8	20 inches	2.8½	26 inches	2.9
8½ inches	2.8½	14½ inches	2.9	20½ inches	2.9½	26½ inches	2.9½
9 inches	3.0	15 inches	3.0	21 inches	3.0	27 inches	3.0
9½ inches	3.2	15½ inches	3.1	21½ inches	3.1	27½ inches	3.1
10 inches	3.3½	16 inches	3.2	22 inches	3.1½	28 inches	3.1½
10½ inches	3.5	16½ inches	3.3	22½ inches	3.2½	28½ inches	3.2
11 inches	3.7	17 inches	3.4	23 inches	3.3	29 inches	3.2½
11½ inches	3.8½	17½ inches	3.5	23½ inches	3.4	29½ inches	3.3
12 inches	4.0	18 inches	3.6	24 inches	3.4½	30 inches	3.3½
12½ inches	4.2	18½ inches	3.7	24½ inches	3.5	30½ inches	3.4
13 inches	4.3½	19 inches	3.8	25 inches	3.6	31 inches	3.4½
13½ inches	4.5	19½ inches	3.9	25½ inches	3.6½	31½ inches	3.5
14 inches	4.7	20 inches	4.0	26 inches	3.7½	32 inches	3.6
		20½ inches	4.1	26½ inches	3.8	32½ inches	3.6½
		21 inches	4.2	27 inches	3.9	33 inches	3.7
		21½ inches	4.3	27½ inches	3.9½	33½ inches	3.7½
		22 inches	4.4	28 inches	4.0	34 inches	3.8
		22½ inches	4.5	28½ inches	4.1	34½ inches	3.8½
		23 inches	4.6	29 inches	4.1½	35 inches	3.9
				29½ inches	4.2½	35½ inches	3.9½
				30 inches	4.3	36 inches	4.0
				30½ inches	4.4	36½ inches	4.1
				31 inches	4.4½	37 inches	4.1½
				31½ inches	4.5	37½ inches	4.2
				32 inches	4.6	38 inches	4.2½
						38½ inches	4.3
						39 inches	4.3½
						39½ inches	4.4
						40 inches	4.4½
						40½ inches	4.5½
						41 inches	4.6

SPACE SETTER CHART—36 INCH FABRICS FOR FULL AND HALF WIDTH DRAPERIES

Number of Widths Per Panel							
3 widths		3–½ widths		4 widths		4–½ widths	
Distance between end pleats	Set space	Distance between end pleats	Set space	Distance between end pleats	Set space	Distance between end pleats	Set space
30 inches	2.7½	36 inches	2.8	42 inches	2.8	48 inches	2.8½
30½ inches	2.8	37 inches	2.8½	43 inches	2.9	49 inches	2.9
31 inches	2.8½	38 inches	2.9½	44 inches	2.9½	50 inches	2.9½
31½ inches	2.9	39 inches	3.0	45 inches	3.0	51 inches	3.0
32 inches	2.9½	40 inches	3.1	46 inches	3.1	52 inches	3.1
32½ inches	3.0	41 inches	3.2	47 inches	3.1½	53 inches	3.1½
33 inches	3.0	42 inches	3.2½	48 inches	3.2	54 inches	3.2
33½ inches	3.+	43 inches	3.3½	49 inches	3.3	55 inches	3.2½
34 inches	3.1	44 inches	3.4	50 inches	3.3½	56 inches	3.3
34½ inches	3.1½	45 inches	3.5	51 inches	3.4	57 inches	3.4
35 inches	3.2	46 inches	3.5½	52 inches	3.5	58 inches	3.4½
35½ inches	3.2½	47 inches	3.6½	53 inches	3.5½	59 inches	3.5
36 inches	3.3	48 inches	3.7	54 inches	3.6	60 inches	3.5½
36½ inches	3.3½	49 inches	3.8	55 inches	3.7	61 inches	3.6
37 inches	3.4	50 inches	3.8½	56 inches	3.7½	62 inches	3.6½
37½ inches	3.4½	51 inches	3.9½	57 inches	3.8	63 inches	3.7½
38 inches	3.5	52 inches	4.0	58 inches	3.9	64 inches	3.8
38½ inches	3.5	53 inches	4.1	59 inches	3.9½	65 inches	3.8½
39 inches	3.5½	54 inches	4.2	60 inches	4.0	66 inches	3.9
39½ inches	3.6	55 inches	4.2½	61 inches	4.1	67 inches	3.9½
40 inches	3.6½	56 inches	4.3½	62 inches	4.1½	68 inches	4.0
40½ inches	3.7	57 inches	4.4	63 inches	4.2	69 inches	4.1
41 inches	3.7½	58 inches	4.5	64 inches	4.3	70 inches	4.1½
41½ inches	3.8	59 inches	4.5½	65 inches	4.3½	71 inches	4.2
42 inches	3.8½			66 inches	4.4	72 inches	4.2½
42½ inches	3.9			67 inches	4.5	73 inches	4.3
43 inches	3.9½			68 inches	4.5½	74 inches	4.4
43½ inches	4.0					75 inches	4.4½
44 inches	4.0					76 inches	4.5
44½ inches	4.+					77 inches	4.5½
45 inches	4.1						
45½ inches	4.1½						
46 inches	4.2						
46½ inches	4.2½						
47 inches	4.3						
47½ inches	4.3½						
48 inches	4.4						
48½ inches	4.4½						
49 inches	4.4½						
49½ inches	4.5						
50 inches	4.5½						

Note: 3+ means set space half way between 3 and 3.1
4+ means set space half way between 4 and 4.1

SPACE SETTER CHART—36 INCH FABRICS FOR FULL AND HALF WIDTH DRAPERIES

Number of Widths Per Panel							
5 widths		5–½ widths		6 widths		6–½ widths	
Distance between end pleats	Set space	Distance between end pleats	Set space	Distance between end pleats	Set space	Distance between end pleats	Set space
54 inches	2.8½	60 inches	2.9	66 inches	2.9	72 inches	2.9
55 inches	2.9	61 inches	2.9½	67 inches	2.9½	73 inches	2.9½
56 inches	2.9½	62 inches	3.0	68 inches	3.0	74 inches	3.0
57 inches	3.0	63 inches	3.0	69 inches	3.0	75 inches	3.0
58 inches	3.1	64 inches	3.+	70 inches	3.+	76 inches	3.+
59 inches	3.1½	65 inches	3.1	71 inches	3.1	77 inches	3.1
60 inches	3.2	66 inches	3.1½	72 inches	3.1½	78 inches	3.1½
61 inches	3.2½	67 inches	3.2	73 inches	3.2	79 inches	3.2
62 inches	3.3	68 inches	3.2½	74 inches	3.2½	80 inches	3.2
63 inches	3.3½	69 inches	3.3	75 inches	3.3	81 inches	3.2½
64 inches	3.4	70 inches	3.3½	76 inches	3.3	82 inches	3.3
65 inches	3.4½	71 inches	3.4	77 inches	3.3½	83 inches	3.3½
66 inches	3.5	72 inches	3.4½	78 inches	3.4	84 inches	3.4
67 inches	3.5½	73 inches	3.5	79 inches	3.4½	85 inches	3.4
68 inches	3.6	74 inches	3.5½	80 inches	3.5	86 inches	3.4½
69 inches	3.6½	75 inches	3.6	81 inches	3.5½	87 inches	3.5
70 inches	3.7	76 inches	3.6½	82 inches	3.6	88 inches	3.5½
71 inches	3.7½	77 inches	3.7	83 inches	3.6½	89 inches	3.6
72 inches	3.8	78 inches	3.7½	84 inches	3.6½	90 inches	3.6
73 inches	3.8½	79 inches	3.8	85 inches	3.7	91 inches	3.6½
74 inches	3.9	80 inches	3.8½	86 inches	3.7½	92 inches	3.7
75 inches	3.9½	81 inches	3.9	87 inches	3.8	93 inches	3.7½
76 inches	4.0	82 inches	3.9½	88 inches	3.8½	94 inches	3.8
77 inches	4.+	83 inches	4.0	89 inches	3.9	95 inches	3.8
78 inches	4.1	84 inches	4.0	90 inches	3.9½	96 inches	3.8½
79 inches	4.2	85 inches	4.+	91 inches	4.0	97 inches	3.9
80 inches	4.2½	86 inches	4.1	92 inches	4.0	98 inches	3.9½
81 inches	4.3	87 inches	4.1½	93 inches	4.+	99 inches	4.0
82 inches	4.3½	88 inches	4.2	94 inches	4.1	100 inches	4.0
83 inches	4.4	89 inches	4.2½	95 inches	4.1½	101 inches	4.+
84 inches	4.4½	90 inches	4.3	96 inches	4.2	102 inches	4.1
85 inches	4.5	91 inches	4.3½	97 inches	4.2½	103 inches	4.1½
86 inches	4.5½	92 inches	4.4	98 inches	4.3	104 inches	4.2
		93 inches	4.4½	99 inches	4.3½	105 inches	4.2
		94 inches	4.5	100 inches	4.3½	106 inches	4.2½
		95 inches	4.5½	101 inches	4.4	107 inches	4.3
				102 inches	4.4½	108 inches	4.3½
				103 inches	4.5	109 inches	4.4
				104 inches	4.5½	110 inches	4.4
						111 inches	4.4½
						112 inches	4.5
						113 inches	4.5½

Note: 3+ means set space half way between 3 and 3.1
4+ means set space half way between 4 and 4.1

SPACE SETTER CHART—36 INCH FABRICS FOR FULL AND HALF WIDTH DRAPERIES

Number of Widths Per Panel							
7 widths		7–½ widths		8 widths			
Distance between end pleats	Set space	Distance between end pleats	Set space	Distance between end pleats	Set space	Distance between end pleats	Set space
78 inches	2.9	84 inches	2.9	90 inches	2.9½	134 inches	4.3½
79 inches	2.9½	85 inches	2.9½	91 inches	2.9½	135 inches	4.4
80 inches	3.0	86 inches	3.0	92 inches	3.0	136 inches	4.4
81 inches	3.0	87 inches	3.0	93 inches	3.0	137 inches	4.4½
82 inches	3.+	88 inches	3.+	94 inches	3.+	138 inches	4.5
83 inches	3.1	89 inches	3.1	95 inches	3.1	139 inches	4.5½
84 inches	3.1½	90 inches	3.1	96 inches	3.1	140 inches	4.5½
85 inches	3.1½	91 inches	3.1½	97 inches	3.1½		
86 inches	3.2	92 inches	3.2	98 inches	3.2		
87 inches	3.2½	93 inches	3.2½	99 inches	3.2		
88 inches	3.3	94 inches	3.2½	100 inches	3.2½		
89 inches	3.3	95 inches	3.3	101 inches	3.3		
90 inches	3.3½	96 inches	3.3½	102 inches	3.3		
91 inches	3.4	97 inches	3.3½	103 inches	3.3½		
92 inches	3.4½	98 inches	3.4	104 inches	3.4		
93 inches	3.4½	99 inches	3.4½	105 inches	3.4		
94 inches	3.5	100 inches	3.4½	106 inches	3.4½		
95 inches	3.5½	101 inches	3.5	107 inches	3.4½		
96 inches	3.6	102 inches	3.5½	108 inches	3.5		
97 inches	3.6	103 inches	3.6	109 inches	3.5½		
98 inches	3.6½	104 inches	3.6	110 inches	3.5½		
99 inches	3.7	105 inches	3.6½	111 inches	3.6		
100 inches	3.7	106 inches	3.7	112 inches	3.6½		
101 inches	3.7½	107 inches	3.7	113 inches	3.6½		
102 inches	3.8	108 inches	3.7½	114 inches	3.7		
103 inches	3.8½	109 inches	3.8	115 inches	3.7½		
104 inches	3.8½	110 inches	3.8	116 inches	3.7½		
105 inches	3.9	111 inches	3.8½	117 inches	3.8		
106 inches	3.9½	112 inches	3.9	118 inches	3.8½		
107 inches	4.0	113 inches	3.9	119 inches	3.8½		
108 inches	4.0	114 inches	3.9½	120 inches	3.9		
109 inches	4.+	115 inches	4.0	121 inches	3.9½		
110 inches	4.1	116 inches	4.0	122 inches	3.9½		
111 inches	4.1½	117 inches	4.+	123 inches	4.0		
112 inches	4.1½	118 inches	4.1	124 inches	4.0		
113 inches	4.2	119 inches	4.1½	125 inches	4.+		
114 inches	4.2½	120 inches	4.1½	126 inches	4.1		
115 inches	4.3	121 inches	4.2	127 inches	4.1		
116 inches	4.3	122 inches	4.2½	128 inches	4.1½		
117 inches	4.3½	123 inches	4.2½	129 inches	4.2		
118 inches	4.4	124 inches	4.3	130 inches	4.2		
119 inches	4.4½	125 inches	4.3½	131 inches	4.2½		
120 inches	4.4½	126 inches	4.3½	132 inches	4.3		
121 inches	4.5	127 inches	4.4	133 inches	4.3		
122 inches	4.5½	128 inches	4.4½	1			
		129 inches	4.4½				
		130 inches	4.5				
		131 inches	4.5½				

4+ means set space half way between 4 and 4.1

SPACE SETTER CHART—36 INCH FABRICS FOR FULL AND HALF WIDTH DRAPERIES

Number of Widths Per Panel							
8–½ widths				9 widths			
Distance between end pleats	Set space	Distance between end pleats	Set space	Distance between end pleats	Set space	Distance between end pleats	Set space
96 inches	2.9½	138 inches	4.2	102 inches	2.9½	144 inches	4.1½
97 inches	2.9½	139 inches	4.2½	103 inches	2.9½	145 inches	4.1½
98 inches	3.0	140 inches	4.2½	104 inches	3.0	146 inches	4.2
99 inches	3.0	141 inches	4.3	105 inches	3.0	147 inches	4.2
100 inches	3.+	142 inches	4.3	106 inches	3.+	148 inches	4.2½
101 inches	3.1	143 inches	4.3½	107 inches	3.1	149 inches	4.3
102 inches	3.1	144 inches	4.4	108 inches	3.1	150 inches	4.3
103 inches	3.1½	145 inches	4.4	109 inches	3.1½	151 inches	4.3½
104 inches	3.2	146 inches	4.4½	110 inches	3.1½	152 inches	4.3½
105 inches	3.2	147 inches	4.5	111 inches	3.2	153 inches	4.4
106 inches	3.2½	148 inches	4.5	112 inches	3.2	154 inches	4.4
107 inches	3.2½	149 inches	4.5½	113 inches	3.2½	155 inches	4.4½
108 inches	3.3			114 inches	3.3	156 inches	4.5
109 inches	3.3			115 inches	3.3	157 inches	4.5
110 inches	3.3½			116 inches	3.3½	158 inches	4.5½
111 inches	3.4			117 inches	3.3½		
112 inches	3.4			118 inches	3.4		
113 inches	3.4½			119 inches	3.4		
114 inches	3.5			120 inches	3.4½		
115 inches	3.5			121 inches	3.5		
116 inches	3.5½			122 inches	3.5		
117 inches	3.5½			123 inches	3.5½		
118 inches	3.6			124 inches	3.5½		
119 inches	3.6½			125 inches	3.6		
120 inches	3.6½			126 inches	3.6		
121 inches	3.7			127 inches	3.6½		
122 inches	3.7			128 inches	3.7		
123 inches	3.7½			129 inches	3.7		
124 inches	3.8			130 inches	3.7½		
125 inches	3.8			131 inches	3.7½		
126 inches	3.8½			132 inches	3.8		
127 inches	3.8½			133 inches	3.8		
128 inches	3.9			134 inches	3.8½		
129 inches	3.9½			135 inches	3.9		
130 inches	3.9½			136 inches	3.9		
131 inches	4.0			137 inches	3.9½		
132 inches	4.0			138 inches	3.9½		
133 inches	4.+			139 inches	4.0		
134 inches	4.1			140 inches	4.0		
135 inches	4.1			141 inches	4.+		
136 inches	4.1½			142 inches	4.1		
137 inches	4.1½			143 inches	4.1		

Note: 3+ means set space half way between 3 and 3.1
4+ means set space half way between 4 and 4.1

SPACE SETTER CHART—36 INCH FABRICS FOR FULL AND HALF WIDTH DRAPERIES

Number of Widths Per Panel							
9–½ widths				10 widths			
Distance between end pleats	Set space	Distance between end pleats	Set space	Distance between end pleats	Set space	Distance between end pleats	Set space
108 inches	2.9½	150 inches	4.1	114 inches	2.9½	157 inches	4.+
109 inches	3.0	151 inches	4.1	115 inches	2.9½	158 inches	4.+
110 inches	3.0	152 inches	4.1½	116 inches	3.0	159 inches	4.1
111 inches	3.+	153 inches	4.1½	117 inches	3.0	160 inches	4.1
112 inches	3.+	154 inches	4.2	118 inches	3.+	161 inches	4.1½
113 inches	3.1	155 inches	4.2	119 inches	3.+	162 inches	4.2
114 inches	3.1	156 inches	4.2½	120 inches	3.1	163 inches	4.2
115 inches	3.1½	157 inches	4.2½	121 inches	3.1½	164 inches	4.2½
116 inches	3.1½	158 inches	4.3	122 inches	3.1½	165 inches	4.2½
117 inches	3.2	159 inches	4.3½	123 inches	3.2	166 inches	4.3
118 inches	3.2	160 inches	4.3½	124 inches	3.2	167 inches	4.3
119 inches	3.2½	161 inches	4.4	125 inches	3.2½	168 inches	4.3½
120 inches	3.2½	162 inches	4.4	126 inches	3.2½	169 inches	4.3½
121 inches	3.3	163 inches	4.4½	127 inches	3.3	170 inches	4.4
122 inches	3.3	164 inches	4.4½	128 inches	3.3	171 inches	4.4
123 inches	3.3½	165 inches	4.5	129 inches	3.3½	172 inches	4.4½
124 inches	3.4	166 inches	4.5	130 inches	3.3½	173 inches	4.4½
125 inches	3.4	167 inches	4.5½	131 inches	3.4	174 inches	4.5
126 inches	3.4½			132 inches	3.4	175 inches	4.5
127 inches	3.4½			133 inches	3.4½	176 inches	4.5½
128 inches	3.5			134 inches	3.4½		
129 inches	3.5			135 inches	3.5		
130 inches	3.5½			136 inches	3.5		
131 inches	3.5½			137 inches	3.5½		
132 inches	3.6			138 inches	3.5½		
133 inches	3.6			139 inches	3.6		
134 inches	3.6½			140 inches	3.6		
135 inches	3.7			141 inches	3.6½		
136 inches	3.7			142 inches	3.6½		
137 inches	3.7½			143 inches	3.7		
138 inches	3.7½			144 inches	3.7		
139 inches	3.8			145 inches	3.7½		
140 inches	3.8			146 inches	3.7½		
141 inches	3.8½			147 inches	3.8		
142 inches	3.8½			148 inches	3.8		
143 inches	3.9			149 inches	3.8½		
144 inches	3.9			150 inches	3.8½		
145 inches	3.9½			151 inches	3.9		
146 inches	4.0			152 inches	3.9		
147 inches	4.0			153 inches	3.9½		
148 inches	4.+			154 inches	3.9½		
149 inches	4.+			155 inches	4.0		
				156 inches	4.0		

Note: 3+ means set space half way between 3 and 3.1
4+ means set space half way between 4 and 4.1

CONCLUSION

If you have read all of the preceding chapters and studied them carefully, you will have a rather complete knowledge of custom draperies. You will have learned how complex the subject is and will realize that the only way you will become completely familiar with it is to work with the many aspects of draperies—designing, measuring, estimating, and arranging for fabrication.

If you are a student, you will have learned much that can help you to include draperies in your design schemes with know-how and perhaps with confidence. You will at least know the proper steps to take and where to go for help. You will know the correct terms to use and how to communicate with the client and the workroom.

As a design school teacher you have a tool for teaching. If you do not want to make this book a part of your course, you can recommend that your students use it as a reference to let them find out for themselves the bewildering variety of factors they will face when dealing with custom draperies.

For those of you already working in the field as designers or specifiers for an architectural or design firm or as independent designers or decorators, you may feel fairly confident about what you are doing, but it doesn't hurt to brush up on a subject. New members of the firm would certainly welcome the guidance the book offers. Just remember that there are many experienced designers who have never been near a workroom, measured for draperies, estimated yardage, or observed an installation. When this is true, they have been exceedingly lucky in those who carried out their designs, and they have probably created gigantic problems for those people at some time or other. The knowledge you have gained here should ease the situation for everyone.

For those who operate a workroom or anticipate setting one up, you have learned the basics and some of the specifics. This should be a foundation. It can only be that since the variables in the business are endless, and many times you must improvise as you go along. If only a few of the designers and decorators you deal with have read the section on workrooms and understood even a little of it, you are very lucky and some of your problems may be diminished.

My final advice to those who are new in the field is to start with a large organization where you can learn as you go. To take care of a sample room for a design firm is a real eye-opener not only for familiarizing yourself with fabrics and sources, but for learning about price changes, back orders, discontinued fabrics, and the like. Spending time with someone who measures and estimates will give you an excellent background even if you don't intend to do these tasks yourself. Any time spent in a workroom observing the various steps in making draperies allows you to speak knowledgeably about this process to your clients. And certainly to spend some time observing installations should make you realize that even if all other things have been done correctly, this final step can ruin the whole job if it was not planned properly by you, the designer.

It is unimportant where your knowledge of the many aspects of custom draperies originates, whether from studying this book, experience, observation, or a combination of all. What is important is that you have this knowledge and use it to make any jobs where you use custom draperies better and easier for all concerned—you, your client, and your workroom.

INDEX